The Cold War in Asia 1945–93

VIVIENNE SANDERS

SECOND EDITION

access to history

The Cold War
in Asia 1945–93

VIVIENNE SANDERS

SECOND EDITION

HODDER
EDUCATION
AN HACHETTE UK COMPANY

The Publishers would like to thank Nicholas Fellows for his contribution to the Study Guide.

The Publishers would like to thank the following for permission to reproduce copyright material:

Photo credits: p4 Library of Congress, LC-USZ62-32833; **p5** Library of Congress, LC-USZ62-117122; **p6** https://upload.wikimedia.org/wikipedia/commons/c/cf/Mao_Zedong%2C_1935.jpg; **p7** Library of Congress, LC-USZ62-39907; **p17** Library of Congress, LC-USZ62-21027; **p24** Library of Congress, LC-DIG-npcc-10140 ; **p38** Library of Congress, LC-DIG-hec-26756; **p39** https://upload.wikimedia.org/wikipedia/commons/5/5c/Kim_Il_Sung_Portrait-2.jpg/Creative Commons Attribution-Share Alike 3.0 Unported license; **p69** Hulton-Deutsch Collection/Corbis; **p77** Keystone/Getty Images; **p97** https://en.wikipedia.org/wiki/Ho_Chi_Minh#/media/File:Ho_Chi_Minh_1946.jpg; **p101** Library of Congress, LC-USZ62-104961; **p103** Topham Picturepoint; **p111** https://commons.wikimedia.org/wiki/File:Ngo_Dinh_Diem_-_Thumbnail_-_ARC_542189.png/This image or file is a work of a U.S. Air Force Airman or employee, taken or made as part of that person's official duties. As a work of the U.S. federal government, the image or file is in the public domain; **p121** Library of Congress, LC-USZ62-117124; **p122** Corbis; **p128** AP/TopFoto.co.uk; **p136** Library of Congress, LC-USZ62-13036 ; **p152** AP Photo/Huynh Cong Nick Ut; **p156** AFP/AFP/Getty Images; **p166** Eddie Adams/AP/Press Association Images; **p175** Library of Congress, LC-USZ62-13037; **p183** Topham Picturepoint; **p209** Rob C. Croes/Anefo/Nationaal Archief/Creative Commons Attribution-Share Alike 3.0 Netherlands; **p215** Bettmann/Corbis; **p224** Topham/AP.

Acknowledgements: are listed on page 258.

Every effort has been made to trace all copyright holders, but if any have been inadvertently overlooked the Publishers will be pleased to make the necessary arrangements at the first opportunity.

Although every effort has been made to ensure that website addresses are correct at time of going to press, Hodder Education cannot be held responsible for the content of any website mentioned in this book. It is sometimes possible to find a relocated web page by typing in the address of the home page for a website in the URL window of your browser.

Hachette UK's policy is to use papers that are natural, renewable and recyclable products and made from wood grown in well-managed forests and other controlled sources. The logging and manufacturing processes are expected to conform to the environmental regulations of the country of origin.

Orders: please contact Hachette UK Distribution, Hely Hutchinson Centre, Milton Road, Didcot, Oxfordshire, OX11 7HH. Telephone: +44 (0)1235 827827. Email education@hachette.co.uk. Lines are open from 9 a.m. to 5 p.m., Monday to Friday. You can also order through our website: www.hoddereducation.com

© Vivienne Sanders
Second edition © Vivienne Sanders 2015

First published as *The USA in Asia 1945–75* in 2010 by
Hodder Education
An Hachette UK Company
Carmelite House, 50 Victoria Embankment
London EC4Y 0DZ

Impression number   10 9 8 7
Year   2021

Cover photo © Jon Arnold Images Ltd/Alamy
Produced, illustrated and typeset in Palatino LT Std by Gray Publishing, Tunbridge Wells
Printed and bound by CPI Group (UK) Ltd, Croydon CR0 4YY

A catalogue record for this title is available from the British Library

ISBN 978 1471838798

Contents

Dedication

Keith Randell (1943–2002)

The *Access to History* series was conceived and developed by Keith, who created a series to 'cater for students as they are, not as we might wish them to be'. He leaves a living legacy of a series that for over 20 years has provided a trusted, stimulating and well-loved accompaniment to post-16 study. Our aim with these new editions is to continue to offer students the best possible support for their studies.

CHAPTER 1

The Western powers and Asia before 1950

Prior to the Second World War, most Asian countries were colonies belonging to Western powers (the United States, France, Britain and the Netherlands) and to Japan. After the war, nationalist movements seeking independence gained strength in these colonies. The development of these movements in East and Southeast Asia was frequently affected by US Cold War policies.

These issues are covered in the following sections in this chapter:

★ The Western powers and East and Southeast Asia to 1945

★ The US containment policy

★ US policies in Asia, 1945–50

Key dates

1900		The Philippines (USA), Indochina (France), Malaya, Borneo, Hong Kong (Britain) and the Dutch East Indies were Western colonies
1910		Korea became a Japanese colony
1931		Japan conquered Manchuria
1937		Japanese conquest of coastal China began
1939		German attack on Poland started Second World War in Europe
1940		Hitler conquered most of Western Europe (except Britain)
1941	June	Germany invaded Russia
	Dec.	Japan attacked Pearl Harbor, soon controlled British, French, Dutch and US Pacific colonies
1945	Feb.	Yalta conference
	May	Germany surrendered
1945	July	Potsdam conference
	Aug.	US atomic bombs led to Japanese surrender and US occupation
1946		Philippines became independent
		Communist forces opposed Filipino and French Indochinese regimes
1948	June	Communist insurgency prompted British declaration of state of emergency in Malaya
	Aug.	Anti-Communist state of South Korea established
	Sept.	Communist state of North Korea established
	Dec.	US stopped aiding Chinese Nationalists against Chinese Communists
1949	Oct.	China became Communist

The Western powers and East and Southeast Asia to 1945

▶ *How and why were the Western powers involved in Asia before 1945?*

Before 1941, five **imperialist** powers possessed **colonies** in East Asia and Southeast Asia. Four were **Western** (the United States, Britain, France and the Netherlands) and one was Asian (Japan):

- The United States acquired the Philippines after its war with Spain in 1898, but in 1934 President **Franklin Roosevelt** (1933–45) promised the Philippines independence in 1946.
- From the late nineteenth century, Indochina (Vietnam, Cambodia and Laos) was French, Malaya, Borneo and Hong Kong were British, and the Netherlands had the Dutch East Indies.
- Japan controlled Korea from 1905, and conquered Manchuria (1931) and much of coastal China (1937 onwards).

The Second World War (1939–45)

The outbreak of war in Europe in 1939 forced Britain, France and the Netherlands to focus their attention upon the threat from Nazi Germany. This made their East and Southeast Asian colonies vulnerable. In 1940, Nazi Germany took control of the Netherlands and France, leaving Britain isolated in the struggle against Hitler's **expansionism**. These events in Europe gave Japan the opportunity to acquire the Pacific territories and their resources from the Western powers.

The Japanese preoccupation with resources had grown in proportion to the increasing restrictions that the United States placed upon its exports to Japan. The **US** restrictions were a response to Japanese expansionism in China, a country towards which the United States was sympathetic. The US attitude led Japan to make a pre-emptive strike upon America's Pacific naval base at Pearl Harbor in December 1941. Pearl Harbor brought the United States into the war in the Pacific and, days later, Hitler's declaration of war on the United States brought it into the war in Europe and into an alliance with Britain and the **Soviet Union**.

Japan followed Pearl Harbor with the conquest and occupation of the Philippines, Indochina, Malaya, the Dutch East Indies and Borneo. Many of the inhabitants of these Western colonies would gladly have been free of Western **imperialism** and some gave a tentative welcome to the Japanese before Japanese policies made them conclude that Japanese imperialism was even worse than Western imperialism.

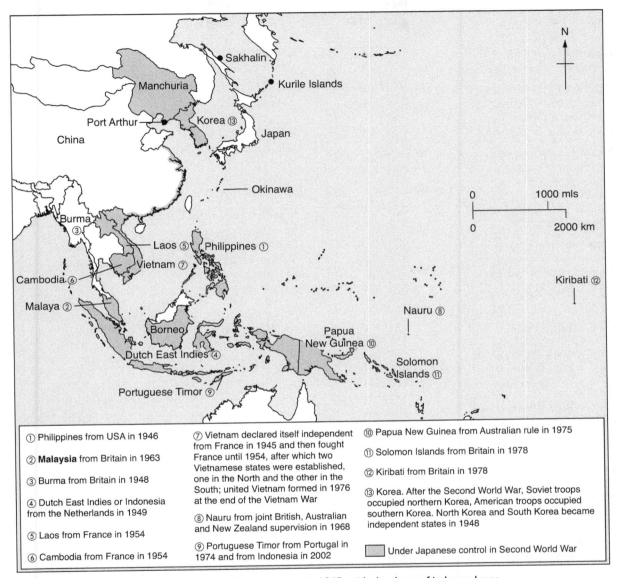

Figure 1.1 Colonial possessions in East and Southeast Asia in 1945, with the dates of independence.

① Philippines from USA in 1946

② **Malaysia** from Britain in 1963

③ Burma from Britain in 1948

④ Dutch East Indies or Indonesia from the Netherlands in 1949

⑤ Laos from France in 1954

⑥ Cambodia from France in 1954

⑦ Vietnam declared itself independent from France in 1945 and then fought France until 1954, after which two Vietnamese states were established, one in the North and the other in the South; united Vietnam formed in 1976 at the end of the Vietnam War

⑧ Nauru from joint British, Australian and New Zealand supervision in 1968

⑨ Portuguese Timor from Portugal in 1974 and from Indonesia in 2002

⑩ Papua New Guinea from Australian rule in 1975

⑪ Solomon Islands from Britain in 1978

⑫ Kiribati from Britain in 1978

⑬ Korea. After the Second World War, Soviet troops occupied northern Korea, American troops occupied southern Korea. North Korea and South Korea became independent states in 1948

 Under Japanese control in Second World War

During the war, the United States, the Soviet Union and Britain discussed the future of the Japanese-occupied nations, for which they had different and sometimes competing plans and hopes.

US, Soviet and British ideas for post-war Asia

Roosevelt opposed territorial imperialism and particularly resented the exclusion of American manufactured goods from the colonial possessions of the Europeans. He said that 'white nations could not hope to hold onto these areas

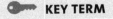 **KEY TERM**

Malaysia From 1963, British Malaya and associated territories were independent and known as Malaysia.

3

Josef Stalin

1879	Born in Georgia
c.1926–53	Dominated Soviet politics
1939	Initial collaboration with Hitler in the Second World War
1941	Nazi Germany attacked USSR
1941–5	USSR and USA allied in the Second World War
1944–8	Took control of Eastern Europe, antagonising the USA and triggering the Cold War
1950	Recognised Ho Chi Minh's Democratic Republic of Vietnam (January)
	Supported Kim Il Sung's attack on South Korea (June)
	Encouraged Communist China to enter the Korean War (October)
1953	Died

Background

Born to a peasant family, Stalin opposed the Russian monarchy from 1899. One of the leading Communists by 1912, he worked quite closely with Lenin during and after the 1917 Russian Revolution. After Lenin's death in 1924, Stalin eliminated all potential rivals and led the Soviet Union from c.1926 until his death in 1953.

Achievements

During Stalin's brutal dictatorship, the Soviet Union was rapidly industrialised. Stalin was greatly revered by many Russians for having led the nation successfully through the Second World War, during which he acquired an East European Empire that served to strengthen the Soviet Union's western frontiers.

Significance in the Cold War

Stalin's suspicious nature contributed greatly to the origins and development of the Cold War in Europe and Asia. His approval for Kim Il Sung's attack on South Korea triggered the Korean War. His East European policy antagonised the United States and was an important cause of the US entry into the Korean War. He encouraged Mao Zedong (see page 6) to enter the war after US forces entered North Korea. Although Stalin was far less active in his support of Ho Chi Minh and Communism in Vietnam than in support of Kim and North Korea, the US thought otherwise. The American belief that Ho was Stalin's puppet, coupled with Stalin's actions in Europe and Korea, helped to stimulate the US involvement in Vietnam.

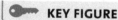 **KEY FIGURE**

Winston Churchill (1874–1965)

British Prime Minister in 1940–5 and 1951–5. While leader of the opposition in 1946, he criticised the Soviet 'Iron Curtain' in Eastern Europe.

as colonies in the long run' and was particularly critical of French imperialism in Indochina (he frequently maintained that France should not be allowed to return there). Although less critical of British imperialism, Roosevelt repeatedly urged British Prime Minister **Winston Churchill** to restore Hong Kong to China and to exit India, but Churchill hoped Britain could retain its imperial possessions for as long as possible.

America, Britain and the Soviet Union differed over China. Roosevelt was frequently hopeful that China would be able to play a major role in the post-war world, but Churchill and the Soviet leader Josef Stalin were sceptical about China's power and potential and by early 1945 Roosevelt was more inclined to agree with them. Stalin was keen to exploit Chinese weakness and to ensure easy Soviet naval access to the Pacific.

The Pacific territories under Japanese occupation were discussed by Roosevelt, Stalin and Churchill at the Yalta conference in February 1945, then by Roosevelt's successor Harry Truman (1945–53), Stalin and the British at Potsdam in July 1945.

Harry S. Truman

1884	Born in Missouri
1935	Elected Senator
1945	Became President in April
1947	'Truman Doctrine' speech
1949	Established NATO
	Republicans said the Democrats Roosevelt and Truman 'lost' China
1950	McCarthy said State Department contained Communists
	Financially assisted French struggle against Vietnamese Communists
1950–3	Korean War
1953	Retired to Missouri
1972	Died

Background

A farmboy from Missouri, Truman first came to national attention by exposing inefficiency in government defence spending in the Second World War. As Vice President, he became President when President Roosevelt died. In 1948, he was elected President in his own right.

Achievements

Truman failed to persuade Congress to undertake meaningful social reforms and was unable to halt the excesses of the Red Scare, but his foreign policy decisions had a lasting impact. He is often praised for establishing NATO, defeating Stalin's Berlin blockade, revitalising Western Europe through Marshall Aid, and for the containment of Communism in Korea.

Significance in the Cold War

Truman's decision to oppose Communism resulted in US involvement in the Cold War and in wars in Korea and Vietnam. That involvement cost a great deal in lives and money. Most people believe Truman had no choice but to oppose Communism in order to maintain American security, but some consider the Cold War an unnecessary war that might have been avoided had the more conciliatory Roosevelt remained in the White House. Truman's decision to send American troops to Korea after North Korea attacked South Korea in 1950 resulted in a war involving many countries that might have led to a third world war. Initially, he aimed only to restore the *status quo* in South Korea. In this he was successful, but he failed in his attempt to reunify the peninsula. When Truman sent American troops into North Korea, it brought China fully into the war and led to nearly three more years of bloody struggle. The conflict between the Chinese and the Americans in Korea confirmed that the Cold War had dramatically arrived in Asia, and ensured that Sino-American relations remained exceptionally hostile until the early 1970s. When Truman aided the French in their struggle to defeat the Communist Ho Chi Minh's fight for Vietnamese independence, he initiated the American involvement in Vietnam, although it could be argued that the commitment was still reversible at his death.

Decisions on Asia at the Yalta conference

Roosevelt, Stalin and Churchill (the 'Big Three') met at the Soviet Black Sea resort of Yalta from 4 to 12 February 1945. Stalin had insisted that the conference take place on Soviet territory, and Churchill and the ailing Roosevelt agreed to make the several thousand-mile journey there in order to discuss winning the war and arrangements for the post-war world.

The war in Europe dominated the agenda at Yalta, but Asia was also discussed. As yet unaware of the massive destructive power of the atomic bomb that would eventually force Japan into reluctant surrender, Roosevelt was desperate for the USSR to enter the war against Japan. He therefore promised the **USSR**:

KEY TERM

USSR Union of Soviet Socialist Republics.

Mao Zedong

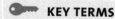

1893	Born to a Chinese peasant family
1921	Became a Communist
1934–5	Established domination over Chinese Communist Party
1930s–45	Simultaneously fought the Chinese Nationalist Party (Guomindang) and Japanese
1949	Established the People's Republic of China in October
1950	In June approved North Korean attack on South Korea
1950–3	Participated in Korean War
1960s	**Sino-Soviet** split
1972	Relations with US improved
1976	Died

Background

Mao felt humiliated by China's disorder and weakness and believed China needed a great political and social revolution to become great again. He said that would inevitably involve violence ('All power grows out of the barrel of a gun'). A founder member of the Chinese Communist Party, he led it from 1935, masterminded the Communist victory over Jiang Jieshi's Chinese Nationalists in the civil war, and established the People's Republic of China in 1949.

Achievements

During his ruthless dictatorship over China (1949–76), Mao contributed greatly to China's modernisation and emergence as a great power. His brutal methods and ideological experiments have been much criticised.

Significance in the Cold War

Mao was a very important factor in US involvement in Asia. When China became Communist in 1949, the United States began to switch its attention from Europe to Asia as the storm centre of the Cold War. Mao gave his assent to Kim Il Sung's invasion of South Korea, which triggered the Korean War. The American belief that Mao and Stalin were behind this invasion helped prompt the US intervention in Korea, which embittered Sino-American relations for the next two decades. The American conviction that Stalin and Mao were behind the Vietnamese Communists helped bring about US intervention in Vietnam.

Mao's relations with the Soviet Union were uneasy from the very beginning. He was a nationalist first and a Communist second, as demonstrated by his willingness to improve relations with the USA in order to counter the USSR after the Sino-Soviet split of the 1960s.

KEY TERMS

Sino-Soviet Chinese–Soviet.

Jiang Jieshi In some books the name Chiang Kai-shek is used instead of Jiang Jieshi.

Communists Believers in economic equality brought about by the revolutionary redistribution of wealth.

Trusteeship In an international context, countries that take responsibility for another country.

- easier Soviet naval access to the Pacific (through the acquisition of the Japanese Kurile Islands, joint control with China of the Manchurian railways and Port Arthur, and the recognition of pre-eminent Soviet interest in the Manchurian port of Dairen, which was to be internationalised)
- the resource-rich island of South Sakhalin.

In return, Stalin promised that he would enter the war against Japan within three months of Germany's defeat and that he would support the government of **Jiang Jieshi**, which was threatened by Mao Zedong and the Chinese **Communists**. Roosevelt and Stalin also agreed to a Soviet–American–British–Chinese **trusteeship** that would steer Korea toward eventual independence from Japan.

Jiang Jieshi (Chiang Kai-shek)

1887	Born to a Chinese middle-class family
1909–11	Supported the revolution against the imperial dynasty
1918	Joined the Nationalist Party (Guomindang)
1925–7	Led the Revolutionary Army; great progress towards Chinese reunification
1930	Converted to Christianity
1930–1	Prioritised Communist threat over Japanese threat
1937	Switched focus to Japanese threat
1941–5	US ally against Japan
1945–9	Defeated by Communists in the Chinese civil war
1949–75	Ruled Taiwan
1950	Korean War improved US–Taiwanese relations
1955	US–Taiwanese defence treaty
1975	Died

Background

The middle-class Jiang Jieshi (Chiang Kai-shek) became a professional soldier, then led the Guomindang from 1925. From the outset, he sought to destroy the Chinese Communist Party (CCP).

Achievements

Although he never managed to defeat the CCP, Jiang played an important part in the defeat of the Japanese. His government was corrupt and ruthless, but it contributed to the modernisation of China. The international community recognised him as the leader of China from the late 1920s to 1949.

Significance in the Cold War

Jiang was important to US policies in East Asia for over half a century. When he seemed likely to reunite China (long torn apart by warlords and foreign invaders), the Americans admired him, and gave him aid to combat the Japanese. During the Second World War, the Americans accepted him as one of the 'Big Four' (USA, USSR, Britain and China), but grew increasingly exasperated because he repeatedly rejected US attempts to get him to co-operate with Mao in the struggle against the Japanese (Mao said he was willing to co-operate). During 1945–9, the Truman administration grew increasingly disillusioned with Jiang and slowly decreased his aid. After China fell to Communism, and Jiang and his Nationalist followers fled to Taiwan, Truman said the USA had little interest in Taiwan. However, when the Korean War broke out, the United States decided that Jiang was an important ally in the struggle against Communism.

Decisions on Asia at the Potsdam conference

The leaders of the USA, the USSR and Britain met in the Berlin suburb of Potsdam on 17 July 1945. Stalin and the new American President, Harry Truman (see page 5), met for the first and only time. Labour Party leader Clement Attlee attended alongside Churchill while awaiting the result of the British election, but when Churchill's Conservative Party lost the election on 26 July, Attlee became Prime Minister and remained at Potsdam until the conference ended on 2 August.

The war in Europe ended in May 1945 and the future of Germany and its European conquests still dominated the discussions at Potsdam. With regard to Asia:

- Stalin reaffirmed his intention to enter the war against Japan
- Truman rejected Stalin's suggestion that they work out the details of the trusteeship of Korea, considering it unlikely that the USSR could mobilise its Far East troops before the war against Japan was over
- it was agreed that following the Japanese surrender, China would occupy northern French Indochina, while the British South East Asia Command (SEAC) would occupy southern Indochina.

While cynical Americans said that SEAC stood for 'Save England's Asian Colonies', the United States had by this time retreated somewhat from its anti-colonial stance. This was partly because the US military wanted to retain control of strategically important Pacific islands such as Okinawa but also because the USSR seemed likely to develop into a greater threat than the European imperialists. Although the Second World War was coming to an end (Japan surrendered after the United States dropped two atomic bombs upon it in August 1945), a Cold War between the United States and the USSR was about to begin. The Cold War would have a massive impact upon East and Southeast Asia.

The Cold War (c.1947–c.1989)

In the half-century of the Cold War era, a state of extreme tension existed between the Western world and the Communist world. The West was led by the United States, which had **allies** such as Britain, France, Italy and West Germany. The Communist world was led by the USSR and, to a lesser extent, China. Although armed to the hilt, the United States and USSR never met directly in combat – hence the 'cold' war.

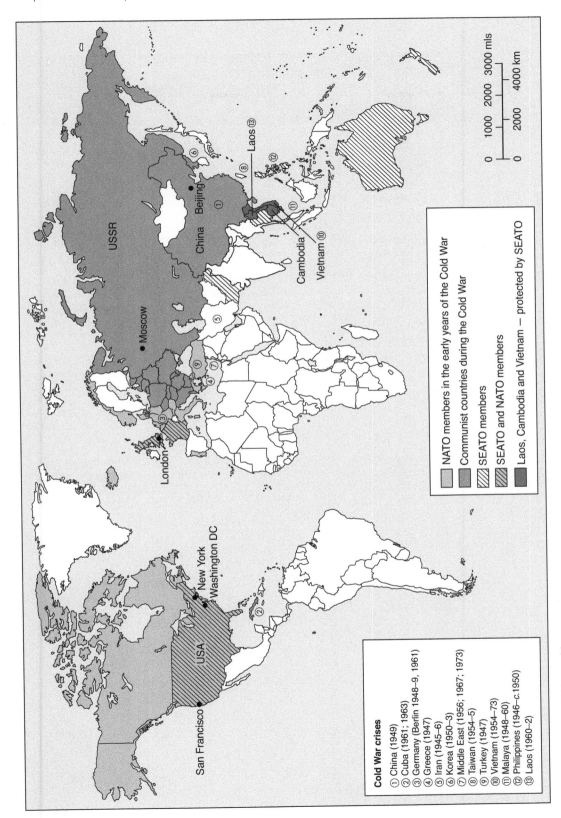

Figure 1.2 The Cold War world.

USSR

China   Beijing

Laos ⑬

Cambodia

Vietnam ⑩

Moscow

London

USA

San Francisco

New York

Washington DC

Cold War crises

① China (1949)
② Cuba (1961; 1963)
③ Germany (Berlin 1948–9, 1961)
④ Greece (1947)
⑤ Iran (1945–6)
⑥ Korea (1950–3)
⑦ Middle East (1956; 1967; 1973)
⑧ Taiwan (1954–5)
⑨ Turkey (1947)
⑩ Vietnam (1954–73)
⑪ Malaya (1948–60)
⑫ Philippines (1946–c.1950)
⑬ Laos (1960–2)

NATO members in the early years of the Cold War

Communist countries during the Cold War

SEATO members

SEATO and NATO members

Laos, Cambodia and Vietnam – protected by SEATO

Summary diagram: The Western powers and East and Southeast Asia to 1945

Asian nation	Pre-Second World War	Second World War	Yalta decisions	Potsdam decisions
Philippines	US colony	Japanese occupation		
Indochina	French colony	Japanese occupation of Vietnam		China to take Japanese surrender in northern Vietnam, British to take it in southern Vietnam
Malaya	British colony	Japanese occupation		
Korea	Japanese colony	Same	A Soviet–American–British–Chinese trusteeship would steer it toward eventual independence	US rejected Soviet initiative to work out trusteeship details
China	Government = Jiang Jieshi's Chinese Nationalists BUT Manchuria and coastal areas conquered by Japan	Same	Roosevelt gave Stalin territorial concessions in China	
Japan	Expansionist	War with USA	Stalin promised to enter war against Japan 3 months after Germany's defeat. Roosevelt promised him South Sakhalin, Kurile Islands, and concessions in Manchuria	Stalin reiterated promise to enter the war against Japan

2 The US containment policy

▶ *When and why did the United States fall out with the USSR?*

Prior to the **Russian Revolution** that began in 1917, relations between the United States and Russia had often been quite friendly. However, relations deteriorated rapidly after the Revolution led to the establishment of a Communist government in Russia (which from 1922 called itself the Soviet Union or USSR).

Ideological opponents

The United States and the USSR had very different **ideologies**:

Table 1.1 The differing ideologies of the USA and USSR

US ideology	Soviet ideology
Americans supported a **capitalist** system, with free trade and minimal government intervention in the economy	Communists favoured a state-controlled economy in which the government promoted economic equality through the redistribution of national wealth
Americans considered a **multi-party state** and free elections the hallmark of democracy	Communists claimed that other parties were unnecessary as the Communist Party was the party of the people and that economic rather than political equality characterised democracy
Americans thought Communist promotion of revolutions might leave the United States without trading partners and allies, and Communist countries might attempt to export revolution to the United States	Many Communists advocated the promotion of Communist revolutions throughout the world

Ideological differences made the USA and USSR suspicious of and hostile towards each other. Each believed its ideology was superior and should be exported, and each perceived the other as an expansionist security threat. The hostility was such that it was not until 1933 that the United States finally gave **diplomatic** recognition to the USSR. Soviet–American relations then improved somewhat. After Hitler invaded the USSR in summer 1941 and declared war on the United States in December 1941, the USA and USSR became wartime allies.

Wartime allies to Cold War enemies

At times, the Soviet–American wartime alliance (1941–5) appeared to work well, despite underlying ideological tensions and disagreements over strategy. However, after the war ended, Soviet–American relations deteriorated, and the two countries embarked on the Cold War. This was due to a range of factors including:

- ideological differences
- US disapproval when the Soviets established domination of Eastern Europe (1944–8)
- the bomb (the Soviets resented America keeping its atomic bomb programme secret while the two countries were supposedly allies in the Second World War, and when the effects of the bomb were demonstrated in 1945, Stalin's fear of US power increased)
- clashes of interest over several countries, including Iran, Germany, Greece, Turkey and Korea

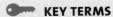

KEY TERMS

Ideology Set of political beliefs, for example, Communism.

Capitalist One who believes in a free market economy with no state intervention – the opposite of the Communist economic philosophy.

Multi-party state Nation in which voters have a free choice between several political parties.

Diplomatic In international relations, 'diplomacy' means relations between nations; a diplomat represents his or her nation abroad; nations that fully recognise each other have diplomatic relations.

- a war of words from 1946 onwards, in which spokesmen from each side were critical of the other
- Stalin's defensive and suspicious personality and Truman's feisty character and determination to prove himself decisive and equal to the job arguably made them more inclined to confrontation than compromise.

George Kennan's Long Telegram and the US containment policy

George Kennan was a leading **State Department** expert on the USSR. In February 1946, the State Department asked him for an explanation of the increasingly anti-American tone of Soviet speeches. He responded in an 8000-word 'Long Telegram' in which he said that Soviet antagonism was not a result of any American actions but due to the Soviet government's need to exaggerate external threats in order to maintain domestic legitimacy (see Source A). Kennan depicted the Soviets as aggressive and this became the orthodox Western interpretation of the origins of the Cold War. Successive US administrations would blame the conflict on Soviet expansionism.

The historian Martin McCauley (2003) described the Long Telegram as 'the decisive factor' in the Truman administration's increasingly tough line against the USSR, but many members of the Truman **administration** had been coming to similar conclusions before the Long Telegram. Soviet designs on the territory of oil-rich Iran had led Truman to write to **Secretary of State** James Byrnes, 'I'm tired of babying the Soviets' – several weeks before Kennan's Long Telegram. Where Kennan was undeniably important was in that he undoubtedly helped clarify and confirm the suspicions and anxieties of leading figures in the Truman administration.

KEY TERMS

State Department
US governmental department with responsibility for foreign affairs.

Administration Rather than refer to a President's 'government', Americans refer to a President's 'administration'.

Secretary of State
The US equivalent of Britain's Foreign Secretary, he had responsibility for foreign policy and was in charge of the State Department.

What influence do you suppose Source A would have had upon US policy toward East and Southeast Asia?

SOURCE A

From George Kennan's Long Telegram to the State Department, 22 February 1946 (available from http://nsarchive.gwu.edu/coldwar/documents/episode-1/kennan.htm**).**

[The Soviets believe] *Everything must be done to advance relative strength of USSR ... [and] to reduce strength and influence ... of capitalist powers ...*

At bottom of Kremlin's neurotic view of world affairs is traditional and instinctive Russian sense of insecurity ... [and] fear of more competent, more powerful, more highly organized societies ... Russian rulers have invariably sensed that their rule was relatively archaic in form fragile and artificial in its psychological foundation, unable to stand comparison or contact with political systems of Western countries. For this reason they have always feared foreign penetration, feared direct contact between Western world and their own, feared what would happen if Russians learned truth about world without or if foreigners learned truth about world within. And they have learned to seek security only in patient but deadly struggle for total destruction of rival power, never in compacts and compromises with it.

… After establishment of Bolshevist regime, Marxist dogma* … became a perfect vehicle for sense of insecurity … In this dogma, with its basic altruism of purpose, they found justification for their instinctive fear of outside world, for the dictatorship without which they did not know how to rule … This is why Soviet purposes most always be solemnly clothed in trappings of Marxism, and why no one should underrate importance of dogma in Soviet affairs. Thus Soviet leaders are driven [by] necessities of their own past and present position to put forward which [apparent omission] outside world as evil, hostile and menacing …

Toward colonial areas and backward or dependent peoples, Soviet policy, even on official plane, will be directed toward weakening of power and influence and contacts of advanced Western nations … so … there will be created a vacuum which will favor Communist-Soviet penetration.

* Karl Marx was the first great Communist theorist; his ideas were followed by Bolsheviks such as Lenin and Stalin during the Russian Revolution.

Already anxious about Soviet domination of Eastern Europe, Truman also perceived the Soviets as aggressive over Iran, Germany, Greece and Turkey between late 1945 and early 1947. As a result, Truman advised **Congress** in March 1947 that the United States would need to support 'free peoples' resisting Communist pressures and attacks. That '**Truman Doctrine**' speech advocated the **containment** of Communism (see Source B).

SOURCE B

From President Truman's 12 March 1947 speech to Congress, in which he asked Congress for financial aid for Greece and Turkey to help them combat Communism (available from http://avalon.law.yale.edu/20th_century/trudoc.asp).

At the present moment in world history nearly every nation must choose between alternative ways of life. The choice is too often not a free one. One way of life is based upon the will of the majority, and is distinguished by free institutions, representative government, free elections, guarantees of individual liberty, freedom of speech and religion, and freedom from political oppression. The second way of life is based upon the will of a minority forcibly imposed upon the majority. It relies upon terror and oppression, a controlled press and radio, fixed elections, and the suppression of personal freedoms. I believe that it must be the policy of the United States to support free peoples who are resisting attempted subjugation by armed minorities or by outside pressures … If we falter in our leadership, we may endanger the peace of the world – and we shall surely endanger the welfare of our own Nation.

🔑 **KEY TERMS**

Congress The US equivalent of the British parliament; Congress makes laws and grants money to fund the President's policies.

Truman Doctrine Truman's declaration of Cold War on the USSR in his March 1947 speech to Congress, in which he said the Soviet threat had to be resisted.

Containment The Truman administration's policy of using counterforce against Soviet expansionism.

What reasons does Source B give in favour of US support for 'free peoples'?

It was Kennan who first popularised the word 'containment' when he expanded upon his Long Telegram in his anonymous 'Mr X' article in the prestigious *Foreign Affairs* journal in July 1947.

Using Source C, what adjectives would you use to describe Kennan's view of the Soviet Union?

SOURCE C

From George Kennan's 'Mr X' article, entitled 'The Sources of Soviet Conduct', published in the journal *Foreign Affairs*, July 1947 (available from www.foreignaffairs.com/articles/23331/x/the-sources-of-soviet-conduct).

It is clear that the main element of any United States policy towards the Soviet Union must be that of a long-term, patient but firm and vigilant containment of Russian expansionist tendencies … It is clear that the United States cannot expect in the foreseeable future to enjoy political intimacy with the Soviet regime. It must continue to regard the Soviet Union as a rival, not a partner, in the political arena. It must continue to expect that Soviet policies will reflect no abstract level of peace and stability, no real faith in the possibility of a permanent happy coexistence of the Socialist* and capitalist worlds, but rather a cautious, persistent pressure towards the disruption and weakening of all rival influence and rival power.

* Communists frequently referred to themselves as Socialists.

Soon after the Mr X article, Kennan advised that there were five centres of power in the world:

- the USA
- the USSR
- Britain
- Germany and Central Europe
- Japan.

He said the United States should aim to keep Britain, Europe and Japan out of Soviet hands, and he emphasised the importance of island bases in the Pacific, especially in Japan and the Philippines. Neither the US armed forces nor the Truman administration needed to be told that Japan and the Philippines were vitally important. From 1946, the United States had been attempting to mould Japan and the Philippines in its own image.

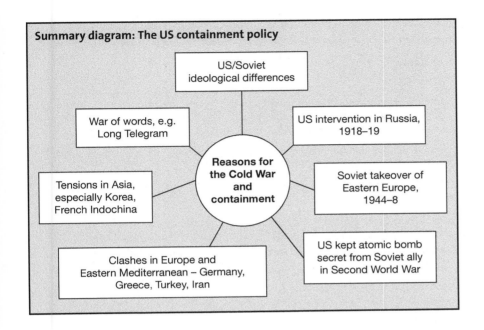

Summary diagram: The US containment policy

US/Soviet ideological differences

War of words, e.g. Long Telegram

US intervention in Russia, 1918–19

Reasons for the Cold War and containment

Tensions in Asia, especially Korea, French Indochina

Soviet takeover of Eastern Europe, 1944–8

Clashes in Europe and Eastern Mediterranean – Germany, Greece, Turkey, Iran

US kept atomic bomb secret from Soviet ally in Second World War

③ US policies in Asia, 1945–50

▶ *Did the United States achieve its aims in Asia, 1945–50?*

After the Japanese defeat in the Second World War,

- the United States occupied Japan (see page 16) and granted Filipino independence (see page 22)
- China was torn apart by a civil war between Communists and non-Communists (see page 30)
- the British returned to Malaya (see pages 34–5)
- the French returned to Indochina, where the Vietnamese Communists led the opposition to French colonialism (see Chapter 3)
- the Soviets took the Japanese surrender in northern Korea and the Americans took it in southern Korea (see page 37).

US policies toward Japan, the Philippines, China, Indochina and Korea were increasingly affected by the developing Cold War. The United States had acquired the islands of the Philippines after the Spanish–American War of 1898. As Americans had long considered their political and economic system the best in the world, they worked to mould the islands in their own image. Then, after the Second World War, the US attempted to remould defeated Japan. There were similar efforts to create US-style states in South Korea (see page 39) and South Vietnam (see page 112). Prior to the Cold War, the US emphasis upon the export of the American political and economic system was based upon a belief in American superiority and the desire to influence and trade with other powers. With the advent of the Cold War, creating states in America's image suddenly seemed essential to US national security.

The US creation of model states

Stalin had promised at Yalta that he would enter the war against Japan three months after Germany was defeated. However, once Germany was defeated and US forces neared Japan, Truman did not want the Soviets to muscle in and claim any spoils of victory, especially as Stalin demanded full Soviet control of Dairen and that Japanese industry in Manchuria be confiscated as 'trophies of war'.

After the US dropped the first atomic bomb on Japan, the Soviet Union duly declared war on Japan, three months to the day after Germany was defeated. Truman therefore rushed US troops to Japan and made it clear that the occupation of Japan was to be a strictly American affair. General Douglas MacArthur, the US commander in the Pacific during the Second World War, took the Japanese surrender and was Truman's choice to command the occupation force in Japan.

The occupation and reconstruction of Japan

The stated aim of the US occupation was 'to ensure that Japan will not again become a menace to the peace and security of the world'. This would be achieved through:

- disarmament and demilitarisation
- the punishment of those responsible for the war
- the development of a liberal democratic political system and economic and social change that would transform Japanese values and behaviour and ensure that it would be pro-American in future.

Several US government departments had been planning the occupation since 1942, but detailed implementation of the US plans for a demilitarised democracy in Japan was left to the occupation force.

The establishment of SCAP

Although MacArthur's title was Supreme Commander of the Allied Powers (**SCAP**) in Japan, SCAP was a totally American organisation for which over 3000 US military and civilian personnel were working by 1948.

In October 1945 the State-War-Navy Coordinating Committee sent MacArthur the planning document SWNCC-228. It tasked SCAP with producing a constitution that would set up a democratic government for Japan with **Emperor Hirohito** as a **constitutional monarch** and promote:

The emancipation of women; the encouragement of the unionization of labor; the opening of schools to more liberal education; the abolishment of systems

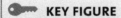

Douglas MacArthur

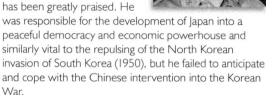

1880	Born in Little Rock, Arkansas
1941–5	Commanded US Army in the Far East in the Second World War
1945–51	Allied Commander of the Japanese occupation
1950	In June, appointed Commander of US/UN/ROK forces in Korea
	In September, after Inchon, drove North Koreans from South Korea
	Chinese entered Korean War in October, MacArthur retreated
1951	Controversially sacked by President Truman
1964	Died

Background

Born into a military family, Douglas MacArthur had a distinguished career in the American Army until he retired in 1937. Military Adviser to the Commonwealth Government of the Philippines from 1937 to 1941, he was recalled to active duty after Pearl Harbor and given command of the US Army in the Far East.

Achievements

General MacArthur's supervision of the US occupation of Japan (1945–51) has been greatly praised. He was responsible for the development of Japan into a peaceful democracy and economic powerhouse and similarly vital to the repulsing of the North Korean invasion of South Korea (1950), but he failed to anticipate and cope with the Chinese intervention into the Korean War.

Significance

MacArthur was of particular importance in the Korean War, because his command of the US/UN/ROK (see page 55) forces and his great reputation gave him the opportunity to influence American Cold War policy. President Truman believed in the policy of containment of Communism and favoured limited war in Korea, but MacArthur was keen to take on Communist China and use all available American resources, including atomic weapons. While Truman was a **Europe-firster**, MacArthur was an **Asia-firster**. What added to MacArthur's importance was that he made his opinions public. Public disagreements over US policy greatly damaged Truman, but it was the President's policies that eventually prevailed. There was no all-out war against Communist China.

---

which through secret inquisition and abuse have held people in constant fear; the democratization of Japanese economic institutions to the end that monopolistic industrial controls be revised.

MacArthur sought freedom in the detailed implementation of the reforms and the Truman administration, preoccupied with the developing Cold War in Europe (see page 11), allowed this until 1948.

SCAP's constitution and policies

The American-designed Japanese constitution came into force in May 1947. Under it:

- Japan was to be a democracy with a constitutional monarch as head of state and a cabinet government drawn from and responsible to an elected legislature consisting of two chambers
- human rights were emphasised, including free speech, freedom of religion, 'the right to maintain the minimum standard of wholesome and cultural living', the right to **collective bargaining**, and gender equality.

 KEY TERMS

Europe-Firster Cold War American who believed Europe should take priority over Asia in US foreign policy.

Asia-Firster Cold War American who believed Asia should take priority over Europe in US foreign policy.

Collective bargaining When trade unions are able to organise and to negotiate with management over wages, hours, and so on.

'Discrimination in political, economic or social relations because of race, creed, sex, social status or family origin' was forbidden (Article 14), marriage required 'the mutual consent of both sexes', and there should be 'essential equality of the sexes' in all areas (Article 24)

- war and armed forces were renounced (Article 9).

Many of these provisions constituted revolutionary political and social change for Japanese society. The most revolutionary political provision was the demotion of the Japanese Emperor from his previous god-like status to that of constitutional monarch. The most socially revolutionary proposal was for gender equality, for Japanese women were traditionally subordinated to men. SCAP also worked to reshape Japanese society through several policies:

- nearly 250,000 former military officers and men highly placed in government and business were purged; 25 were tried for war crimes, seven were executed and most of the others received long jail sentences
- the power of the Japanese landowning elite was radically decreased in 1946 through a massive land redistribution programme that helped increase agricultural productivity (enthusiastic new landowners worked harder than ever before)
- the new American-style education system was less elitist than the old Japanese system (7 per cent of Japanese attended high school in 1940 but over 15 per cent by 1955) and played a vital role in producing the highly educated work force behind the subsequent Japanese 'economic miracle'
- SCAP tried to break up the 83 **zaibatsu** companies such as Mitsubishi that had dominated the pre-war Japanese economy and were felt to have been important supporters of militarism and nationalistic expansionism (and, some said, constituted rivals to American companies).

Many of the reforms, such as the introduction of constitutional monarchy, the renunciation of war and the reform of the education system, were highly successful, but others met determined local resistance. For example, while the Americans who drew up the constitution attempted to give local authorities greater power (as in the US federal system), the Japanese were unaccustomed to such devolution and quietly ensured that this proved unworkable by the 1950s. Similarly, the constitution's emphasis on women's rights could not overcome centuries of discrimination against women, even though many women exercised the vote for the first time in 1946 and nearly 40 women were elected to the Japanese parliament.

The Japanese reaction to MacArthur and SCAP

Although Emperor Hirohito had ordered to his people to accept peace, there was some initial opposition to SCAP. The first post-war Japanese cabinet resigned in October 1945 over SCAP's order that political prisoners be freed and military and civilian officials be purged. The cabinet of the new Prime Minister, Shidehara Kijuro, was aghast at two provisions in SCAP's constitution: the

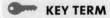
KEY TERM

Zaibatsu Industrial and financial conglomerates or cartels that emerged in late nineteenth-century Japan; under SCAP they developed into looser associations known as keiretsu.

renunciation of war and the dramatic change in the position of the Emperor. However, Hirohito accepted his changed constitutional status and told the cabinet he saw no reason to reject it. The Japanese government therefore accepted the new constitution, although one cabinet member recorded that he 'secretly wept' with rage.

The Japanese people accepted SCAP and its policies because:

- Japan had been humiliatingly and totally defeated in the war and was now occupied by American soldiers.
- Many Japanese were amazed that the US occupation force did not behave as the Japanese had in China, and this contributed to acceptance of the new constitution.
- Although many Americans thought the Emperor Hirohito should be tried as a war criminal, MacArthur insisted upon his retention and used him effectively. SCAP manipulated the war crimes trials to ensure that the Emperor and the royal family were not implicated, and MacArthur sent Hirohito on nationwide tours to encourage positive enthusiasm for SCAP.
- SCAP control of the media enabled it to promote SCAP policies.
- The Japanese were traditionally respectful of authority.
- Liberals, women and union leaders enthusiastically supported SCAP's constitution.
- The lack of Japanese-speakers in SCAP enabled the Japanese authorities to change, delay and even ignore SCAP instructions. For example, the National Public Servants law of 1946 was designed to decrease the powers of the conservative Japanese bureaucracy, which had played an important part in Japanese expansionism from 1931. However, while paying lip service to the acceptance of SCAP policies, the bureaucracy became even more powerful under the occupation and subverted US intent on issues such as devolution.
- Many Japanese thought highly of MacArthur, so much so that the Japanese newspaper editor Itakura Takuzo complained, 'The Japanese people have long been plagued by the mistaken idea that government is something to be executed by some deity, hero or great man.' He felt that projecting this idea of the god emperor upon MacArthur was 'the worst enemy of democracy'.

MacArthur certainly deserved Japanese plaudits:

- He softened the horrors of defeat and gave a welcome sense of continuity by his retention of Emperor Hirohito.
- In 1946, when the Japanese people were near starvation because of food shortages (the result of war and inflation), MacArthur diverted surplus US Army food supplies to Japanese civilians (Japanese acceptance of the occupation enabled the United States to decrease its occupation force from 600,000 to 200,000 so there were fewer American mouths to feed).
- He persuaded the US Congress to grant Japan more financial aid than the Truman administration originally planned.
- He ensured that Japan paid minimal **reparations**.

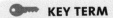 **KEY TERM**

Reparations In this context, compensatory payments from a defeated country to victors and victims.

**Yoshida Shigeru
(1878–1967)**

Prime Minister of Japan from May 1946 to May 1947 and October 1948 to December 1954, he collaborated quite effectively with the US occupation force, oversaw the renaissance of Japanese industry and helped Japan's international rehabilitation.

**George Marshall
(1880–1959)**

A career soldier, he controlled America's war strategy from 1939 to 1945. In 1945, Truman sent him to China to try to reconcile the CCP and GMD, but he failed. He was Truman's Secretary of State from 1947 to 1949, and his Secretary of Defense from 1950 to 1951. He was important in the establishment of Marshall Aid to war-damaged Europe, and of NATO.

Democratic elections

From 1946, democratic elections were held in Japan. In 1946, the Liberal Party won the most seats and **Yoshida Shigeru** became Prime Minister (May 1946 to May 1947). He coexisted reasonably well with the Americans, flattering MacArthur and sending Mrs MacArthur flowers and gifts. He consoled himself by pointing out to others in private that America had once been a British colony but was now more powerful than Britain. SCAP sometimes considered him to be too independent-minded, but when US attitudes toward Japan changed, Yoshida became more acceptable.

Changing US attitudes toward Japan

During the Second World War there had been two differing viewpoints about Japan within the Roosevelt and Truman administrations. The 'China Crowd' regarded Japan as likely to be a permanent threat to the United States, while the 'Japan Crowd' thought Japan could quite easily be moulded into a reliable post-war ally for the United States. During and immediately after the war, the 'China Crowd' was in the ascendant and SCAP policies reflected that. However, the Truman administration soon began to switch to the 'Japanese Crowd' viewpoint that the Japanese economy should be built up because:

- The onset of the Cold War (see page 11) made many in the Truman administration, including Kennan (see page 12), conclude that Japan would be important in the containment of Communism.
- **George Marshall** became Secretary of State in 1947 and he wanted to assert control over MacArthur in Japan and shift the emphasis from liberal reforms to economic revival, so that a rejuvenated Japan would be useful US ally against Communism.
- A more prosperous Japan would make the Japanese more supportive of the new political and social systems and less inclined to turn Communist (the Japanese Communist Party won 3 million votes in the 1949 election).
- Japan was costing the United States a great deal of money. Between September 1945 and June 1948, the United States sent $1 billion to prevent mass starvation and ensure economic activity. This led many in Washington to conclude that it would be cheaper to build up the Japanese economy.

From pro-labour to pro-business

The change in US policy was reflected in the US switch from pro-labour to pro-business policies. SCAP had encouraged the formation of trade unions, but when some became increasingly militant, MacArthur banned a threatened general strike in 1947. In October 1948 Truman ordered MacArthur to

- stop extracting any reparations from Japan (MacArthur had not taken much anyway)

- promote Japanese exports
- eliminate most of the restrictions on Japanese industry.

Following Washington's instructions, zaibatsu-style **cartels** remained intact and new ones emerged, while union rights were restricted. Public servants were forbidden to strike and Communists and left-wing trade unionists were purged from the unions and public services by MacArthur and Prime Minister Yoshida from 1950.

1950 – a turning point

The year 1950 was a great turning point for Japan. After the outbreak of the Korean War (see page 47), most of the American soldiers stationed in Japan were diverted to Korea. SCAP created a 75,000-strong 'Police Reserve', a Japanese Army in all but name. American purchases for the Korean War greatly stimulated Japanese industry (see Table 1.2), the regeneration of which was overseen by SCAP and Yoshida. MacArthur and Yoshida effectively repressed Japanese Communists in the 'Red Purge' that began in 1950. The Korean War also accelerated the process whereby Japan slowly regained international respectability. In September 1951, Yoshida signed a peace treaty and a defence treaty (the US–Japanese Security Treaty) with the United States and the US occupation of Japan came to an end.

Between 1945 and 1950, Japan had developed from defeated and hated enemy into valued friend in the Cold War. MacArthur and SCAP had remade Japan in America's image. It was a model of democracy and capitalism.

SOURCE D

From General Douglas MacArthur's farewell address to Congress on 19 April 1951 (available at www.americanrhetoric.com/speeches/douglasmacarthurfarewelladdress.htm).

The Japanese people since the war have undergone the greatest reformation recorded in modern history. With a commendable will, eagerness to learn, and marked capacity to understand, they have … erected in Japan an edifice dedicated to the supremacy of individual liberty and personal dignity, and in the ensuing process there has been created a truly representative government committed to the advance of political morality, freedom of economic enterprise, and social justice.

Politically, economically, and socially Japan is now abreast of many free nations of the earth and will not again fail the universal trust. That it may be counted upon to wield a profoundly beneficial influence over the course of events in Asia is attested by the magnificent manner in which the Japanese people have met the recent challenge of war, unrest and confusion surrounding them from the outside and checked communism within their own frontiers without the slightest slackening in their forward progress.

KEY TERM

Cartels Monopolistic associations of manufacturers.

Table 1.2 Japan's booming manufacturing industries 1947–50

Year	Value of Japanese exports of manufactured goods
1947	$174 million
1948	$258 million
1949	$510 million
1950	$827 million

How far do you agree with MacArthur's assessment of US achievements in Japan in Source D?

I sent all four of our occupation divisions to the Korean battlefront, without the slightest qualms as to the effect of the resulting power vacuum upon Japan. The results fully justified my faith.

I know of no nation more serene, orderly and industrious, nor in which higher hopes can be entertained for future constructive service in the advance of the human race.

Independence in the Philippines

In 1934 President Roosevelt had promised Filipino independence in 1946, not so much because of any anti-colonialism but because the US Congress

- considered the Philippines an economic burden
- sought to halt Filipino immigration to America and the free importation of Filipino products such as sugar, which threatened American producers.

The United States always considered itself a particularly benevolent colonial power. In 1936, Roosevelt granted the Philippines Commonwealth status under an elected president and Congress with virtually total control over domestic affairs. By 1936, most public servants were Filipino and educational standards were exceptionally high for Asia (around 50 per cent of Filipinos were literate).

However, the domination of agriculture and the political system by a small Filipino elite caused unrest in the 1930s, especially on the island of Luzon. The most densely populated of the Filipino islands, Luzon's population doubled to 1.4 million between 1903 and 1939. Population pressure created an acute land shortage and great landlord pressure for higher crop yields, leading to violent clashes, strikes, and the establishment of peasant political organisations. At this stage, the tiny Filipino Communist Party (PKP) was primarily urban and had little to do with peasant unrest.

The Japanese drove the Americans out of the Philippines early in the Second World War, but MacArthur retook the islands in August 1944. The American return was widely welcomed by the local population. The United States re-established the Philippines Commonwealth government and the Philippines became an independent republic on 4 July 1946.

Roxas and the 1946 elections

The first President of the newly independent Philippines was the experienced Filipino politician Manuel Roxas (1946–8). His election owed much to General MacArthur. As military adviser to the Filipino government in the 1930s and the liberator of the Philippines from the Japanese in 1944, MacArthur had gained Filipino respect. In 1946, MacArthur decreed that Roxas had not collaborated with the Japanese and gave Roxas access to the US Army radio network in the Philippines. Voters assumed that American soldiers on patrol were helping Roxas, but even then he won only 54 per cent of the vote.

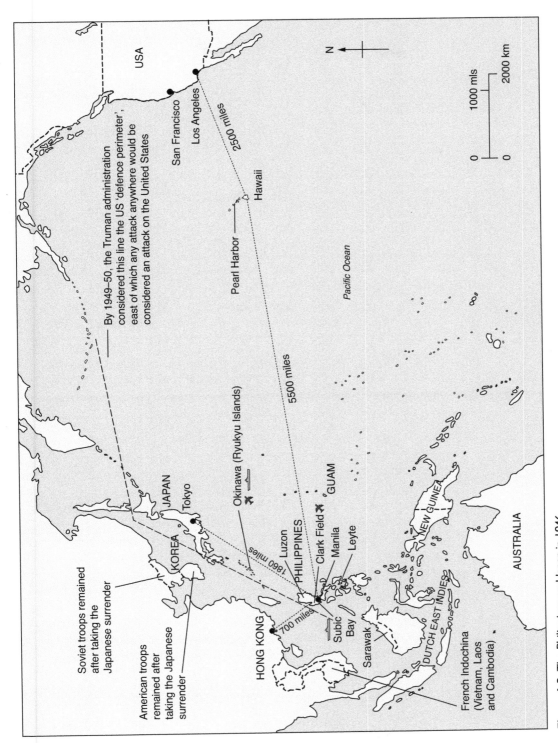

Figure I.3 The Philippines and Japan in 1946.

Soviet troops remained after taking the Japanese surrender

American troops remained after taking the Japanese surrender

By 1949–50, the Truman administration considered this line the US 'defence perimeter', east of which any attack anywhere would be considered an attack on the United States

USA

N

1000 mls
2000 km
0
0

San Francisco
Los Angeles
2500 miles

Hawaii
Pearl Harbor

5500 miles

Pacific Ocean

JAPAN
Tokyo

Okinawa (Ryukyu Islands)

KOREA

GUAM

1860 miles

PHILIPPINES
Luzon
Clark Field
Manila
Leyte

700 miles

HONG KONG

Subic Bay

Sarawak

NEW GUINEA

DUTCH EAST INDIES

French Indochina (Vietnam, Laos and Cambodia)

AUSTRALIA

Manuel Roxas

1892	Born in Capiz (now Roxas City) in the Spanish Philippines
1913	Law degree from the University of the Philippines
1919–22	Youngest ever Governor of his province
1921–38	Served in the Philippines House of Representatives (Speaker from 1922 to 1933)
1941	Elected to the Philippines Senate; liaison officer between Commonwealth government and General MacArthur
1945	Senate President
1946	President of the Commonwealth of the Philippines from 28 May to 4 July
1946–8	First President of the newly independent Republic of the Philippines
1948	Died

Background

Roxas was a member of the Filipino economic, social and political elite. His role during the Second World War was controversial: he collaborated with the Japanese occupation force but also passed on information to the Americans. General MacArthur gave him full support after the war ended so he never suffered for his collaboration.

Achievements

As the first President of the independent Philippines, Roxas gave the Americans military bases and significant economic concessions in exchange for a great deal of financial aid. His corrupt and frequently brutal government helped encourage the Huk rebellion (see page 26).

Significance

Along with Syngman Rhee of South Korea, Ngo Dinh Diem of South Vietnam and Jiang Jieshi of Taiwan, Roxas was one of several post-war US Asian allies who demonstrated US willingness to condone undemocratic but pro-American governments during the Cold War.

The US ambassador to the Philippines, Paul McNutt, told MacArthur a fair election was an impossibility in a country as venal as the Philippines and David Bernstein, an American adviser to the Philippine government, said MacArthur had brought back 'the puppet politicos and the buy-and-sell parasites' and made US policy toward the Philippines look 'stupid, irrational and cynical'. Most Americans and some Filipinos lauded the April 1946 elections, and declared the Philippines the 'showcase of democracy', but Roxas would probably not have been elected without US support. Furthermore, the traditional Filipino elite still held power, and as a result, corruption and social injustice would continue.

Roxas' concessions to the USA

As President of the Commonwealth of the Philippines (28 May 1946 to 4 July 1946) and as first President of the newly independent Republic of the Philippines (4 July 1946 to 15 April 1948), Roxas faced two massive and interconnected problems:

- the Philippines had been devastated by years of occupation and war: the capital, Manila, lay in ruins, while the agricultural areas of Leyte and Luzon were a wasteland

- the United States was willing to give aid but demanded great economic and territorial concessions in return.

To the disappointment of many in the State Department, Congress insisted upon exploiting the Philippines. In 1946, **Republican** Senator Harold Knutson of Minnesota wrote that Americans wanted 'to be helpful to the Philippine people' but that 'we have interests to look after too', while Republican Senator Robert Taft said the Philippines should be 'an American outpost in the Pacific'.

Roxas knew that the **Joint Chiefs of Staff (JCS)** gave Japan, Okinawa, Korea and Guam higher priority than any bases in the Philippines and, fearing a possible US withdrawal and desperate for American aid, he was willing to give the Americans any economic and territorial concessions they desired. While negotiating the defence treaty with the US ambassador in 1946, Roxas told him, 'You can have what you want.'

The economic concessions granted to the United States were enshrined in the Philippine Trade Act of 1946, also known as the Bell Trade Act, after Democrat Congressman C. Jasper Bell, who helped convince Congress that the Philippines should be controlled 'economically even though we lost them politically'. Under the Trade Act,

- the only foreign goods Filipinos could buy were American goods
- Filipinos could not sell any products that might 'come into substantial competition' with American manufactured goods
- quotas were imposed on Filipino products that competed with American products
- the Filipino peso was pegged to the US dollar, which protected American businessmen against currency fluctuations
- Americans shared equal rights with Filipinos over ownership of natural resources such as forests and mines.

These concessions gave the US greater economic power than when the Philippines had been a US territory. The US State Department opposed the Philippines Trade Act – one official declared it a betrayal of the US promise to grant independence. The equal rights concession particularly infuriated the Filipinos, many of whom felt that they had suffered harsher post-war terms than America's defeated enemy Japan.

The territorial concessions that Roxas granted in March 1947 were less unpopular. The United States obtained 99-year leases on 22 military and naval bases, including Clark Field and Subic Bay. These were to be sovereign US territory on which the US had the right to try Americans for any crimes and had jurisdiction over Filipinos who worked there.

While the Trade Act in particular cost the Philippines dearly, the concessions also helped trigger a rebellion.

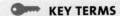

KEY TERMS

Republican Member of one of the two main American political parties; generally opposed to federal government interventionism to assist the less privileged; many in the party were 'Asia-firsters' in the Cold War.

Joint Chiefs of Staff (JCS) The heads of the American Army, Navy and Air Force.

The cost of the concessions

Roxas steered the Trade Act through a reluctant but desperate Filipino legislature two days before independence, because the Commonwealth Constitution only necessitated a straightforward majority of votes. After independence, he had to work far harder to obtain the necessary three-quarters majority in the legislature for the passage of the motion granting equal rights for Americans. He ensured this by depriving eleven opposition members of seats, claiming they had been elected through 'fraud and terror', while simultaneously allowing his own supporters, many of whom were under indictment for treasonous collaboration with Japan, to take their seats. Six of those deprived of their seats belonged to the Democratic Alliance of the **Huks**. A referendum on the issue of US parity rights was held in March 1947: only 40 per cent of Filipinos voted and Roxas made sure that most of them voted the right way. Officials threatened opponents of the amendment with reprisals and polling booths were removed from areas where there was opposition.

The most significant result of Roxas's electoral chicanery was that his refusal to allow the six members of the Democratic Alliance of the Huks to take their seats triggered a Huk rebellion.

Reasons for the Huk rebellion

The pre-war Filipino Communist Party (PKP) was small but its numbers increased during the war, when the anti-Japanese resistance on the island of Luzon was led by the PKP's Luis Taruc and his Hukbalahap (Huk) movement. By September 1944, around 10,000 Huk **guerrillas** fought the Japanese, although they were not supported by the official US resistance organisation, with whom they sometimes clashed. After Japan was defeated, the US ordered the Huks to surrender their arms and used violence against those who refused, but the Huks managed to hide and retain many of their weapons.

The Huks rebelled in mid-1946. The trigger for the rebellion was the way Roxas had deprived the Democratic Alliance of the six legislative seats, but social, political and economic inequality underlay the Huks' grievances. After the war against Japan ended, the power of the landowners was restored and the peasantry were oppressed by Roxas' Military Police, who worked closely with the US Army. The landowners and other members of the governing elite (which included many pardoned wartime collaborators) were all hostile to the Huks. The rebels also sought an end to US economic privileges.

Between 1946 and 1949, the peasant-based Huk rebellion grew. There were around 5000 guerrillas in Central Luzon by 1948. They had considerable popular support from the local peasantry. The Filipino government prolonged the rebellion by using brutal repression and refusing to deal with peasant grievances. Government troops, aircraft and artillery killed many citizens and arrested many others for supposedly supporting the rebels. With the Cold War under way, the Truman administration gave Roxas $7.2 million in military aid to combat the Communist Huks. Even then, the rebellion continued to grow, fuelled by the

- post-war economic dislocation
- domination of the political system by the socio-economic elite
- government's continued and brutal attempts to defeat the rebels.

However, although the number of Huk rebels in Central Luzon had risen to around 12,000 by 1950, they were soon defeated.

Reasons for the defeat of the Huk rebellion

The Huk rebellion was defeated because:

- The rebellion did not spread beyond Central Luzon because other regions lacked Central Luzon's tradition of peasant radicalism and high proportion of tenant farmers. Peasants elsewhere remained apathetic.
- Some Huk recruits alienated villagers with their brutality.
- The Huks had insufficient manpower and food supplies.
- The United States assisted Roxas and his successor President Elpidio Quirino with the Joint United States Military Advisory Group (it numbered 58 military men by 1952) and with over $500 million financial aid from 1951 to 1956.
- In September 1950, President **Quirino** followed US advice and made Ramon Magsaysay Secretary of the Department of National Defence. Magsaysay did sterling work in crushing the rebels.

Ramon Magsaysay

As Secretary of Defence, **Magsaysay**

- immediately persuaded the Americans to step up the financial aid
- reformed the army and revitalised its pursuit of the Huks (he decreased the brutality that had led many peasants to join the Huks and offered amnesty to guerrillas, all of which served to deplete the Huk ranks)
- convinced the government to force landlords to allow peasants to keep more of the harvest, sponsor rural development projects and give financial aid to former guerrillas to get them to settle on land away from Central Luzon
- won great popularity with the peasantry thanks to his policies, his willingness to hear their grievances, and his own simple lifestyle.

Magsaysay was the main reason for the decline of the Huk rebellion after 1950: by 1956, they were reduced to a handful of men. However, while President (1953–7), Magsaysay allowed landlord domination of Central Luzon to continue, which caused problems in the future.

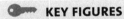

KEY FIGURES

Elpidio Quirino (1890–1956)

A lawyer who entered politics in 1919, he obtained large-scale US economic aid while President of the Philippines (1948–53) and supported the USA in the Korean War. He failed to deal effectively with the Huk rebellion and his administration was corrupt.

Ramon Magsaysay (1907–57)

President Quirino appointed him as Secretary of Defence because his experience as a guerrilla in the Second World War was useful in the Filipino government's struggle against the Huk guerrillas. Elected President in 1953, his administration (1953–7) was relatively free of corruption. Enthusiastically anti-Communist, he joined SEATO in 1954 and supported the USA at the Bandung conference.

Table 1.3 US success with the Filipino and Japanese model states

US aims	US achievements – the Philippines	US achievements – Japan
Political US aim: create a democracy	The US had excessive influence, as in the election of Roxas. Roxas was frequently undemocratic, as when he excluded eleven elected representatives in 1946. Many Filipino politicians were corrupt: an official inquiry in 1947 revealed that $300 million worth of military equipment given by the USA to the Filipino government had been stolen between 1945 and 1947. Amongst those indicted was José Avelino, Speaker of the Senate. In 1949, President Truman urged President Quirino to end corruption and mismanagement. The *New York Times* reported that an investigation into the 'disappearance' of millions of pesos of loans to tenant farmers had discovered 'no tenants and no crops, and the money could not be recovered.' Presumably the US aid had been pocketed by officials and big landowners.	Japanese elections were free and fair. Japanese governments were stable.
Economic US aim: promote capitalism so that the USA would have countries with which to trade and supporters against Communism	Due to the Philippines Trade Act, the Filipino economy was unbalanced. There was no manufacturing industry and the balance of trade with the United States was unfavourable. However, the USA profited from its economic relationship with the Philippines.	After the United States decided to revive the Japanese economy, the Korean War paved the way for a Japanese economic boom.
Social US aim: develop and share American values such as freedom and individualism	Filipino society became Americanised in its materialism and consumerism. Rich Filipino women ceremoniously served American canned fruit as a status symbol – even though the fruit was grown in the Philippines and could be obtained fresh.	SCAP introduced greater equality for women and workers, but long-standing social conservatism restricted women and SCAP turned against unions. On the day the US occupation ended, the left-wing national newspaper the *Asahi Shimbun* published a critical essay saying the occupation had made the Japanese 'irresponsible, obsequious and listless' with 'distorted perspectives' – that certainly suggested that the US had effected great changes in Japanese society.
Military US aim: create a strong anti-Communist ally for the United States	Roxas granted the US vital bases at Clark Field and Subic Bay. The Philippines remained generally pro-American and sent 7500 troops to join the UN force in the Korean War. Filipino Catholicism made great Filipino support for Communism unlikely – significantly, the Huk rebellion owed much to US pressure on Roxas and MacArthur's insistence that the Filipino elite retain their privileges.	Most Japanese were conservative and anti-Communist. The slow remilitarisation of Japan from 1950 was no threat to the USA. With memories of the Second World War still fresh, the United States did not want a huge Japanese army and did not request Japanese participation in the Korean War or the Vietnam War. What the United States wanted and got was the base at Okinawa, which was invaluable in those wars.

The Philippines and Japan – model states?

Overall, the United States was pleased with developments in the Philippines and Japan by 1950. Japan was developing into a model democratic and capitalist state, while the Philippines was half way to democracy and capitalism. Although many Asians nations mocked the Philippines as a 'poor little rich country', awash with American consumer products yet suffering an unfavourable balance of trade and much poverty, the United States got what it wanted out of the Philippines, economically and militarily.

Why had the Philippines and Japan developed so differently between 1945 and 1950? Japan was a defeated and occupied nation, so the Americans and MacArthur had a free hand and were able to introduce liberal reforms and real democracy to Japan in order to ensure that the defeated enemy would be so transformed as to never be a threat again. The Philippines had been an American colony, and in the post-war period the Philippines needed America more than America needed the Philippines. As a result, the Philippines was easy to exploit. MacArthur did not introduce liberal reforms – there was no need to transform the Philippines and the Filipino elite had been his friends since his time as military adviser to the Commonwealth government (see page 17).

US involvement with Jiang Jieshi and China

From the 1930s, the government of the US-educated Jiang Jieshi, head of the Chinese Nationalist Party or **Guomindang (GMD)**, was increasingly challenged by the slowly growing Chinese Communist Party (CCP) under Mao Zedong and by Japanese imperialism. Japan invaded China and conquered Manchuria in 1931, then conquered much of coastal China from 1937. These Japanese conquests owed much to iron and steel imported from the United States. The United States sympathised with China and attempted to halt the conquests by placing economic sanctions on Japan and giving secret military and economic aid to Jiang. Resentment at these sanctions was a major reason behind the Japanese attack on Pearl Harbor that brought the United States into the Second World War and made Jiang and the United States wartime allies.

The United States found Jiang an irritating ally because the GMD–CCP hostility weakened the Chinese war effort against Japan. Although Roosevelt publicly maintained that China was a vital ally, on a par with Britain and the USSR, aid to Jiang was in reality low on the list of US military priorities. Jiang complained that the Americans gave him insufficient aid and treated him badly. US mistreatment was evidenced by Roosevelt's willingness to hand over Chinese territories to Stalin at Yalta without any consultation with Jiang (see page 6).

While some American observers in China were optimistic about Jiang's capabilities, others were highly critical and more impressed by the Communists.

 KEY TERM

Guomindang (GMD)
Also known as the Kuomintang (KMT), the Chinese Nationalist Party was dominated by Jiang Jieshi from the 1920s.

When Roosevelt sent General 'Vinegar Joe' Stilwell to be Jiang's Chief of Staff (1943–5), Stilwell ridiculed the leadership qualities of Jiang, whom he called 'peanut', and dismissed his regime as unpopular and corrupt. Jiang hated Stilwell so Roosevelt eventually replaced him with Ambassador Patrick Hurley, who admired and praised the Nationalist leader, but still failed to persuade him to co-operate with the CCP in the war against Japan.

The United States and the Chinese civil war, 1945–9

After the defeat of Japan, the struggle between Jiang's Nationalists and Mao's Communists escalated into full-scale civil war. Initially, the US continued financial and military aid to Jiang. Two months after the Japanese surrender, Truman gave Jiang $450 million and sent 50,000 US Marines, ostensibly to transport GMD troops to take the Japanese surrender, but in reality to prevent CCP gains in northern China. Over 400,000 GMD troops were transported to north China in American ships and planes. Some US Marines even clashed with CCP troops when they protected communication lines in order to help GMD troops.

In late 1945, the Truman administration seemed on the brink of large-scale military intervention in China, but the State Department strongly opposed the idea and the American public would not have approved any reversal of the ongoing demobilisation of American troops. The disillusioned pro-Jiang Ambassador Hurley resigned, criticising the Truman administration and claiming that the State Department contained some subversive Communists. That generated Republican criticism of Truman's China policy, so Truman sent the highly respected General George Marshall to China in December 1945. Marshall organised a CCP–GMD truce, but it collapsed in April 1946 and he despaired of China. The State Department advocated totally abandoning Jiang, and arms shipments to him were halted.

The State Department believed areas such as Western Europe, the Middle East and Japan were far more important than China, but the Republican outcry about abandoning Jiang led to the lifting of the arms embargo in May 1947 and the sale of military equipment to him at a 90 per cent discount. The China Aid Act of April 1948 granted Jiang $125 million but in December 1948, the Truman administration cancelled all aid, convinced Jiang could never defeat the Communists. Republican criticisms prompted the Truman administration to produce a 'China White Paper' (August 1949) that aimed to show that even US intervention could never have saved the GMD.

A few months after the United States halted all aid to Jiang, Mao's Communist forces were triumphant. On 1 October 1949, Mao declared the establishment of the People's Republic of China (PRC), the world's second great Communist state. Jiang and the remnants of his Nationalist forces fled to the island of Formosa, now more commonly called Taiwan.

Reasons for the fall of China to Communism in 1949

After China became Communist, Republicans claimed the **Democrats** 'lost China' through Roosevelt's concessions to Stalin at Yalta and insufficient aid to Jiang Jieshi. However, more important reasons were:

- the Japanese invasion
- the Communist appeal to the peasantry
- Jiang's loss of middle-class support
- the differing military strategies and performances of the GMD and the CCP
- the leadership of Mao Zedong.

The Japanese invasion

Prior to the major Japanese offensive of 1937, Jiang and the GMD were in the ascendancy, which suggests that the Japanese played a crucial role in Mao's rise to power. The Japanese distracted Jiang: they cost him many of his best troops and much of his money, and they enabled the CCP to establish itself more fully in the countryside. Probably most important of all, the Japanese damaged Jiang's reputation as a nationalist leader who could defend China. His refusal to co-operate with the CCP when China was in mortal danger during the war against Japan made him look less patriotic than Mao.

Communist appeal to the peasantry

Mao came from peasant stock and understood and wooed the peasantry in a way that the middle-class Jiang never did. Landlords and richer peasants constituted 10 per cent of China's population in the first half of the twentieth century, but owned 70 per cent of the land. Many of the poorer peasants were forced to give between 50 per cent and 80 per cent of their crops as rent and were chronically in debt. The Communist emphasis on the equal distribution of wealth naturally held great appeal to China's poor. The importance of peasant support was demonstrated in the final crucial battle of Xuzhou (1949), in which the CCP was aided by 2 million peasant labourers mobilised by **Deng Xiaoping**.

Jiang's loss of middle-class support

Jiang Jieshi and the GMD rose to prominence on a tide of middle- and upper-class exasperation with decades of poor government. However, once in power the GMD lost its revolutionary dynamism and employed many of the corrupt bureaucrats who had served previous unpopular regimes. The GMD secret police were repressive and Jiang reneged on promises of democratic government. Many of his supporters were further disillusioned when he refused to co-operate with the CCP in the struggles against Japan and post-war economic dislocation. It was perhaps Jiang's unsuccessful economic policy that most cost the GMD middle- and upper-class support.

The printing of vast quantities of banknotes fuelled **hyperinflation**: prices rose to 6000 times the level of 1937 during the Japanese War era (1937–45). By April

KEY TERMS

Democrats One of the two main US political parties; from the 1930s, favoured increased federal government interventionism to help the less privileged.

Hyperinflation When governments print excessive quantities of banknotes, the currency can become worthless.

KEY FIGURE

Deng Xiaoping (1904–97)

One of the early CCP members, Deng Xiaoping led China from 1978 to 1992. He introduced many elements of capitalist economic practices.

1949, a grain of rice cost 2500 Chinese dollars. Jiang made no attempt to stabilise the currency, and as a result different cities had different exchange rates. The hyperinflation hit urban dwellers badly and lost him their support. His government responded by raising taxes, particularly upon the peasantry, which serve to further increase peasant allegiance to the CCP.

Jiang's Army

The GMD Army contributed to the Communist victory because:

- It was riddled with corruption, so much so that it provoked a rebellion in Taiwan in 1947. Jiang's officers sold food on the black market, leaving the ordinary soldiers underfed (their rice sacks were frequently filled up with sand).
- After years of war, Jiang lost hundreds of thousands of men through death and desertion: desertion rates often ran at 70 per cent – some GMD units had to tie up their soldiers overnight to stop them going home or joining the Communists.
- Jiang's conscription policies hit the peasantry hardest and encouraged many to switch allegiance to the CCP.
- Morale was low by the final phase of the war in 1949. For example, Jiang's generals surrendered Beijing to the CCP general Lin Biao without a fight.

Jiang's strategy and generals

Jiang made frequent, crucial strategic errors. For example, after 1946 he concentrated too many of his troops in the battle for Manchuria, without first gaining control of the parts of northern and central China that lay between Manchuria and GMD-held southern China. When Jiang's generals warned him about such dangers he refused to listen. He was always deeply suspicious of any of his generals who were too successful, but insufficiently suspicious of Communist spies in his camp, such as his Assistant Chief of Staff, General Liu Fei, who ensured the Communists knew all forthcoming GMD military movements.

The Communist military performance

Mao's 'Eight Rules of Conduct' ensured that the Communist soldiers had better relations with the peasantry than GMD soldiers had: for example, Communist soldiers were told to help the villagers, to pay for what they damaged, not to put molest women, and not to dig latrines near homes. Mao's Red Army was better at mobilising the whole population, using peasants who could not fight to help distribute propaganda.

The Communists knew better than to try to resist the Japanese head-on, relying for the most part on guerrilla warfare. Consequently, they lost fewer men than the GMD. Mao repeatedly used the effective strategy of withdrawal, enticing the enemy into over-extension of its forces in hasty and ill-judged pursuit, as in 1946.

While Jiang lacked brilliant generals and treated his best with suspicion, Mao knew when to defer to an able general. For example, in the crucial 65-day battle of Xuzhou in the winter of 1948–9, Mao's veteran commander Zhu De employed excellent tactics, but Jiang proved his strategic incompetence when he chose to attack where his forces could be attacked from three sides, lost 500,000 men, and interfered with the battle from 200 miles away because he distrusted his generals.

Mao's leadership

Probably the main reason why the Communists won the Chinese civil war was because Mao

- won more supporters than Jiang through his social and economic policies
- was more flexible than Jiang, adjusting his land reform policies in order to maximise support
- played more effectively upon Chinese nationalism than Jiang
- had a superior military strategy and trusted able generals such as Lin Biao
- seemed far more democratic than Jiang in his willingness to participate in coalitions and to listen to the people.

Mao's propaganda rightly emphasised that he was a superior leader to Jiang Jieshi.

The impact of US and Soviet intervention

Truman's Republican opponents maintained that the Communist victory was due to ample Soviet aid to Mao and to inadequate US aid to Jiang. Neither assertion was correct. Although the Soviets helped the CCP to acquire Japanese arms after the Japanese surrender in 1945, Stalin was often a great handicap to Mao. For example, in 1949 Moscow ordered the Communists not to cross the Yangtze River. Mao ignored the advice, proceeded south and finished off GMD resistance. Furthermore, the Soviet ambassador was one of the very last to recognise that the Communists were on the verge of victory in 1949, remaining with Jiang until a very late stage. Basically, Stalin remained true to his Yalta promise to support Jiang's government and he was neither keen on nor helpful to the CCP in the Chinese civil war.

The Truman administration (1945–53) always knew that nothing short of full US military intervention would save Jiang and that such intervention was not feasible because

- the American public demanded the speedy demobilisation of American troops after the defeat of Japan
- the containment of the USSR in Europe was the administration's priority between 1945 and 1949
- too many American observers considered Jiang a hopeless case.

British policies in Malaya

There was little opposition to British rule before and immediately after the Second World War. The key feature of Malayan history in the immediate post-war period was not so much the struggle for independence but rather the ethnically mixed population, which greatly affected the relationship between the colonial power and the inhabitants of the colony. Mid-twentieth-century British Malaya contained indigenous Malays, Chinese and Indians.

The Chinese and Indians had been brought to Malaya to work in the rubber plantations and tin mines and some became very successful in trade and business. Some demanded equal citizenship rights but were not granted them because pre-war British rule favoured the indigenous Malays. The British protected the impoverished Muslim Malay peasantry and many of the English-educated Malay aristocracy worked in the government. During the Japanese occupation (1942–5), the Malays remained docile, but the Sino-Japanese War (see page 31) encouraged Japanese brutality toward the Malayan Chinese. Many Chinese joined the Malayan People's Anti-Japanese Army (MPAJA). The MPAJA was dominated by the predominantly Chinese Malayan Communist Party (MCP), established in 1930. The British gave the MPAJA military support during the war and in 1945 the MPAJA did not oppose the British return. Most of the indigenous Malay population welcomed the return of the British, particularly as the British had always favoured them over the Chinese population of Malaya.

Antagonism between the indigenous Malays and the Chinese increased dramatically in 1945 because:

- the Malays did not want the Chinese to have citizenship rights because the Chinese outnumbered them (in 1947, the population of British Malaya was 43.5 per cent Malay, 44.7 per cent Chinese and 10.3 per cent Indian)
- in the Second World War, ethnic groups had competed for jobs and food and the Chinese had resented the lack of Malay resistance to the Japanese (during the last months of 1945, the MPAJA murdered Malay collaborators and Malays retaliated by attacking Chinese)
- the British now seemed more favourably inclined toward the Chinese, because they had resisted the Japanese.

The British Military Administration, 1945–6

After the defeat of the Japanese, the British Military Administration (BMA) was established in order to facilitate the return of civilian rule. Confidence in Britain was damaged by the British surrender to the Japanese and by the BMA, which failed to stop a minority of British soldiers engaging in plunder and rape, and was ineffective in handling economic problems and communal violence.

The Malayan Union, 1946–8

Keen to restore civilian rule, Britain proposed a Malayan Union consisting of the Malay Peninsula states (but not the important port of Singapore with its majority Chinese population), in which non-Malays would have equal citizenship rights. Britain made these proposals because

- a more centralised government would help revitalise the economy and prepare Malaya for independence
- Britain appreciated Chinese opposition to the Japanese occupation
- the British feared that without full citizenship, the Chinese might transfer their loyalty to China
- equal citizenship seemed to be the only way forward for a future independent Malayan state.

The Malayan Union came into being on 1 April 1946, but most Malays opposed it because it removed the powers of their traditional rulers, who had high religious, political and social status and granted equal citizenship rights to non-Malays. The British then dropped the idea of the Malayan Union because of

- mass, peaceful Malay protests against it and anxiety lest the Malays turn anti-British (in May 1946, the United Malay National Organisation or UMNO, established to oppose the Union, gained considerable support)
- the unenthusiastic Indian and Chinese response to the Union (some Chinese did not want to lose their Chinese nationality).

The British then replaced the ill-fated Malayan Union with the Federation of Malaya Agreement (February 1948).

The Federation of Malaya

The Federation of Malaya Agreement restored the power of traditional Malay rulers and made universal citizenship rights dependent upon fifteen-year residence in Malaya for non-Malays (rather than the original five years). This increased Malay support for the proposal, especially as many were growing doubtful about maintaining the British connection. For their part, the British anticipated and hoped that independence would be a long way off because the Malays were politically inexperienced and, more importantly, Malaya's tin and rubber earned the British much-needed American dollars.

The Malayan Communist uprising

The Chinese-dominated Malayan Communist Party (MCP) did not oppose the return of the British in 1945, because they had few and poorly equipped forces and the British assured them of a role in political planning. The MCP therefore collaborated in the united front policy to work non-violently for independence, but simultaneously encouraged working-class discontent about food shortages and low wages, and organised a series of strikes throughout 1946. When the BMA used military force against strikers and arrested strike leaders, the MCP backed down and focused on gaining greater grassroots support amongst the Chinese population, especially through the Chinese language schools that had inculcated Malayan Chinese nationalism since the 1920s.

In June 1948 the MCP decided on armed struggle because

- the British Administration was making life difficult for the Chinese trade unions and deporting Chinese Communist leaders
- it was inspired by the CCP's military progress in China
- MCP leader Lai Teck, who had masterminded the peace strategy, disappeared (along with the MCP funds) in March 1947 while under investigation for having worked with the British, and was replaced by more radical leaders who used his disgrace to discredit co-operation with the British
- the Federation of Malaya had restored Anglo-Malay collaboration and domination
- after three British planters were murdered by the MCP's Malayan Races Liberation Army (MRLA), the government declared a State of Emergency, under which membership of the MCP was illegal.

Initially, the MRLA had around 2300 front-line fighters (their numbers peaked at over 7000 in 1951). They used weapons that the MPAJA had not surrendered in 1945. At first, the British believed that this armed uprising was part of the Soviet-backed anti-colonial strategy because there were simultaneous Communist insurgencies in British Burma, the Dutch East Indies, French Indochina and the Philippines, but by 1951 the British concluded that the MCP had no foreign support.

Aiming to destroy the Malayan economy and the government, the MRLA targeted mines, plantations and communications, and assassinated owners, managers and members of the public. The campaigns were directed from jungle camps situated near Chinese squatter areas where they had a great deal of support. There were possibly 250,000 Chinese squatters who had fled Malayan cities during the Great Depression and now lived in the forests and in European plantations abandoned during the war.

The Emergency

Under the Emergency, the British had strong powers of arrest and large numbers of police and soldiers at their disposal. In 1948, the Communist insurgents were outnumbered by 9000 Malay police and ten British infantry battalions, who were supported in their search for insurgents by army reinforcements, armoured cars, artillery and aircraft. By early 1950, there were 16,220 police, whose performance was greatly improved by Colonel W.N. Gray. The Malay police guarded plantations and mines and protected Malay villages.

The defeat of the Communists in Malaya

The Communists were effectively defeated by 1955 and the Emergency was officially declared at an end in 1960. The Communists were defeated because of:

- government force and power
- the isolation of the MCP through economic and political concessions to other Chinese, for example, the introduction of elected local government from 1952
- opposition to the MCP amongst moderate Chinese
- the government's detention of 6343 Chinese squatters, resettlement of many in areas free of MCP influence, and repatriation of 9062 to China
- Sir Gerald Templer's counterinsurgency campaign, conducted from 1952 (his tactics included strategic hamlets, see page 127, that defended villages and cut them off from Communist guerrillas)
- Communist divisions over leadership and doctrine
- the Korean War, which generated demand for Malayan tin and rubber and caused a Malayan economic boom
- the British announcement in 1952 that independence was imminent
- Malay support for Britain, which was the main reason for the Communist defeat.

Independence

In 1957, the Federation of Malaya gained independence from Britain. In 1963, the Federation of Malaya combined with British territories in Borneo (including Sarawak) and Singapore to form the state of Malaysia (see page 3). Fear of Chinese domination led to the Malaysian parliament's separation of Singapore from the Federation in 1965. There again, as so often in post-war Malayan/Malaysian history, anxiety about the Chinese population was a major factor.

US policy and British Malaya

Events in Malaya impacted upon US policy in several ways. Some British and American historians have argued that US policy towards Vietnam owed much to Truman administration concerns about the British and Malaya. The administration believed Britain's post-war recovery depended upon British access to the natural resources of Southeast Asia, especially Malayan rubber and tin, which earned the British invaluable US dollars at a time when US imports to Britain greatly exceeded British exports to the USA.

While it is arguable that Malaya was a major cause of US entry into the Vietnam War, due to American concerns about Britain, there is no doubt that the Communist insurgency in Malaya was an important factor in convincing the Truman administration that Communism was on the march in Asia and needed to be contained.

Malaya had a further influence on US policy in that the successful suppression of the Communist insurgency impressed many in Washington and in the government of South Vietnam and encouraged them to introduce strategic hamlets. The strategy of isolating peasant villages from Communist insurgents worked in Malaya because the insurgents were predominantly ethnic Chinese who were detested by the Malay villagers, but failed in Vietnam because both villagers and insurgents were Vietnamese.

US reactions to the fall of China to Communism

The 'fall' of China to Communism dramatically affected US domestic politics. President Truman was a victim of his own 'Truman Doctrine' of 1947 (see page 13), which depicted a frightening world in which the United States faced an evil, expansionist Communist ideology. As most Americans were fully persuaded by the Truman Doctrine, many then wondered why Truman had allowed China to fall to Communism if the Communists were such a threat. Jiang was surely beyond salvation, but Republicans, exasperated by more than a decade of Democrats in the White House, made a great deal of political capital out of Truman's 'loss' of China. Republican attacks exacerbated the post-war **'Red Scare'** and contributed to great changes in US foreign policy.

As early as June 1949, the Truman administration concluded that,

> *The extension of communist authority in China represents a grievous political defeat for us … If Southeast Asia is also swept by communism, we shall have suffered a major political rout, the repercussions of which will be felt throughout the rest of the world … The colonial-nationalist conflict provides a fertile field for subversive movements, and it is now clear that Southeast Asia is the target for a coordinated offensive directed by the Kremlin.*

The combination of the

- loss of China
- Republican attacks on Truman for losing China
- Huk rebellion in the Philippines (see page 26)
- Communist activity in British Malaya (see page 34)
- Communist opposition to the colonial regime in French Indochina (see page 96)
- desire to maintain Japan as a bulwark against Communism (see page 20)

led Truman, in 1950, to get involved in the Korean War and with Jiang Jieshi's Taiwan (see page 30) and the French colonial regime in Vietnam. The memory of those Republican attacks helped ensure that subsequent Democrat Presidents escalated US involvement in the Vietnam War.

In short, China's fall to Communism brought the Cold War to Asia with a vengeance.

The occupation of a divided Korea and UN involvement, 1945–9

A small country, Korea was always vulnerable to foreign influence and domination. From the late nineteenth century, Japan controlled Korea. The Korean nationalist politician Syngman Rhee sought US support against Japanese colonialism, but when US President Woodrow Wilson (1912–21) called for the rights of people to decide their own political destiny, he meant Europeans, not Asians.

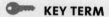

KEY TERM

Red Scare Period of anti-Communist hysteria.

Korea and the Second World War

During the Second World War, the 'Big Three' (see page 5) discussed the future of Korea after the defeat of Japan:

- The 1943 Cairo Declaration stated that Korea was to become independent 'in due course' (Roosevelt defined that as a period of up to 40 years). British Foreign Secretary Anthony Eden was cynical about the professed anti-colonialism of the Roosevelt administration. In 1943, he opined that Roosevelt 'hoped that former colonial territories, once free of their masters, would become politically and economically dependent upon the United States and had no fear that others might fill that role'.
- At Yalta in February 1945, it was agreed that post-war Korea would be governed by a four-power trusteeship (the USA, the USSR, Britain and China). Roosevelt believed this offered the opportunity for US domination and would help restrict Soviet influence in East Asia.
- At Potsdam in July–August 1945, the United States rejected Soviet proposals that a detailed trusteeship plan be drawn up, confident that the Soviets would not be able to mobilise troops in the Far East before the Japanese surrendered.

On 8 August, Stalin declared war on Japan and by 10 August, Soviet forces approached the northern part of Korea. On the same day, the US proposed the 38th parallel as a temporary dividing line between the American and Soviet armies taking the Japanese surrender in Korea. That division put two-thirds of the Korean population and the Korean capital, Seoul, under US administration. Several American officials urged Truman to send US forces to occupy the northern part of Korea, but then Stalin agreed to the 38th parallel proposal.

Plans for Korea in late 1945

Unaware of Soviet–American discussions, Koreans celebrated the Japanese surrender (15 August) and established a Korean People's Republic (KPR). The KPR included some Communists and Syngman Rhee was elected as its chairman in his absence. However, the Americans and the Soviets had different plans.

Washington perceived the KPR as a Communist-dominated organisation and ordered the head of the US forces in southern Korea, Lieutenant-General John Hodge, to ignore it. Hodge knew little of Asia and disliked Asians (he described Koreans and Japanese as 'all the same breed of cat'). He feared Korean left-wingers and favoured the conservative elite, many of whom had long collaborated with the Japanese. While Hodge used the old elites to help govern southern Korea, the Soviets purged collaborators.

At the Moscow conference in December 1945, US Secretary of States **James Byrnes** and Soviet Foreign Minister **Vyacheslav Molotov** agreed to establish a Soviet–American Joint Commission, which was to consult with Korean parties and make recommendations for a Korean provisional government that would

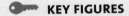

KEY FIGURES

James Byrnes (1879–1972)

Byrnes served in Congress (1911–41), on the Supreme Court (1941–2) and as Truman's Secretary of State (1945–7). After his personal relationship with Truman deteriorated, he resigned, and went on to be Governor of South Carolina (1951–5).

Vyacheslav Molotov (1890–1986)

Close ally of Stalin until they fell out in 1949; Foreign Minister 1939–49 and 1953–6. Disgraced after he opposed the repudiation of some Stalinist policies by Stalin's successor, Nikita Khrushchev.

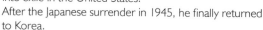

Syngman Rhee

1875	Born in Whanghae, Korea
1898–1904	Imprisoned for nationalist activities
1904–10	Lived in USA; received a degree from Princeton University
1912–45	In exile in the USA
1945	Returned to Korea; built up mass following
1948–60	Repeatedly elected President of South Korea
1950–3	Needed US/UN aid to survive North Korean invasion
1953	Hindered peace talks
1960	Resigned after demonstrations and violence; exile in Hawaii
1965	Died

Background
Rhee came from a middle-class rural family. His first occupation was journalism. Always militantly nationalistic, he organised protests against Japanese and Russian influence in the late nineteenth century. His political activities forced him into exile in the United States. After the Japanese surrender in 1945, he finally returned to Korea.

Achievements
Rhee's South Korean regime was undemocratic and authoritarian, but under his leadership, South Korea received large quantities of US aid and enjoyed economic prosperity.

Significance
As the leader of the US-sponsored state of South Korea, Rhee was an important Cold War figure. His pursuit of his ambition for a reunified Korea contributed to the US involvement in the Korean War and to the prolongation of that war. Despite his fervent anti-Communism, Rhee was a frequent embarrassment to the United States, as his government was usually unpopular and dictatorial.

KEY FIGURE

Kim Ku (1876–1949)
A long-time opponent of Japanese domination, Kim headed the China-based Korean opposition to Japan from 1927 to 1945. Upon returning to Korea in 1945, he opposed the development of two Korean states. His assassination remains a mystery.

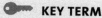

KEY TERM

Coup A *coup d'état* is the illegal overthrow of a government, usually by violent and/or revolutionary means.

work alongside a four-power trusteeship towards Korean independence within a period of five years.

Meanwhile, two esteemed and popular Korean nationalists had arrived back in Korea. Kim Il Sung arrived first, in September 1945, and received a great welcome. In February 1946 he was declared leader of an 'Interim People's Committee' that, in collaboration with the Soviet occupation force, governed the northern part of Korea and repressed non-leftist nationalists.

Syngman Rhee arrived in southern Korea in November 1945 and immediately denounced the KPR. Rhee had a rival in **Kim Ku**. Kim had led the wartime Korean Provisional Government in China, in alliance with Jiang Jieshi and the Guomindang. Kim opposed trusteeship and demanded immediate Korean independence. In late December 1945, Kim's attempted **coup** against the American Military Government (AMG) prompted Hodge to threaten to kill him. Hodge disliked Rhee but considered him preferable to Kim, so Rhee emerged as the American-backed Korean leader in the south. In February 1946, a rightist Representative Democratic Council (RDC) was established in southern Korea under the leadership of Rhee. It worked closely with the AMG.

Kim Il Sung

1912	Born near Pyongyang, Korea
1930s	Joined Korean guerrilla resistance movement against Japanese colonialism in Manchuria
1941–5	Led a Korean contingent in the Soviet Army
1945	Returned to Korea; established a Communist government backed by the USSR in northern Korea
1948	First Prime Minister of North Korea
1950–3	Invasion of South Korea triggered the Korean War; US/UN saved South Korea
1953–94	Oppressive dictator of an increasingly isolated and impoverished country
1994	Died; his son succeeded him as ruler

Background

Kim said he was born into a lower middle-class family. The family relocated to Manchuria, where he joined the CCP (see page 29) and participated in anti-Japanese guerrilla activities. He spent the Second World War in the USSR and served in the Red Army. The Soviets supported his leadership in the north of Korea from the first.

Achievements

He was a dictator who achieved a remarkable cult of personality in North Korea and ensured that his son, Kim Jong-il, succeeded him as ruler. By 1980, his North Korean state was in great economic difficulty and faced increasing international isolation.

Significance

Kim was an important Cold War figure in that his nationalism and Communism triggered off the only Cold War conflict in which the armies of two major powers (the USA and the People's Republic of China) clashed directly. After the Korean War, in which Kim failed in his attempt to reunify the peninsula, his North Korean state was a poor advertisement for Communism.

The development of two Korean states

The Soviet–American Commission met again in March 1946 but still could not agree upon a Korean government. Meanwhile, the Americans rejected Rhee's suggestion of an anti-Communist campaign in the north, but responded favourably to his suggestion of a new south Korean state. In late 1946, the AMG supervised elections for an interim assembly. Hodge appointed half of the new 90-strong legislative assembly and the AMG and the Korean police increasingly repressed southern Communists.

Meanwhile, northern Korea was developing into a Communist state in which Kim Il Sung was slowly increasing his power. Communist **cadres** indoctrinated the population and by late 1946, the press was Communist-dominated. Opposition from non-leftists and Christians was met with violence. In early 1947, 30,000 Korean Communists were sent to help the CCP in Manchuria (see page 30): the aim was to gain military experience in preparation for a war to regain southern Korea.

The Soviet–American positions on Korea during 1946–7 were clearly different and antagonistic. Within weeks of the Truman Doctrine speech (see page 13), Secretary of State **Dean Acheson** was planning the establishment of a separate South Korean government and the encouragement of the South Korean economy through large-scale American financial aid. He envisaged South Korea as being of great assistance to Japan. The Soviet–American Joint Commission

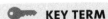

KEY TERM

Cadres Communist activists.

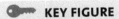

KEY FIGURE

Dean Acheson (1893–1971)

A lawyer by profession and a keen Democrat, Acheson served in the State Department under Roosevelt then under Truman. As Truman's Secretary of State (1949–53), he was highly influential in Truman's Cold War policies. He was a leading member of the 'Wise Men' who advised President Johnson on Vietnam.

met again in summer 1947, but still failed to reach agreement. In September 1947, the JCS advised Truman against keeping American troops in Korea because Korea lacked strategic significance. However, as Cold War tensions increased, Truman feared Republican criticism and damage to US credibility should the troops be withdrawn and therefore turned to the **United Nations (UN)**.

The US use of the UN

In September 1947, the United States referred the Korean issue to the United Nations, hoping to gain UN support for US policies in Korea. In November, the Americans persuaded the UN General Assembly to pass a resolution establishing the United Nations Temporary Commission on Korea (UNTCOK). UNTCOK comprised representatives from Australia, Canada, El Salvador, France, India, Nationalist China (Taiwan), the Philippines and Syria. It was supposed to observe nationwide Korean elections, but the US knew that the Soviets and North Koreans would not allow elections in the northern part of Korea. When UNTCOK was refused access to the north, the UN ordered UNTCOK to oversee elections in the south alone. Although Canada and Australia opposed this on the grounds that it would lead to the creation of two Korean states, both reluctantly remained on UNTCOK.

South Korea's first election was held in May 1948, but many leftists, moderates and even the rightist Kim Ku refused to participate (he was assassinated in 1949). These were clearly not model democratic elections. UNTCOK members could not speak a word of Korean, but nevertheless in December 1948, the UN General Assembly passed a resolution

- agreeing with UNTCOK that the South Korean elections had been free and fair
- declaring the **Republic of Korea** to be the lawful government of South Korea.

Two Korean states

Truman's containment policy had brought the authoritarian Syngman Rhee to power in a new US-dominated state that had the support of the international community as represented in the General Assembly of the United Nations. The conservative Korean Democratic Party dominated the National Assembly of South Korea, which on 15 July 1948 elected Syngman Rhee as President. South Korea, officially entitled the Republic of Korea (**ROK**), came into formal existence on 15 August 1948.

Kim Il Sung's northern regime was even more repressive and authoritarian. Elections were held on 25 August 1948 and the new state of North Korea, officially entitled the Democratic People's Republic of Korea (**DPRK**), was formally established on 9 September 1948. The Soviet occupation force withdrew from North Korea in December 1948, and the American force left South Korea in June 1949.

KEY TERMS

United Nations (UN)
The UN was set up in 1945. The 50 nations that signed its founding charter pledged to assist any other member that was a victim of aggression.

Republic of Korea Anti-Communist South Korean state.

ROK The Republic of Korea, also known as South Korea.

DPRK The Democratic People's Republic of Korea, also known as North Korea.

North Korea versus South Korea

Kim Il Sung and Syngman Rhee both sought to reunify the Korean peninsula. Each dreamt of ruling a reunited Korea. Communist guerrillas caused problems in South Korea, although all but 3000 of them were exterminated by spring 1950. Their activity prompted Rhee to ask the United States to approve an invasion of North Korea in early 1949, but the United States refused. Similarly, Kim Il Sung pressed the USSR and China for aid for a military offensive against South Korea. In spring 1949, Mao responded that he was preoccupied with the Chinese civil war for the moment, but that once it was over, 'We can throw in Chinese soldiers for you; all black, no one will notice.' Mao felt sufficiently confident of victory to allow the Korean soldiers to leave China in order to help their homeland. Stalin was far less amenable. In March 1949, he told Kim that the Americans would never abandon South Korea:

> The Americans will never agree to be thrown out of there and because of that, to lose their reputation as a great power. The Soviet people would not understand the necessity of a war in Korea, which is a remote place outside the sphere of the USSR's vital interests.

Stalin was right: the United States would stand by South Korea. Although the Americans refused to countenance an attack on North Korea, they nevertheless proceeded with nation-building in South Korea. Americans supervised the economic and military development of the new nation: 500 soldiers in the Korean Military Advisory Group trained the South Korean Army, while 2000 bureaucrats helped the South Korean regime in Seoul. If South Korea were to fall to Communism, it would damage US prestige and containment efforts worldwide. As a State Department memorandum said,

> Since Korea is another area in which United States influence should show results in the social and economic life of the country, it is important that we not let the Republic fail.

Furthermore, the United States had developed a defensive perimeter strategy in which Korea played a significant role.

Korea and the US defensive perimeter strategy, 1949

The Truman administration and the armed forces had been committed to a Pacific defensive perimeter strategy since at least March 1949, when General MacArthur articulated it. The US defence perimeter ran from the Aleutians to Japan, through the Ryukus Islands then the Philippines. In a speech on 12 January 1950, Secretary of State Dean Acheson made a public declaration of this defence perimeter strategy. Although Korea was West of the defensive perimeter, Acheson made it clear that if there was an attack on South Korea, the 'entire civilized world under the Charter of the United Nations' would aid any 'people who are determined to protect their independence.' In other words, if there was a Communist attack on South Korea, the United States would encourage and participate in UN intervention.

In what ways does Source E both suggest and not suggest that the United States would defend South Korea if it were attacked?

SOURCE E

From Secretary of State Dean Acheson's 12 January 1950 speech to the National Press Club (available from http://teachingamericanhistory.org/library/document/speech-on-the-far-east/).

The defeat and the disarmament of Japan has placed upon the United States the necessity of assuming the military defense of Japan ... in the interest of our security and ... the security of the entire Pacific area and ... of Japanese security ...

The defensive perimeter runs along the Aleutians to Japan and then goes to the Ryukyus [and] ... the Philippine Islands ... So far as the military security of other areas in the Pacific is concerned ... Should ... an attack occur... the initial reliance must be on the people attacked to resist it and then upon the commitments of the entire civilized world under the Charter of the United Nations ...

There are other problems that press, and these other problems are not capable of solution through military means. These other problems arise out of the susceptibility of many areas, and many countries in the Pacific area, to subversion and penetration ... because ... there are new governments which have little experience in governmental administration and have not become firmly established or perhaps firmly accepted in their countries. They grow, in part, from very serious economic problems ...

There is a new day which has dawned in Asia ... It is a day in which the old relationships between east and west are gone, relationships which at their worst were exploitations, and which at their best were paternalism. That relationship is over, and the relationship of east and west must now be in the Far East one of mutual respect and mutual helpfulness.

Although the foreign patrons of both North Korea and South Korea had rejected the idea of war in 1949, there were border clashes between the ROK and the DPRK after May 1949. Then, in spring 1950, Stalin agreed on a North Korean attack. The combination of

- the ambitions of Kim and Rhee
- Stalin's agreement to an attack on South Korea
- US determination to defend South Korea

made an internationalised Korean War inevitable.

Table 1.4 Western policies and East and Southeast Asia before 1950

Asian nation	Western role in government before 1941	Government 1941–5	Western role in government 1945–50	Western response to Communist activity 1945–50
Philippines	US Commonwealth	Japanese	US Commonwealth to 1946, then independence from, but concessions to, USA	US helped Philippines government crush rebellion, 1946–*c.*1956
Indochina	French colony	Japanese	French continued to rule	French struggled against Communist/nationalist uprising, US financial aid to French
Malaya	British colony	Japanese	British ruled but gave indigenous Malays some power	British and Malays crushed ethnic Chinese Communist insurgency, 1948–*c.*1955
Korea		Japanese	Soviets took Japanese surrender in north; Communist state of North Korea established (1948). Americans took Japanese surrender in south; pro-American, anti-Communist state of South Korea established (1948)	Communist North Korea and non-Communist South Korea repeatedly clashed. North Korea attacked South Korea, 1950, and US and Western allies helped South Korea in Korean War
Japan		Self-governing	US occupation	US halted Communist influence in trade unions
China	US aided Jiang Jieshi's government but Japan conquered Manchuria and coastal areas	Stayed same except for Japanese-occupied areas	US gave Jiang intermittent aid but he lost the civil war to Mao Zedong's Communists, by 1949	US gave limited aid to Jiang, but USSR less helpful to Mao

Summary diagram: US policies in Asia, 1945–50

Country	US policy	Success or failure
Japan	Create a peaceful, anti-Communist, capitalist democracy	9/10
Philippines	Ensure the independent Philippines: • gave the US military concessions • gave the US economic concessions and advantages • was anti-Communist • was a democracy • was 'in our image'	10/10 7/10 7/10 6/10 8/10
China	• Get GMD and CCP co-operation • Help GMD defeat CCP • Dump Jiang without any Republican backlash	0/10 1/10 0/10
Malaya	Hope for British defeat of Communists	10/10
Korea	• Create a strong, anti-Communist South Korean state • Gain UN support for South Korea	5/10 8/10
French Indochina	Support the French financially in their struggle against Communism	5/10

Chapter summary

Prior to the Second World War the Western powers and Japan appeared secure in their Asian Pacific colonies. However, the inevitable demise of European colonialism was evidenced when the Japanese conquered the European Pacific empires with ease and when the destruction of the Japanese empire was left to the United States.

Despite their humiliation at the hands of the Japanese in 1941–5, the European powers returned to their Pacific colonies after the Japanese surrender, but from now on the fate of the nations in East and Southeast Asia was frequently affected by US attitudes. American interest in the region was greatly increased by their rivalry with the Soviet Union, a rivalry that distorted what Roosevelt had expected to be the inevitable rise of an Asian nationalism that would force Western powers out of the region. With the advent of the Cold War, Asian nationalism became associated in Western minds with Communist expansionism and it affected Western attitudes and policies toward French Indochina, the Philippines and British Malaya.

Preoccupied by the threat from the Soviet Union and Communism, the Americans proceeded between 1945 and 1950 to create Japanese and South Korean states in their own image, to give the Philippines the promised independence while nevertheless making the new nation grant humiliating concessions, and to conclude from the Huk rebellion in the Philippines, from British struggles against Communism in Malaya, from French struggles against Communism in Indochina, and from the fall of China to Communism, that Communism was dangerously expansionist in Asia and would need to be contained there soon. As a result, in the summer of 1950, the United States entered the war against Communism in Korea. Asian hopes that there would be freedom from Western intervention had come to naught.

Refresher questions

Use these questions to remind yourself of the key material covered in this chapter.

1 Which countries had empires in the Pacific in 1939 and what colonies did they have?

2 What decisions on Asia were made at Yalta and Potsdam?

3 Why were the United States and the USSR antagonists by 1949?

4 Which diplomat was important in the development of the containment policy?

5 In which four Asian states did the USA attempt nation-building after 1945?

6 What policies did SCAP adopt?

7 How and why had US attitudes to Japan changed by 1950?

8 Why did the Huks rebel?

9 Why were the Huks defeated?

10 Why did China fall to Communism?

11 What was the US reaction to the fall of China to Communism?

12 Why was there a Communist insurgency in Malaya?

13 Why was the Malayan Communist rebellion unsuccessful?

14 How and why did two Korean states develop?

15 What role did the United Nations play in Korea between 1945 and 1949?

 Question practice

ESSAY QUESTIONS

1 Which of the following was of more importance to the United States before 1950? i) Roxas. ii) Jiang Jieshi (Chiang Kai-shek). Explain your answer with reference to both i) and ii).

2 To what extent did the US successfully create model states in Japan and the Philippines in 1945–52?

3 'The Truman administration's failure to fully support Jiang Jieshi [Chiang Kai-shek] was the main reason for the fall of China to Communism.' How far do you agree?

CHAPTER 2

The Korean War 1950–3

When North Korea attacked South Korea in June 1950, the United States mobilised the United Nations in support of South Korea. US/UN/ROK forces drove the North Koreans out of South Korea, then entered North Korea. Their invasion of North Korea triggered Chinese intervention in the war, which led to a bloody two-year stalemate until the armistice of July 1953. The causes, course and consequences of the Korean War are covered under the following headings:

★ The causes and outbreak of the Korean War

★ US and UN involvement in the war in 1950

★ Reasons for Truman's dismissal of MacArthur

★ Causes of stalemate 1951–3

★ The outcome for the participants

★ The impact of the Korean War to 1977

The key debate on *page 55* of this chapter asks the question: Who or what caused the Korean War?

Key dates

1945	Feb.	Roosevelt and Stalin agreed on four-power trusteeship
	Aug. 10	Soviet–American agreement on dividing line between their armies in Korea
	Dec.	Soviet–American talks on Korean independence began
1946		Rhee and Kim emerging as leaders
1947	Nov.	UN involvement (UNTCOK)
1948	May	South Korea established
	Sept.	North Korea established
1948–9		Border clashes. Soviet then American troops departed
1950	Jan.	Acheson's 'defence perimeter' speech
	Feb.	McCarthy's speech
	March	Stalin approved North Korean attack on South Korea
	April	NSC-68

1950	June 25	North Korea attacked South Korea
	June 27	UN Security Council resolution supported South Korea
	June 30	Truman sent US troops
	July 3	US 7th Fleet arrived in Taiwan Strait
	Aug.	US/UN/ROK behind Pusan Perimeter
	Sept. 15	Successful US assault on Inchon
	Sept. 30	US/UN/ROK troops crossed the 38th parallel
	Oct.	Chinese attacked US/UN/ROK in North Korea, soon forced retreat
1951	March	Ridgway drove Chinese from South Korea
	April	Truman dismissed MacArthur
	June	Armistice talks began
1953	July	Armistice signed

The causes and outbreak of the Korean War

▶ *Why did North Korea attack South Korea in June 1950?*

The underlying reason for the outbreak of war in Korea in June 1950 lay in the great power decisions made in the Second World War, which led to the creation of two Korean states (see pages 37–9).

The aims of Kim Il Sung and Syngman Rhee

On the eve of the Korean War, North Korea was Communist, pro-Russian and pro-Chinese, while South Korea was anti-Communist and pro-American. North Korea had been armed to the hilt by the USSR and was militarily superior to South Korea. The USA had given South Korea far less military aid because they feared Rhee might attack North Korea. The creation of two Korean nations moulded in the image of the two great Cold War protagonists made a Korean War very likely, especially as Syngman Rhee and Kim Il Sung were both ambitious nationalists. Both wanted reunification, but each wanted it on his own terms.

Rhee aimed for a reunified Korea with himself as leader. He favoured a pro-American yet independent country with a capitalist economy and 'democracy' – so long as the electorate and legislature recognised that he should rule as he pleased. Rhee sought American support for an attack on the North.

Kim also aimed for a reunified Korea with himself as leader. He favoured a pro-Soviet and pro-Chinese yet independent Korea, with a state-controlled economy. Kim believed that only one party was necessary in his Korea: the Communist Party, the party of the people. Kim asked the Soviets and the Chinese for support, advice and materiel for a North Korean attack on South Korea.

Although the USA and the USSR both refused to back an offensive by their Korean protégé, there were frequent border clashes. Most were initiated by South Korea. They began in the summer of 1948 and peaked in the summer of 1949. Thousands of Korean troops were involved in these border skirmishes. Most historians now agree that the two Koreas were already waging civil war before North Korea's invasion of South Korea led to the full-scale **internationalised Korean War**. The Korean civil war was caused by the nationalism and ambition of Kim Il Sung and Syngman Rhee, both of whom aimed for Korean reunification. It seems that Kim thought that his June 1950 invasion would inspire a popular rebellion against the autocratic Rhee.

In June 1950, the United States was convinced that the USSR and China were behind what the West perceived as an aggressive North Korean attack on

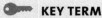 **KEY TERM**

Internationalised Korean War What began as a Korean civil war changed in nature when foreign nations joined in.

South Korea. In some ways, the Americans, Soviets and Chinese all bore some responsibility for the outbreak of the Korean War, although the most significant factor was the nationalism and ambition of Kim Il Sung and Syngman Rhee.

The US contribution to the outbreak of the Korean War

The American historian Bruce Cumings (1981) claimed the United States bore great responsibility for the outbreak of war because it supported Rhee's unpopular, authoritarian regime in South Korea. However, it could be argued that Rhee (like Kim) was initially popular but lost support through growing authoritarianism. The British historian Peter Lowe (2000) also attributed great responsibility to the United States, through what he described as an 'unquestionably foolish' combination of US statements and acts:

- In his 12 January 1950 speech (see page 42), Secretary of State Dean Acheson failed to specify Korea as one of the areas beyond the US defence perimeter that would get UN support if attacked.
- The Democrat chairman of the influential **Senate Foreign Relations Committee**, Senator Connally, made a speech that suggested acceptance of a possible Communist takeover of the whole peninsula. Rhee criticised the speech as foolish.
- In January 1950, the Republican-dominated Congress rejected a **bill** for aid for Korea. The Republicans were not opposed to aid to Korea (the bill passed in February) but were trying to make the point that they opposed the Democrat President Truman's China policy (see page 30).

These words and deeds might have suggested to some Communists that Korea mattered little to the United States and that an attack on South Korea would not be opposed. However, there is no incontestable evidence that the Soviets or Chinese knew of or paid attention to the speeches of Acheson and Connally and Republican machinations in Congress. Furthermore, Stalin and Mao had their own good reasons to assist and encourage Kim.

Soviet support for Kim Il Sung

Kim needed Stalin's approval for the invasion of South Korea because he viewed Stalin as the leader of world Communism and he wanted Soviet military aid (especially fighter planes). Throughout 1949, Stalin was unenthusiastic and repeatedly stopped Kim from attacking South Korea, probably because he feared an attack might prompt US intervention.

However, Stalin gave Kim the go-ahead in March 1950. Many reasons have been suggested for Stalin's change of mind:

- After China became Communist in late 1949, Communist parties worldwide wanted a reunified and Communist Korea. As Stalin told a Chinese visitor

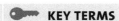

KEY TERMS

Senate Foreign Relations Committee Highly influential body of recognised specialists in foreign policy in the US Senate.

Bill In order to make a measure law, the suggested measure has to be presented to Congress. Once this bill is passed by both houses of Congress, and assented to by the President, the bill becomes an act or law.

in spring 1949, 'the centre of the world revolution is transferring to China and East Asia'. The Soviet Union needed to demonstrate its Communist credentials, lest other Asian nations looked to Mao rather than Stalin for inspiration and leadership.

- Stalin felt the establishment of the People's Republic of China and the Soviet atomic bomb test in autumn 1949 had tilted the world balance of power in favour of Communism. The Sino-Soviet alliance of February 1950 had greatly strengthened the Communist bloc and Stalin and Mao believed it would deter Western aggression.
- The Yugoslav representative at the UN said Stalin encouraged Kim in order to get the US embroiled with Communist China. With China and the United States occupied and weakened, the USSR would become more powerful. A Korean War would distract the United States from Europe and enable Stalin to feel more secure there.
- Stalin feared a resurgent Japan, which seemed to be developing from US foe to friend and was only about 100 miles from Korea. The Soviet Union and Communism would be safer if the whole Korean peninsula were Communist.
- On 28 January 1950, Stalin received intelligence information indicating that the United States would not defend South Korea if South Korea were attacked. That information might have been based upon Acheson's defence perimeter speech.
- Stalin wanted to pre-empt a South Korean attack on North Korea.
- The North Korean attack would not cost Stalin much: he warned North Korea it 'should not expect great assistance and support from the Soviet Union, because it had more important challenges to meet than the Korean problem'.

Stalin provided Kim with the tanks that were crucial to the North Korean advance in summer 1950, air support and Soviet military advisers, but no Soviet soldiers fought in Korea and the Soviet Navy remained inactive.

Chinese support for Kim

The United States believed that Moscow and Beijing colluded in the North Korean attack on South Korea. Mao feared a resurgent Japan and was concerned about American influence in Korea, which bordered China's industrial heartland in Manchuria. In spring 1949, Mao promised Kim eventual support (see page 41) and when he met Kim in May 1950, he was even more enthusiastic. He even offered to send Chinese forces to the Sino-Korean border, but Kim reportedly told him that the Koreans could take care of themselves.

However, this was neither 'Mao's war' nor 'Stalin's war'. It was Kim who persuaded and pushed until they gave him their support. Even then, Stalin's support was limited.

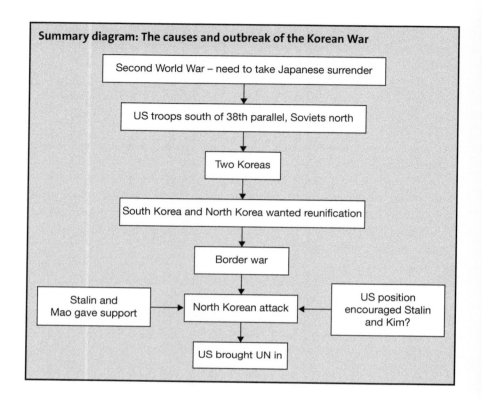

Summary diagram: The causes and outbreak of the Korean War

Second World War – need to take Japanese surrender

US troops south of 38th parallel, Soviets north

Two Koreas

South Korea and North Korea wanted reunification

Border war

Stalin and Mao gave support → North Korean attack ← US position encouraged Stalin and Kim?

US brought UN in

2 US and UN involvement in the war in 1950

▶ *Why and with what results did the United States enter the Korean War?*

🔑 **KEY TERM**

Security Council The UN chamber that contained the great powers; the other members were only represented in the General Assembly.

When North Korea attacked South Korea on 25 June 1950, UN Secretary-General Trygve Lie asserted, 'This is war against the United Nations.' At the request of the United States, the attack was debated in the UN **Security Council**. With US encouragement and in the absence of the Soviets, who were boycotting the UN in protest that Communist China had no UN seat, the Security Council passed a resolution requesting that North Korea withdraw. Two days later, on 27 June, another Security Council resolution declared that the UN should oppose North Korea.

When North Korea attacked South Korea, the USA had 500 advisers in South Korea as part of its Korea Military Advisory Group (KMAG). These advisers joined South Korean forces and civilians in such a rapid retreat that they nicknamed KMAG 'Kiss My Ass Goodbye'. On hearing of the North Korean attack, President Truman told Secretary of State Dean Acheson, 'We've got to

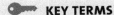

stop the sons of bitches, no matter what.' Truman responded to the 27 June UN resolution with an **executive order** authorising US air and naval forces to aid South Korea. He told the nation:

> *The attack upon Korea makes it plain beyond all doubt that Communism has passed beyond the use of subversion to conquer independent nations and will now use armed invasion and war.*

When General Douglas MacArthur (see page 17) warned Truman that without American troops the Communists would take over the whole of Korea, Truman sent US troops to Korea on 30 June and ordered the US 7th Fleet to the **Taiwan Strait**, where it arrived on 3 July. On 7 July, a UN Security Council resolution called for the creation of a United Nations Command (**UNC**) to defend South Korea. The UN asked Truman to select a UNC commander, and Truman appointed MacArthur.

Why Truman entered the Korean War

Anti-Communism underlay all the other reasons for the US entry into the Korean War. Fearful of an ideology that rejected capitalism and political democracy, Americans believed their security would be greatly threatened in a world where increasing numbers of countries went Communist. Communist nations might refuse to trade with the United States and damage the US economy, or use persuasion or force to export their ideology to other countries – including the United States and its allies.

The world balance of power

Prior to the Second World War, the USSR was the world's sole Communist country. However, as Soviet troops marched across Eastern Europe towards Germany in 1944–5, they began to create pro-Soviet regimes in Poland, Romania, Bulgaria, Hungary and Czechoslovakia. By 1950, all of Eastern Europe and the Soviet half of Germany had become Communist and disappeared behind Stalin's '**Iron Curtain**'.

US resentment and fear at the loss of Eastern Europe was exacerbated by several events that suggested that the world balance of power was tilting in favour of expansionist Communism in 1948–9:

- In early 1948, opposition to Communism in Czechoslovakia was quashed and Stalin's **Berlin blockade** blocked Western road, rail and canal access to West Berlin.
- Americans felt greatly threatened when the Soviet atomic bomb test in August 1949 ended the US atomic monopoly.
- China became Communist in October 1949. Truman had depicted Communism as a terrifying evil in his 'Truman Doctrine' speech of March 1947 (see page 13) and was now vulnerable to Republican accusations that he had 'lost China' (see page 36). This left Truman on the defensive and keen to prove his anti-Communist credentials.

- The fall of China, the North Korean attack on South Korea, and Communist insurgencies in Vietnam, the Philippines and Malaya, seemed to confirm that Communism was on the march in Asia.
- Many in the Truman administration believed US Cold War credibility was at stake in Korea. The US ambassador to the USSR, Alan Kirk, cabled Washington on 25 June 1950, that the attack represented 'a clear-cut Soviet challenge which US should answer firmly and swiftly as it constitutes direct threat our leadership of free world against Soviet Communism'.

McCarthyism and domestic political concerns

The United States was already in the grip of a 'Red Scare' when Republican Senator Joseph McCarthy declared in February 1950 that there were Communists in Truman's State Department. This generated hysterical anti-Communism and Truman feared if he were not seen to oppose the Communist threat, the Republicans might win a great victory over the Democrats in the Congressional elections of November 1950.

NSC-68

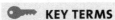

KEY TERMS

National Security Council
Established in 1947 to co-ordinate US government work on internal and external security; members included the President, Vice President, Secretary of State, Secretary of Defence, and the chiefs of the CIA and JCS.

Conventional forces
Soldiers, sailors and so on, as opposed to nuclear or high-tech weaponry.

Early in 1950 a beleaguered Truman, haunted by the Soviet bomb, the establishment of the People's Republic of China and McCarthy, commissioned the **National Security Council** (NSC) to produce a planning paper. He wanted this paper to summarise where the United States stood in relation to Communism and in which direction it should move.

NSC-68 was a classic Cold War document in that it described a polarised world, in which the enslaved (in Communist countries) faced the free (in countries such as the USA). This 68th planning paper of the NSC (hence 'NSC-68') claimed that the USSR had a 'fanatic faith' and that its leaders wanted total domination of Europe and Asia. The paper recommended:

- the development of a hydrogen bomb even more powerful than the atomic bombs dropped on Japan, so that the United States could resist Communist attempts at world domination
- the build-up of American **conventional forces** in order to defend the nation's shores and enable the USA to fight limited wars abroad
- higher taxes to finance the struggle
- alliances to gain help for the United States
- the mobilisation of the American public in order to create a Cold War consensus.

The recommendations of NSC-68 make it easy to see why the United States was ready to intervene in Korea.

Fears for Japan

The post-war American occupation had revitalised Japan, which was increasingly perceived as a potentially valuable US ally in the Cold War (see page 20). Japan was only 100 miles from South Korea and within Acheson's defence perimeter. The safety of Japan would be jeopardised in the face of a Communist Korean peninsula with Communism apparently on the march. The Defence Department told Truman that Japan was vital for the defence of the West against Communism and in June 1950, several of Truman's leading advisers said Communist control of South Korean airbases would greatly threaten Japanese security.

The United Nations and lessons from history

Collective security had been tried in the years between the two world wars in the form of the League of Nations. The League's failure was thought to have played a role in the outbreak of the Second World War. A keen student of history, Truman felt that the 1930s had taught that collective security should be supported and appeasement (as when Britain and France gave concessions to Hitler) should be avoided. The North Korean attack led Truman to believe that the League's successor was being tested: if he failed to support the United Nations and appeased aggressors, another world war might result. He was certain of support from Western allies such as Britain and France: they were anxious about Communist unrest in their colonial possessions (see pages 34 and 100) and they needed US protection in Europe.

US world domination?

From the viewpoint of the Communists (and of a few Western historians), the American entry into the Korean War was part of the US attempt at world domination. Some Western historians attribute US actions to ambitions to mould other nations in their own image (see page 15) or to ensure a capitalist-dominated world economy (see page 57).

The significance of the US entry into the Korean War

Truman took great risks in entering into the Korean War. His administration was very conscious that events in Korea might somehow lead to a third world war if the USSR and China got involved. JCS chairman General Omar Bradley was reasonably confident that they would not, but US allies such as Britain considered US policy towards China and Taiwan in 1950 provocative.

US policy toward China and Taiwan in 1950

When Truman sent American forces to Korea, he also dispatched the US 7th Fleet to the Taiwan Strait. His stationing of the fleet between mainland China and Taiwan was motivated by the US fear that a Chinese Communist takeover of Taiwan or an aggressive move by Jiang Jieshi would threaten US security, but Communist China naturally interpreted it as reinjection of the United States into the Chinese civil war. Chinese fears were confirmed when, to State Department dismay, General MacArthur made a high-profile visit to Taiwan to see Jiang on 30 July and publicly praised him. Secretary of State Dean Acheson had declared

KEY TERM

Collective security
An international system whereby all countries agree to collectively protect any one of their number that is a victim of aggression. The League of Nations served as the first worldwide collective security organisation between the two world wars, and the United Nations took up the role after 1945.

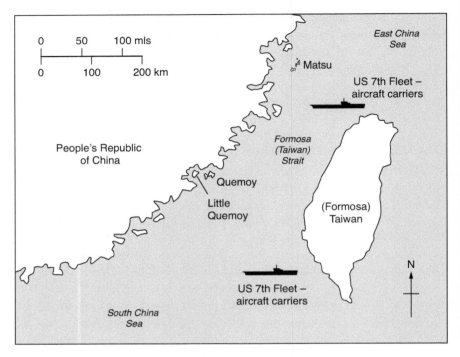

Figure 2.1 The Taiwan Strait in July 1950.

on 10 July 1950 that the US war aim in Korea was simply to restore the *status quo* by evicting North Korea from South Korea. However, the British criticised the dispatch of the 7th Fleet as constituting a US extension of the Korean War to China. Britain pointed out that the combination of the fleet deployment and MacArthur's public support for Jiang suggested that the US aimed at something more than the restoration of the Korean *status quo*. At the very least it suggested that America aimed to defend Jiang and perhaps even to promote his aggression against the People's Republic of China.

US public opinion

A second great risk that Truman took in entering the Korean War was a hostile public reaction. Initially, the war had considerable popular support. Polls showed three-quarters of Americans approved of aiding South Korea. Second World War hero General Dwight D. Eisenhower (see page 101) said, 'We'll have a dozen Koreas soon if we don't take a firm stand.' Members of Congress stood up and cheered when Truman's decision to send in troops was announced and when he asked them for $10 billion in July 1950. A *Christian Science Monitor* reporter said, 'Never before have I felt such a sense of relief and unity pass through the city [Washington].'

Despite the cheers in Congress, Truman asked Senator Tom Connally, head of the influential Senate Foreign Relations Committee, whether he needed a congressional declaration of war. Senator Connally thought not, even though Truman pointed out it was stipulated by the US Constitution. Connally said:

> *If a burglar breaks into your house, you can shoot at him without going down to the police station and getting permission. You might run into a long debate by Congress, which would tie your hands completely. You have the right to do so as Commander in Chief and under the UN Charter.*

Subsequently, however, when the war went badly, Truman's failure to get a congressional declaration of war caused him great political difficulties, and gave his opponents the opportunity to call the Korean War 'Truman's war'.

MacArthur

Another risk in entering the Korean War lay in the appointment of General Douglas MacArthur to command the **US/UN/ROK** forces in Korea. MacArthur's military record and success in Japan made him seem the logical choice, but he was potentially problematic. John Foster Dulles (see page 105), the leading Republican spokesman on foreign affairs, warned Truman that the UN commander would need tact – not MacArthur's strong point. JCS Chairman Omar Bradley considered MacArthur domineering, vain and arrogant (MacArthur was convinced that he understood what he called the 'mind of the Oriental' better than anyone else and he surrounded himself with sycophants and friendly members of the press who he could be sure would take flattering pictures of him). Truman himself had reservations: in his diary in 1945, he described MacArthur as 'Mr Prima Donna, Brass Hat', a 'play actor and **bunco man**'.

From the first, there were major tensions between MacArthur and Truman. Truman believed in containment and wanted a limited, defensive war in South Korea in order to forestall Soviet or Chinese intervention; MacArthur wanted to go all out in North Korea and, later, against Communist China.

Key debate

For roughly two decades after the end of the Korean War, American historians demonstrated relatively little interest in what some christened 'the forgotten war', 'the war before Vietnam' or 'the unknown war'. Subsequently, the war generated considerable debate – although far less than the Vietnam War.

Was it a war of Communist aggression?

For many years, the traditional **orthodox viewpoint** on the Korean War among Western historians was that it was a war of Communist aggression (especially Stalin's). Not surprisingly, this was the viewpoint presented by President Truman and Secretary of State Dean Acheson in their memoirs.

 **KEY TERMS**

US/UN/ROK The forces of the United States, United Nations and Republic of Korea (South Korea) that opposed North Korea in the Korean War.

Bunco man A con man.

Orthodox viewpoint Historians who see the Korean War as a war of Communist aggression and blame the Soviets for the Cold War have the orthodox viewpoint.

Who or what caused the Korean War?

EXTRACT 1

From Harry Truman, *Years of Trial and Hope, Memoirs by Harry S. Truman*, Doubleday, 1965, pp. 378–9.

In my generation, this was not the first occasion when the strong had attacked the weak. I recalled some earlier instances: Manchuria, Ethiopia, Austria.* I remembered how each time that the democracies failed to act it had encouraged the aggressors to keep going ahead. Communism was acting in Korea just as Hitler, Mussolini, and the Japanese had acted 10, 15 and 20 years earlier. I felt certain that if South Korea was allowed to fall, Communist leaders would be emboldened to override nations close to our own shores. If the Communists were permitted to force their way into the Republic of Korea without opposition from the free world, no small nation would have the courage to resist threats and aggression by stronger Communist neighbors. If this was allowed to go unchallenged it would mean a third world war, just as similar incidents had brought on the Second World War. It was also clear to me that the foundations and the principles of the United Nations were at stake unless this unprovoked attack on Korea could be stopped.

* The Japanese attacked Chinese Manchuria (1931); Mussolini's Italy attacked Ethiopia (1935); Nazi Germany occupied Austria (1938).

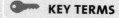

KEY TERMS

Revisionist Historians critical of US motives in the Cold War as aggressive and acquisitive. The revisionist view of the Korean War is that it was a Korean civil war.

Post-revisionist Following orthodox or traditional interpretations of an event such as the Korean War, historians usually come up with an opposing viewpoint – the revisionist viewpoint. Usually, the majority of historians will then combine the best of the orthodox and revisionist viewpoints.

Was it a Korean civil war?

In 1981, the US historian Bruce Cumings presented a **revisionist** viewpoint on the Korean War, emphasising that this was initially a Korean civil war that had been underway since violent border clashes began in 1948. The **post-revisionist** consensus that has emerged since then is that the North Korean attack was motivated more by Korean nationalism and by the desire for the reunification of the peninsula than by Communist aggression.

EXTRACT 2

From William Stueck, 'Revisionism and the Korean War', *Journal of Conflict Studies*, volume 22, number 1, 2002.

We now have a substantial body of documentation from Russia that shows Kim consulting – indeed, urging – Soviet Premier Joseph Stalin over and over again regarding an attack on the South. The first occasion was during Kim's March 1949 visit to Moscow. When Kim proposed the use of military means to unite his country, his host demurred, saying, among other things, that 'one should not forget that the agreement on the 38th parallel is in effect between the USSR and the United States. If the agreement is broken by our side, it is more of a reason to believe that the Americans will interfere.' By April 1950, Stalin had changed his mind regarding a North Korean military offensive, but he agreed with Kim's idea of commencing operations on the remote Ongjin peninsula to create uncertainty as to the initiator. Only then, with Stalin's approval and subsequent military assistance and Chinese leader Mao Zedong's blessing, did Kim proceed to launch the attack. Key elements of the attacking forces were ethnic Koreans who had recently returned from China after fighting on the Communist side in the civil war there. This evidence by no means negates the civil aspect of the Korean War: in all likelihood, Stalin would not have come up with the idea of an attack on his own, nor approved it without Kim's persistent and determined advocacy. Yet the new evidence certainly demonstrates the critical nature of the conflict's international dimension. And the explicit documentation of that dimension, even in retrospect, adds weight to the legitimacy of US intervention.

How far was the United States responsible for the outbreak of the Korean War?

Bruce Cumings and Peter Lowe emphasised that US policies in Korea after 1945 bore a great deal of responsibility for the Korean civil war and therefore for the internationalised Korean War. According to Cumings, this was partly because the United States stopped a left-wing revolution in Korea in 1945 and imposed the unpopular Syngman Rhee's reactionary regime on the south. Kim Il Sung decided that his invasion of South Korea had an excellent chance of success because of Rhee's unpopularity. Also, according to Lowe, the United States made some serious errors (see page 48).

EXTRACT 3

From Peter Lowe, *The Origins of the Korean War*, Routledge, 2014, pp. 72–4.

Dean Acheson's address to the National Press Club deeply concerned Rhee for [it] seemed to show that South Korea was expendable or, at any rate, that American intentions towards South Korea were ambiguous. Equally disturbing was the fact that the House of Representatives voted narrowly on 19 January 1950, by 193 votes to 191, to reject the administration's Korean Aid Bill … Soon afterwards an unfortunate press interview was given by Senator Tom Connally … chairman of the Senate Foreign Relations Committee … Connally did not regard Korea as vitally important to American strategy … It was unquestionably foolish to convey the impression that Korea was expendable. North Korea and the Soviet Union could only have drawn encouragement in the belief that America would most likely not act with vigour if North Korea moved against the south to reunify the peninsula.

Was it a war of US aggression?

While orthodox Western historians see the US intervention in Korea as motivated by the desire to oppose aggression, revisionist historians attribute the US intervention to more selfish motives, such as the desire to promote American political and economic hegemony. That hegemony required a massive increase in US defence expenditure and, amongst other things, the rebuilding of the Japanese economy. Revisionists often emphasise Dean Acheson's need for a crisis such as the Korean War to persuade Americans to finance increased defence expenditure, and also his economic concerns. In contrast, Acheson himself emphasised that US intervention was motivated by concern for 'the security of American-occupied Japan' and the damage to 'the power and prestige of the United States' that would be done if America were not to live up to 'our internationally accepted position as the protector of South Korea'.

EXTRACT 4

From Bruce Cumings, *Still the American Century*, British International Studies Association, 1999.

The war in Korea was the lever ('Korea came along and saved us', in Acheson's famous words) through which Washington finally found a reliable method that would pay the bills for hot and cold wars on a global scale … For Acheson, however, the struggle with Communism was but one part, and the secondary part, of a project to revive the world economy from the devastation of the global depression and World War II … The Korean War, seen by North Koreans as a war of national liberation in the face of American attempts to re-stitch South Korea's economic linkages with Japan, turned into the crisis that built the American national security state and pushed through the money to pay for it.

> ? How far do Extracts 1–4 agree on the reasons for the outbreak of the Korean War?

US/UN/ROK retreat, June–September 1950

With the advantage of surprise, the North Korean forces quickly took the South Korean capital, Seoul, and drove South Korean and American forces into retreat. The main reason for the retreat of the South Korean and American forces in June and July 1950 was unpreparedness.

Some revisionist historians have claimed that the South Koreans' rapid retreat in summer 1950 was due to the unpopularity of Syngman Rhee's regime, but their poor initial performance was due primarily to the shortage of heavy artillery pieces and the lack of tanks. US military planners had previously decided that the mountains and rice paddies of Korea made the Korean landscape unsuitable for tanks, so none had been given to Syngman Rhee (see page 39). Without tanks of their own, the South Koreans and then the Americans struggled in the face of the North Korean Soviet-built T-34 tanks.

The US Army was equally unprepared. Rapidly run down after the Second World War, it had gone soft on occupation duty in Japan. Official US Army historian Roy Appleman said the occupation divisions 'were not trained, equipped or ready for battle', and that 'the great majority of the enlisted men were young and not really interested in being soldiers'.

Early in the war, co-ordination between the air force and troops on the ground was very poor and an American soldier wounded by an attack by his own air force asked, 'What kind of screwy war is this?'

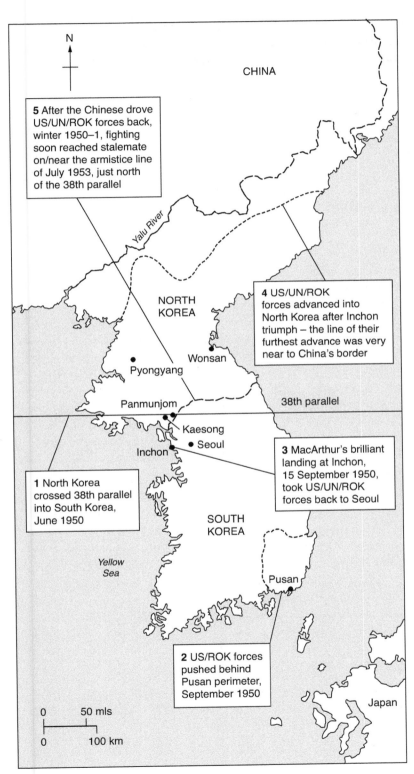

Figure 2.2 The course of events in Korea in 1950.

CHINA

N

5 After the Chinese drove US/UN/ROK forces back, winter 1950–1, fighting soon reached stalemate on/near the armistice line of July 1953, just north of the 38th parallel

Yalu River

NORTH KOREA

4 US/UN/ROK forces advanced into North Korea after Inchon triumph – the line of their furthest advance was very near to China's border

Wonsan

Pyongyang

Panmunjom

38th parallel

Kaesong

Seoul

Inchon

3 MacArthur's brilliant landing at Inchon, 15 September 1950, took US/UN/ROK forces back to Seoul

1 North Korea crossed 38th parallel into South Korea, June 1950

SOUTH KOREA

Yellow Sea

Pusan

2 US/ROK forces pushed behind Pusan perimeter, September 1950

Japan

0   50 mls

0   100 km

Study Source A. What did Michaelis see as the weaknesses of the American Army in 1950?

From Lieutenant Colonel John 'Iron Mike' Michaelis's 1950 interview with the *Saturday Evening Post*, quoted in Max Hastings, *The Korean War*, Simon & Schuster, 1987, p. 267.

When they [American soldiers in Korea] started out, they couldn't shoot. They didn't know their weapons. They have not had enough training in plain-old-fashioned musketry. They'd spent a lot of time listening to lectures on the difference between Communism and Americanism and not enough time crawling on their bellies on manoeuvres with live ammunition singing over them … The US Army is so damn roadbound that the soldiers have almost lost the use of their legs. Send out a patrol on a scouting mission and they load up in a three-quarter ton truck and start riding down the highway.

Morale

American morale was high at first: 'We thought they would back off as soon as they saw American uniforms', said one soldier. General George Barth said the US troops had 'overconfidence that bordered on arrogance'. However, American confidence was soon dissipated as the US forces failed to halt the North Korean tanks. The retreat became chaotic, and inexperienced American troops frequently fled, a phenomenon that became known as **'bugout fever'**. In this humiliating retreat in summer 1950 and then as the war dragged on (see page 78), there was little to motivate the Americans who fought in Korea. Retreat and fighting a limited war against an ideological enemy in a faraway country made it difficult to maintain morale. There had been no attack on American soil, as at Pearl Harbor, nor were there strong ancestral links to Korea as there had been for many Americans fighting in Europe in the Second World War.

Morale was further damaged when Americans found what Colonel Paul Freeman called 'this God-awful country' a particularly unpleasant place in which to fight. In August the temperature was over 38°C, which accentuated the smells that characterised Korea, such as the *kimchi* (fermenting cabbage) buried along the roadsides and the 'honey wagons', ox-drawn carts of human excrement used to fertilise Korean rice paddies. Thirsty American soldiers, ignorant of Korean agricultural methods, drank water from those rice fields, and caught chronic dysentery. Unable to tell who was North Korean or South Korean or, later, Chinese, **GIs** began to call all Asians 'gooks', from the Korean word for 'Korean people', *han'guk saram*. The word 'gooks' began to take on an increasingly derogatory tone.

At first then, the only things that inspired many American soldiers were the determination to stay alive and not to let their fellow American soldiers down.

 **KEY TERMS**

Bugout fever The tendency of inexperienced and frightened American troops to flee the battlefield out of formation in the early days of the Korean War.

GIs US soldiers were issued with certain equipment by their superiors. 'GI' stood for 'government issue' and was used to describe American soldiers.

'There will be no more retreating'

With battle-hardened divisions who had participated in the Chinese civil war, the North Koreans proved a tough enemy. From the first there was great American bitterness about North Korean tactics and atrocities. For example, the North Koreans hid soldiers among streams of South Korean civilians fleeing southward from the North Korean advance. That tactic enabled the North Koreans to get behind the US defences and fire at unsuspecting Americans, often using South Korean refugees as human screens from behind which they could throw hand grenades.

The fighting was brutal and the number of casualties very high. For example, in late July, the US **ground commander**, the experienced and aggressive Major General Walton 'Bulldog' Walker, had to make a stand at Taejon, because it had an airstrip and was the hub of roads that were desperately needed to cope with the men and equipment pouring in from Japan. Of the 4000 Americans who fought at Taejon, one in three ended up dead, wounded or missing.

During August 1950, the retreating US and ROK troops were pinned behind the **Pusan Perimeter**, an area 100 miles by 50 miles in the southeastern corner of the Korean peninsula, within which were the only remaining port and airfield for the US to land more troops and supplies. 'There will be no more retreating', Walker told his troops.

Luckily for the Americans, the North Koreans also had problems by late August. They were outnumbered (they had lost 58,000 men in their charge to the south) and down to around 40 tanks. The Americans still controlled the skies and seas, and North Korean supply lines were overstretched. Within the Pusan Perimeter, the North Koreans could not use their favourite tactic of flanking the enemy, because the Americans and South Koreans were bordered by the sea to the south and the east. The Americans and South Koreans now had less territory to defend and more troops with which to defend it. Furthermore, the arrival of six US tank battalions soon made a massive difference.

The Inchon landing

By September the United States had suffered 8000 casualties, and although 50 countries had pledged some kind of support, only the British had arrived. The military situation naturally aroused doubts back home as to the wisdom of the involvement, but supporters of the war remained in the majority in Washington. Then, on 15 September 1950, the military situation was suddenly and miraculously revolutionised by a stroke of MacArthur genius. Against the advice of other military experts, MacArthur undertook what proved to be a highly successful assault on Inchon.

In September 1950, MacArthur advocated a landing 200 miles behind the North Korean lines at Inchon. Generals, admirals, staff officers and the JCS produced countless objections (for example, Inchon had no beach, just a 15-foot sea wall

KEY TERMS

Ground commander While MacArthur was in charge of US forces in the Pacific, Walker then Ridgway commanded the American troops in Korea.

Pusan Perimeter The area on the southeastern corner of the Korean peninsula, into which the US/UN/ROK forces were forced in the early weeks of the Korean War.

that would need to be scaled or blown up), but MacArthur contended that the 'impracticalities involved will tend to ensure for the element of surprise', won the backing of President Truman and the assault went ahead.

MacArthur was lucky. Despite every South Korean and American seeming to know and talk freely about the landing, the North Koreans were still taken by surprise and Inchon was soon taken. One nervous Marine had reported the smell of poisonous gas, but it turned out to be Korean garlic.

As the Americans who had landed at Inchon advanced towards Seoul, other Americans and South Koreans worked their way out of the Pusan Perimeter by late September. By now, they had been joined by some British troops. As the US/UN/ROK forces advanced from behind the Pusan Perimeter, they came across more North Korean atrocities, including two American **POWs** who had been put into shallow trenches, and shot and buried there. The two Americans pretended to be dead, and were buried alive, but they punched air holes in the soil above them and waited until they were rescued.

MacArthur retook the South Korean capital, Seoul, and on 27 September ceremoniously handed the capital building over to a grateful Syngman Rhee. Rhee thanked MacArthur profusely on behalf of the South Korean people for saving their nation, saying, 'We love you.' Inchon had proved MacArthur right. His triumph would have dramatic political and military implications in the months to come.

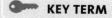

KEY TERM

POWs Prisoners of war.

A US or UN war?

There is much evidence that the Korean War was a UN war. One of President Truman's declared aims was to support the UN and he had the support of the Security Council and the General Assembly. He frequently maintained that the Korean War was a UN war or UN 'police action', and American troops painted 'Harry's police' on the sides of their tanks and jeeps. The pronouncements of the Truman administration and official UN statements all claimed that this was a UN war.

The contributions of UN members

Fifteen other members of the United Nations fought alongside the American and South Korean troops: Britain, Australia, New Zealand, South Africa, Canada, France, the Netherlands, Belgium, Colombia, Greece, Turkey, Ethiopia, the Philippines, Thailand and Luxembourg. Roughly 4000 of their soldiers died in Korea. Other UN members helped in different ways. For example, India, Italy, Norway, Denmark and Sweden sent medics, while Chile, Cuba, Ecuador, Iceland, Lebanon, Nicaragua, Pakistan and Venezuela sent food and economic aid. Panama provided transportation. On the other hand, as the Soviets always said, the 'UN' efforts in Korea were triggered and dominated by the Americans.

The United States and South Korea provided 90 per cent of the fighting men, and although the UN asked that the UNC commander have direct access to the UN, Truman insisted that MacArthur communicate only with Washington. Furthermore, there was disagreement among America's allies over many issues on which the US acted without reference to anyone else. For example, Britain and Canada were critical and anxious over:

- the dispatch of the US 7th Fleet to the Taiwan Straits, which they viewed as America reinjecting itself into the Chinese civil war (see page 30)
- the US decision to cross the 38th parallel (see page 64), which they considered a threat to the moral superiority of the UN
- American talk of using atomic weaponry in Korea (see page 69)
- the May 1953 American bombing of North Korean dams and irrigation systems, which adversely affected civilians.

There is no doubt that throughout the war the US always did what it wanted to do, usually without reference to the UN and its allies. Significantly, Truman had shown little interest in the UN prior to the Korean War, only using it to legitimise elections in South Korea (see page 40).

UN co-ordination problems

In some ways, MacArthur's refusal to deal with the UN is understandable, as there were difficulties enough in co-ordinating the war effort. Around 40,000 troops from other UN countries joined American troops in Korea and communications between forces of different nationalities proved difficult. Some of the problems were simply irritating. General Matt Ridgway recalled:

> … a thousand petty headaches. The Dutch wanted milk where the French wanted wine. The Muslims wanted no pork and the Hindus no beef. The Orientals wanted more rice and the Europeans more bread. Shoes had to be extra wide to fit the Turks. They had to be extra narrow and short to fit the men from Thailand and the Philippines. Only the Canadians and Scandinavians adjusted easily to United States rations and clothes.

However, other problems were more serious. For example, a British brigade took a hill, then called for an American air strike against North Korean positions. The British identified themselves with white panels on the ground, but the North Koreans did that too, so the Americans bombed the British. American **'friendly fire'** caused 60 British casualties. There were further communication problems when the British Commonwealth Brigade tried to free some ambushed Americans: the Americans did not know the British radio frequency. While the Americans and British just about spoke the same language (in the rapid retreat of late November 1950, the British did not know that the American phrase 'haul ass' translated as 'retreat fast'), the Turks could not understand what the US commanders were telling them and sometimes captured South Koreans instead of Chinese.

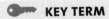 **KEY TERM**

Friendly fire When a force's own side or an ally fires on the force by mistake.

The US/UN/ROK crossing of the 38th parallel and advance to the Yalu River

The United States had declared its war aim to be the restoration of the Korean *status quo*. However, the UN had declared its war aim to be, 'To repel armed invasion and restore peace and stability in the area', wording sufficiently vague to give respectability to the US/UN/ROK crossing of the 38th parallel into North Korea on 30 September. The US/UN/ROK now aimed to destroy the North Korean forces and to reunify the Korean peninsula. Indeed, South Korean forces did not wait for UN approval before crossing. 'We will not allow ourselves to stop', said Syngman Rhee.

There were several reasons why US/UN/ROK war aims changed in September 1950 from the restoration of the *status quo* in Korea to the destruction of North Korea:

- After Inchon and retaking Seoul, military momentum and a surge of optimism made most Americans and South Koreans consider stopping at the 38th parallel ridiculous and certain to damage their national morale.
- Americans and South Koreans sought revenge against the North Korean aggressor: there had been so many casualties and North Korean atrocities had been well publicised.
- Syngman Rhee and General MacArthur were desperately keen to reunify the Korean peninsula. Subsequently, when the invasion of North Korea went wrong, the Truman administration 'tried to deflect blame' (historian James Matray, 2002) by emphasising MacArthur's role in changing the war aims. MacArthur's advice was certainly taken very seriously, especially after his Inchon triumph.
- Republican attacks for his 'loss' of China (see page 51), coupled with the McCarthy scare (see page 52), made Truman anxious to maintain his anti-Communist credentials. If he were seen to be failing to push home the advantage against the Communists, it might adversely impact upon Democratic candidates in the forthcoming congressional elections.
- The war had come to represent US determination to stand up to Communism. It was felt that American credibility and prestige would be best served by the defeat of North Korea.

The new war aims caused problems. First, although the UN approved the decision to invade North Korea, some American allies were unenthusiastic. For example, Britain felt that while the initial aim (the restoration of the *status quo*) was clearly defensive, this new aim (the destruction of North Korea) could be perceived as aggressive. A minority in Washington were also unhappy. For example, George Kennan (see page 12) recommended that the US get out of Korea as soon as possible because Korea was not that important and the US could get into trouble there.

Second, MacArthur's orders were not very clear during September and October. On 27 September, the JCS gave him a modified version of a UN Security Council resolution, which said his military objective was 'the destruction of the North Korean Armed Forces' and authorised him to conduct military operations in North Korea. On 29 September, new Secretary of Defence George Marshall told MacArthur, 'We want you to feel unhampered tactically and strategically to proceed north of the 38th parallel', but Truman ordered that only South Korean forces were to be used near the Chinese border. A UN resolution of 7 October, passed by a margin of 45 to 7, said, 'all appropriate steps [should] be taken to ensure conditions of stability throughout Korea', but there was no clarification of 'appropriate steps'.

As yet though, MacArthur was optimistic. At a 15 October meeting on Wake Island, a US base in the middle of the Pacific Ocean, MacArthur assured Truman, 'Formal resistance will end in North and South Korea by Thanksgiving [23 November].' He said there was 'very little' chance of Chinese or Soviet intervention, and that if the Chinese did intervene, they would not fight very well anyway. MacArthur's optimism seemed justified: on 19 October, American and South Korean forces 'liberated' the North Korean capital, Pyongyang. This was the first (and last) time a Communist capital was liberated by the West in the Cold War and MacArthur's reputation soared further.

On 24 October, MacArthur reversed Washington's orders that only ROK forces should operate near the Chinese border and US forces headed for the Yalu River, the border between North Korea and China. MacArthur said this was a military necessity, but it represented a great change in US policy. The JCS said it was 'a matter of concern', but did not stop him. 'It was really too late', said Bradley (see page 55). It was at this point that the Chinese stealthily moved 150,000 men into North Korea.

Chinese intervention in Korea and its impact

Soon after Inchon, the Communist position had so deteriorated that Stalin was considering whether to abandon North Korea or to encourage Chinese intervention. He chose the latter. The Chinese proved willing to intervene because the triumphant Americans had dramatically changed their war aims. On several occasions the Chinese warned the United States that if American troops crossed the 38th parallel, China would intervene in the war. Truman ignored those warnings.

Why China intervened

Without access to Chinese sources, Western historians found it easy to believe the contemporary Chinese diplomats who said that Chinese intervention was motivated by security reasons:

- the US had sent the 7th Fleet to Taiwan
- MacArthur had defied orders that said he should not send US troops too close to the Yalu River
- MacArthur had publicly declared his support for Jiang and his opposition to Communist China.

However, Chinese historians such as Chen Jian (2001), Zhang Shu Guang (1995) and Shen Zhihua (2000), with unprecedented access to their national archives, emphasised factors other than security:

- China traditionally believed that it was a superior power, to which others (including Korea) were supposed to defer. After China had been exploited, dominated and humiliated by other countries during the nineteenth and early twentieth centuries, the Korean War offered an opportunity for China to re-establish its prestige and status on the world stage.
- When the Communists fought the Nationalists in the Chinese civil war, North Korea had sent thousands of soldiers to help, so Mao felt an obligation to help North Korea.
- Stalin pressed and encouraged Mao to enter the war, probably because he knew that a **Sino-American** conflict would strengthen his position in relation to both of them. China would rely on Soviet financial and material aid, and China and the United States would be weakened by the conflict. Entering the Korean War was not a decision that was taken lightly. Mao had a very difficult job in obtaining **politburo** unanimity, as the new Communist regime had only recently been established.

It would soon become clear that China's entry into the war would greatly change its course and consequences.

The impact of China's entry

When US/ROK forces reached the Yalu River, the Chinese sent 150,000 men into North Korea. The US was blind to all the signals:

- On 12 October, despite Chinese troop movements to the border and statements and charges of border violations, the **CIA** said 'there are no convincing indications of an actual Chinese Communist intention to resort to full-scale intervention in Korea'.
- American air surveillance struggled to detect Chinese troop movements, because they marched overnight, had no cumbersome artillery and very few trucks, and used mountain trails, not roads.
- When Walton Walker (see page 61) was faced with the first Chinese POWs, he thought they were Chinese who lived in Korea: 'After all, a lot of Mexicans live in Texas.'

The battle-hardened Chinese troops, who had fought a bitter civil war for many years, proved to be formidable opponents.

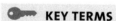

KEY TERMS

Sino-American Chinese–American.

Politburo The Chinese Communist government's equivalent of the British or US cabinet.

CIA The Central Intelligence Agency was established in 1947; it was responsible for collecting and evaluating intelligence data for the US federal government.

MacArthur's response

On 1 November, the Americans, already surprised to find themselves having to build defensive lines, found themselves surrounded by Chinese, some of whom marched into the middle of American positions wearing ROK clothing discarded in the rapid South Korean retreat in the face of the Chinese advance.

Despite JCS opposition, MacArthur persuaded Truman to allow him to bomb the Yalu bridges in order to halt the Chinese troops at the Chinese border, but after one month of bombing, only four of the twelve bridges had been destroyed and by then the Yalu River was frozen and the Chinese just walked across it. Persuading himself that the Chinese were in retreat, MacArthur decided that a big offensive would end the Korean War. He wanted it to begin on 15 November, but General Walker knew he had insufficient supplies. The attack was therefore delayed until 25 November, but even then Walker's forces remained short of ammunition, winter equipment and rations. MacArthur talked of getting American boys back home by Christmas but made speedy victory unlikely when he broadcast the battle plan on Armed Forces Radio. That infuriated his commanders and made the Chinese task a lot easier. In the broadcast, MacArthur reiterated US war aims.

Looking back on the failed offensive, Acheson explained that although the President's advisers knew that MacArthur should have been restrained, they did nothing, because 'It would have meant a fight with MacArthur, charges by him that they had denied his victory.'

US/UN/ROK retreat, November 1950

Although Truman tried to reassure the Chinese that there was no threat to Chinese territory, the Chinese thought otherwise and took advantage of the November delay to prepare an offensive. Faced with 300,000 Chinese and 100,000 North Koreans, the 270,000 US/UN/ROK forces were outnumbered. They were also out-generalled, as when the Chinese pretended to retreat then awaited them with eager anticipation. The Chinese believed that:

> [American] infantry is weak. Their men are afraid to die … They depend on their planes, tanks and artillery … Their habit is to be active during the daylight hours. They are very weak at night … When transportation comes to a standstill, the infantry loses the will to fight.

The Chinese considered the South Koreans even weaker than the Americans, describing them as puppets 'deficient' in warfare. As a result, the Chinese focused their attack on the South Koreans and opened up the UN lines. MacArthur now admitted that he faced 'an entirely new war', an 'undeclared war by the Chinese', which necessitated more US forces. Colonel Paul Freeman said the Chinese were 'making us look a little silly in this God-awful country'.

The American troops in that 'God-awful country' were astounded by the North Korean winter, which had arrived before the US/UN/ROK forces received the proper winter clothing. It was sometimes –30°C and motor oil and weapons frequently froze. Warming tents had to be used to defrost the men before they were sent out into the cold again. Hair oil and urine kept frozen rifles going some of the time. Plasma froze in the tubes of the medics, who had to dip their fingers into patients' blood in order to keep their hands warm. 'The only way you could tell the dead from the living was whether their eyes moved. They were all frozen stiff as boards', said one American surgeon. The Chinese suffered even more. Many froze to death in their foxholes. One Chinese officer was surprised to see thousands of snowmen on the horizon: on closer inspection, they turned out to be entire platoons of Chinese soldiers who had frozen to death on the spot.

Frozen Chosin

One of the hardest fought battles was waged by 25,000 Americans surrounded by 120,000 Chinese in the mountains of North Korea, near the Chosin Reservoir. Their chief of staff criticised the 'insane plan' that had sent them there. One captain felt as if they had run 'smack into what seemed like most of the Chinese from China. I always wonder why they sent us up into all that.' US air supremacy saved many American lives at 'frozen Chosin', but twelve GIs were burned by **napalm** dropped from their own planes. 'Men all around me were burned. They lay rolling in the snow. Men I knew, marched and fought with begged me to shoot 'em. I couldn't', said one private. In one division, 'Many were crying and hysterical. Some were sick and vomiting. Some had so many wounds you could hardly touch them.' Of the 25,000 American troops who fought in the Chosin Reservoir campaign, 6000 were killed, wounded or captured, while 6000 others suffered from severe frostbite. This 50 per cent casualty rate was far higher than that of the Second World War. Survivors of 'frozen Chosin' told the American press the Chinese burned wounded POWs alive and danced around the flames, then bayoneted others who tried to surrender.

The US/UN/ROK retreat would have been even worse without their superior mobility. The Chinese were on foot and could not keep up with the pace of the retreat, which the Americans christened 'the big bugout'. Colonel Freeman was despondent:

> Look around here. This is a sight that hasn't been seen for hundreds of years – the men of a whole United States Army fleeing from a battlefield, abandoning their wounded, running for their lives.

However, General Oliver P. Smith scolded the press when they used the word 'retreat': 'We are not retreating. We are merely attacking in another direction.'

KEY TERM

Napalm Flammable liquid used in warfare.

SOURCE B

A group of Marines struggling through the snow at Chosin Reservoir in 1950, carrying a wounded colleague to be flown from the battle zone for medical treatment.

> What can you infer from Source B about the physical difficulties facing forces in Korea?

Western divisions

The Chinese intervention and subsequent US/UN/ROK retreat gave Truman several great problems in late 1950:

- His poll ratings were falling and his Democratic Party suffered losses in the November 1950 elections.
- Washington was in a state of panic: the JCS feared a Soviet attack in Europe, and on 15 December 1950, Truman declared a state of national emergency.
- When Truman told a press conference he had 'always' considered using atomic weapons in Korea, and that 'the military commander in the field will have charge of the use of weapons, as he always has', British Prime Minister Clement Attlee (see page 7) rushed to Washington, fearful that MacArthur had his finger on the nuclear button. Truman had to hastily reassure everyone that he was in ultimate control of the use of all weapons.
- General MacArthur was publicly critical of his policies.

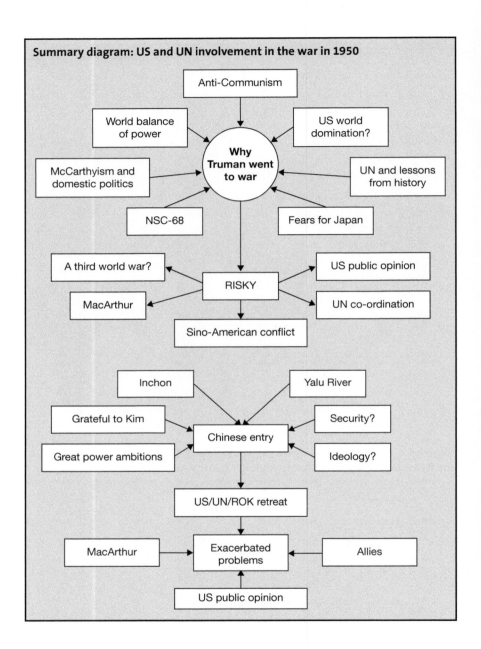

Summary diagram: US and UN involvement in the war in 1950

3 Reasons for Truman's dismissal of MacArthur

▶ *Why did President Truman dismiss General MacArthur?*

Instead of being 'home for Christmas', as MacArthur had promised, the forces of the United States and its allies were once more behind the 38th parallel by early December 1950. The US/UN/ROK forces had abandoned Pyongyang, and MacArthur seemed to be a beaten general. One of his officers wrote home that 'when a gambler pulls one off', as MacArthur had at Inchon, 'he is hailed as a genius, and when he fails, he is a bum. This time,' the officer opined, MacArthur had 'failed and he has to take the consequences of failure as I see it.'

MacArthur blamed everyone but himself for the US/UN/ROK retreat. Full of complaints in the winter of 1950–1, he

- insisted in vain that he should be allowed to use atomic weapons
- repeatedly demanded more troops, but none were available in the US or in any other UN nation
- wanted to use Jiang Jieshi's forces, but Washington did not want to crank up the war with China and Jiang's army had already been bested by Mao's in the Chinese civil war
- complained that he was having to fight with 'an enormous handicap … without precedent in military history' when denied permission to bomb Chinese territory.

SOURCE C

From the writings of Harry Truman, published in *Life* magazine, 13 February 1956, pp. 68 and 71.

I should have relieved General MacArthur then and there. The reason I did not was that I did not wish to have it appear as if he were being relieved because the offensive failed. I have never believed in going back on people when luck is against them, and I did not intend to do it now. Now, no one is blaming General MacArthur, and I certainly never did, for the failure of the November offensive … [But] I do blame General MacArthur for the manner in which he tried to excuse his failure.

Why, according to Source C, did Truman sack MacArthur?

The Chinese offensive of the late 1950s greatly shocked both MacArthur and those under his command but the early months of 1951 saw great changes that led to a US/UN/ROK revival and the dismissal of MacArthur. The revival was due not to MacArthur but to Chinese errors and to the new US ground commander, Matt Ridgway.

Table 2.1 Assessing MacArthur

Positives	Negatives
Usually praised as a Second World War hero	Accused of waging 'war by remote control' in Korea (he spent most of the war in Japan)
Success with SCAP and still responsible for Japan throughout the Korean War	Did not relieve ineffective officers in Korea
Brilliant success at Inchon	Overconfident that the Chinese would never intervene in Korea then mismanaged their onslaught
Truman chose and retained him (on his desk, Truman had a sign saying, 'The buck stops here')	Too old by Korea (over 70 years)
Confused orders from Washington to Korea (during October 1950, he was ordered not to use US troops near the Chinese border, but he was also told by Secretary of Defence George Marshall that he could do as he liked)	Too powerful: his great prestige, his command of US forces in the Pacific, his role in Japan and his command of UNC combined to make it difficult for any politician or military leader to oppose him, and help to explain the Truman administration's ambiguity in handling him and MacArthur's own temerity in publicly attacking the President's wartime policies

Ridgway's brilliance

Just before Christmas 1950, Walton Walker presented a Silver Star medal to his soldier son. Hours later, Walker was killed when his jeep collided with a truck (Truman declined Syngman Rhee's offer to put the South Korean truck driver to death). Walker had defended the Pusan Perimeter brilliantly, but had always been intimidated by MacArthur and his accidental death brought an even better leader to the forefront: far from being intimidated by MacArthur, Matt Ridgway proved willing to challenge him.

The 55-year-old Ridgway had earned great praise in the Second World War, and was the army's Deputy Chief of Staff in December 1950. The JCS told the new ground commander that his brief was basically to secure South Korea. Ridgway faced daunting problems:

- the Chinese onslaught
- the morale of the 365,000 US/UN/ROK troops
- MacArthur.

By now the Chinese were caught up in the same kind of optimistic military momentum that had encouraged the Americans to cross the 38th parallel in September 1950. In January 1951, the Chinese crossed the 38th parallel into South Korea – 'just walking there' would take it, said Peng, the top Chinese general. Nearly half a million Chinese drove toward Seoul, in the vicinity of which were American, ROK, British, British Commonwealth, Greek and Filipino forces. The Chinese aimed at the ROK forces, whose panicky retreat shocked Ridgway. Seoul was lost to the Communists yet again, and hundreds of thousands of South Korean refugees poured southward for the second time in six months.

Ridgway and morale

The US/UN/ROK troops had been in retreat for months and Ridgway found morale low. 'This was a bewildered army, not sure of itself or its leaders, not sure what they were doing there', he wrote later. 'There was obviously much to be done to restore this army to a fighting mood.' Ridgway managed to do it because:

- The troops liked him: he had a hand grenade taped on the right side of his chest, and a first-aid kit on the left, so they nicknamed him 'Iron Tits'. He made them feel he cared, as when he handed out the extra winter gloves or stationery for writing home that he carried in his jeep. His actions became legendary. 'Thanks, pal', said a radio operator, burdened by equipment and stuck in the mud, when a man bent down to tie up his bootlaces for him. The radio man was surprised to see it was a three-star general – Ridgway.
- Ridgway kept his officers on their toes, sacking one who gave him a plan for a second retreat to the Pusan Perimeter.
- Ridgway was a thorough and imaginative commander who improved reconnaissance and the supply system, and initiated a series of carefully thought-out counter-attacks. By February 1951, American troops were moving forward again. Michaelis (see page 60) said, 'Ridgway took that defeated army and turned it around. He was a breath of fresh air, a showman, what the army desperately needed.'
- The Chinese had overstretched themselves and their supply lines had reached their outer limits. The flatter lands of South Korea favoured the tanks and artillery that the Chinese lacked but Ridgway possessed in abundance.

Ridgway and the JCS versus MacArthur

By this time, the disastrous retreat of late 1950 had somewhat diminished MacArthur's influence. While the JCS had told Ridgway, 'Korea is not the place to fight a major war', and that fighting the Chinese in Korea constituted an 'increased threat of general war', MacArthur disagreed. He wanted to:

- destroy North Korea
- unleash Jiang Jieshi's forces on China
- institute an American blockade of China.

JCS chairman Omar Bradley subsequently guessed at MacArthur's motivation:

The only possible means left to MacArthur to regain his lost pride was now to inflict an overwhelming defeat on those Red Chinese generals who had made a fool of him.

Tensions began to develop between MacArthur and Ridgway. For example, MacArthur tried to claim credit for initiating '**Operation Killer**', which was Ridgway's idea. By March, when Seoul was retaken and American forces were back at the 38th parallel, the MacArthur problem was about to come to a head.

Truman versus MacArthur

Truman and MacArthur had long had major disagreements over:

- the relative strategic importance of Asia and Europe
- the use of nuclear weapons in the Korean War
- whether or not the United States should further provoke Communist China.

Basically, Truman was committed to waging limited war in Korea, while MacArthur was spoiling for an all-out fight against Communist China. They had clashed as early as August 1950, when MacArthur issued an unauthorised statement on the need for the United States to defend Taiwan – a highly sensitive foreign policy question (see pages 53–4). Truman subsequently said he should have sacked MacArthur then and there. Then, in December 1950, MacArthur told journalists that Asia was the main Cold War battleground and that 'limited' war was wrong. When Ridgway asked the air force chief why the JCS did not tell MacArthur what to do, the chief replied, 'What good would that do? He would not obey the orders. What can we do?' Shocked, Ridgway replied, 'You can relieve any commander who won't obey orders, can't you?' In spring 1951, MacArthur committed two acts of insubordination that saw him relieved of command.

MacArthur and Truman's peace initiative

By March 1951, the Truman administration recognised that the war had stalemated and, under pressure from Western allies, was willing to discuss peace. Truman had made it clear that no one was to release policy statements without State Department clearance, because the situation was highly delicate. Some felt that when MacArthur then issued a **communiqué** that publicly insulted China as facing 'imminent military collapse', he had sabotaged Truman's plan. He certainly upset American allies. Horrified Canadian Foreign Minister Lester Pearson said the days 'of relatively easy and automatic' Canadian–American relations were over. Truman later recalled that MacArthur had issued that controversial communiqué:

> *in open defiance of my orders as President and **Commander-in-Chief**. By this act, MacArthur left me no choice. I could no longer tolerate his insubordination.*

Privately, Truman told a Democratic senator, 'I'll show that son of a bitch who's boss. Who does he think he is? God?' For the moment though, he simply reprimanded MacArthur.

MacArthur's message to Congress

MacArthur committed his second act of insubordination of spring 1951 when he sent a letter to Republican congressman Joseph W. Martin and gave Martin permission to read it out in Congress. In it, MacArthur wrote that 'if we lose this war to Communism in Asia', the fall of Europe would inevitably follow. The letter made it very clear that he opposed Truman's doctrine of containment (which he likened to appeasement) and policy of limited war in Korea: 'There is no substitute for victory.' In allowing this letter to be read out in public, MacArthur violated the JCS directive of 6 December 1950, which said all government officials had to obtain clearance before they published any comments on the war. At last, in April 1951, Truman relieved MacArthur of his command in the Far East.

SOURCE D

From President Truman's statement, released 10 April 1951 (available at www.pbs.org/wgbh/amex/macarthur/filmmore/reference/primary/officialdocs02. html).

With deep regret I have concluded that General of the Army Douglas MacArthur is unable to give his wholehearted support to the policies of the United States government and of the United Nations in matters pertaining to his official duties. In view of the specific responsibilities imposed upon me by the Constitution of the United States and the added responsibilities entrusted to me by the United Nations, I have decided that I must make a change of command in the Far East.

Does Source D contradict Source C (on page 71)?

Truman versus US public opinion

The Chinese intervention in the Korean War dramatically affected American public opinion. Although public support for the Korean War was initially great, the US/UN/ROK retreat polarised it. Some turned against Truman's way of waging the war: for example, in December 1950, Republican Senator William Knowland, whose support for Jiang Jieshi earned him the nickname 'the Senator from **Formosa**', and General Curtis ('Mr Atom Bomb') LeMay supported MacArthur in demanding tougher actions against China. Others turned against the war itself: when the Chinese took Seoul in January 1951, a poll revealed that 49 per cent of Americans felt sending troops to Korea had been a mistake, and 66 per cent believed the United States should abandon South Korea. However, Truman had no intention of getting out. Truman and the JCS told MacArthur the bottom line:

It is important to United States prestige worldwide, to the future of UN and NATO organisations, and to efforts to organize anti-Communist resistance in Asia that Korea not be evacuated unless actually forced by military considerations, and that maximum practicable punishment be inflicted on Communist aggressors.

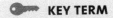 **KEY TERM**

Formosa Taiwan was more commonly known as Formosa in the 1940s and 1950s.

American public opinion had played a very important part in the war:

- Truman had entered the war in June 1950 partly because he feared looking 'soft' on Communism
- Truman decided upon crossing the 38th parallel partly because he anticipated a public outcry if he failed to follow up the US/UN/ROK advantage
- the main reason Truman took so long to relieve MacArthur was the general's popularity back home.

When Truman finally dismissed MacArthur, it further damaged his popularity. Truman's **approval rating** sank as MacArthur and his admirers engaged in dramatic and emotional farewells.

MacArthur's farewells

When MacArthur left Tokyo for the last time, around 2 million Japanese people lined his route to the airport, to demonstrate their respect. A leading Japanese newspaper lamented, 'We feel as if we have lost a kind and loving father.' Then, when the old general returned to the United States, he was met by over half a million supporters in San Francisco and given a record-breaking **ticker-tape parade** in New York City. An unprecedented 3249 tons of ticker-tape, shredded paper and confetti rained down on him in his triumphal motorcade through the city. His 20 April 1951 speech to Congress is rightly famous. In that speech, he gained impressive and repeated congressional applause with his references to 'your sons' whom he had just left on the battlefields of Korea, to the 'feisty' South Koreans who had begged him 'don't scuttle the Pacific', and to his lifetime of service to his country. His final flourish was brilliantly dramatic:

> I am closing my 52 years of military service. The world has turned over many times since I took the oath at West Point, but I still remember the refrain of one of the most popular barracks ballads of that day which proclaimed most proudly that, 'Old soldiers never die; they just fade away.' And like the old soldier of that ballad, I now close my military career and just fade away – an old soldier who tried to do his duty as God gave him the light to see that duty. Goodbye.

The applause was rapturous. Some congressmen wept openly. A conservative Republican said, 'We heard God speak here today, God in the flesh, the voice of God.' Ex-President Hoover described MacArthur as a 'reincarnation of St Paul'. One poll revealed 69 per cent of Americans believed Truman was wrong to sack him. Truman, who described the speech as '100 per cent bullshit', received 27,000 letters and telegrams, the vast majority of which criticised him. Over 100,000 letters reached Congress, many demanding Truman's **impeachment**. Senator McCarthy (see page 52) called Truman a 'son of a bitch' and blamed the firing on Truman's Missouri friends, all 'stoned on bourbon and Benedictine [a liqueur]' (the President was famous for entertaining old friends from his home state in the White House).

KEY TERMS

Approval rating American pollsters continually check the public's opinion (approval) of the President's performance.

Ticker-tape parade When national heroes returned to the United States, the citizens of New York City would shower them with bits of paper (ticker-tape) as they drove through the streets of the city in an open-top car.

Impeachment Process whereby Congress has the constitutional power to remove an errant President.

SOURCE E

MacArthur, standing, being driven along Broadway, New York, on 23 April 1951. Many contemporaries thought the ticker-tape parade demonstrated MacArthur's popularity.

Support for MacArthur's dismissal

Some contemporaries supported Truman. Democrat Senator Robert Kerr said:

> *I do not know how many thousand American GIs are sleeping in unmarked graves in North Korea. But most of them are silent but immutable evidence of the tragic mistake of 'The Magnificent MacArthur' who told them that the Chinese Communists just across the Yalu would not intervene.*

Leading newspapers, some of which had been hostile to Truman, felt that the President had preserved the constitutional principle of civilian control over the military.

The JCS fully supported Truman, fearing that MacArthur might deliberately provoke an incident in order to widen the war into an all-out conflict between the United States and Communist China. The JCS position was evident in the congressional hearings on the war in May 1951. JCS chairman Omar Bradley explained that he disagreed with MacArthur over the importance of China and Secretary of Defence George Marshall registered his disapproval of MacArthur's rejection of a limited war strategy. After the JCS testimonies, the MacArthur controversy died down.

> Would you agree with those who thought the parade in Source E demonstrated MacArthur's popularity? **?**

The significance of MacArthur's dismissal

MacArthur's dismissal was significant in three ways:

- It demonstrated Truman's commitment to his doctrine of containment of Communism and to limited war. Truman rejected MacArthur's desire to enter into a full-scale war with China as likely to lead to a third world war.
- Truman successfully asserted the constitutional principle of civilian control over the military.
- It signalled that Western Europe remained vital to US security, as JCS chairman Omar Bradley attested before Congress in May 1951. In a clear attack on MacArthur and other Republican Asia-firsters, Bradley denied that China was the greatest threat to the United States. For Bradley and for other Europe-firsters, the Soviet Union was the greatest enemy and Europe the greatest prize. Nevertheless, it can reasonably be argued that the Korean War had shifted the storm centre of the Cold War from Europe to Asia.

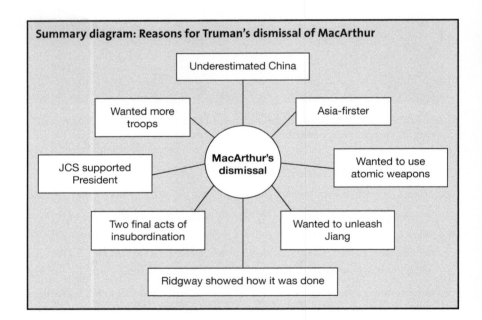

Summary diagram: Reasons for Truman's dismissal of MacArthur

Underestimated China

Wanted more troops

Asia-firster

JCS supported President

MacArthur's dismissal

Wanted to use atomic weapons

Two final acts of insubordination

Wanted to unleash Jiang

Ridgway showed how it was done

Causes of stalemate 1951–3

▶ *Why did the Korean War last so long?*

Between summer 1951 and summer 1953 there was stalemate on the battlefield and in the peace talks.

The changing nature of the war

Prior to spring 1951, the Korean War had been characterised by rapid advances and retreats, as illustrated when the South Korean capital Seoul changed hands five times between June 1950 and March 1951. In the hope of another swift advance, the Chinese launched another offensive on South Korea on 22 April 1951, but the cost in lives proved too high: 12,000 Chinese troops died on the first day alone.

The military situation was about to reach stalemate. The combatants' front lines stabilised near the 38th parallel and both sides dug in and engaged in trench warfare. The main reason for the stalemate was that the two sides appeared equally matched. First, while the Americans had by far the more advanced technology and weaponry, the Chinese had a seemingly inexhaustible supply of manpower. Second, the Americans and the Soviets were unwilling to use their full military capability. Ridgway's replacement, General Matt Clark, wanted to attack Chinese Manchuria and use atomic weapons in order to end the stalemate, but Washington rejected that option. The Soviets were even more careful. While encouraging the Chinese efforts (in December 1950, Stalin urged Mao to 'liberate Seoul'), the Soviets always limited their own involvement. Although Stalin gave Kim war materiel, advisers and Soviet pilots to fly Soviet planes, he kept Soviet troops and the Soviet navy out of the conflict.

The war was further prolonged by the slow progress in the peace talks that took place between 1951 and 1953. In those two years, the bitter fighting continued and it was calculated that two soldiers died for every minute the peace talks were on.

Prolonged peace talks

In December 1950, the UN proposed peace talks. China told the UN it would only consider peace talks if:

- US/UN forces got out of Korea
- the US 7th Fleet left the Taiwan Strait
- Communist China obtained the UN seat for China, currently held by Jiang Jieshi and Taiwan.

Under US pressure, and to the irritation of some American allies such as Britain, the UN denounced China as an aggressor in February 1951. That made the prospects for peace talks recede, until the failure of the spring 1951 offensive helped prompt China to request an armistice in June 1951. China now modified its aims and concentrated upon an armistice that might remove most of the American troops from Korea. By this time, both sides wanted peace.

Why the combatants wanted peace

The United States wanted peace because:

- The war was expensive. In 1953, the Secretary of the Treasury told Truman's successor President Eisenhower (see page 101) that the expenditure was damaging US government finances.
- The war had cost many American lives, and the American public had turned against what was frequently referred to as 'Truman's war'. In an autumn 1951 poll, a majority agreed that the Korean War was 'an utterly useless war'.
- There was pressure from America's allies and from **non-aligned nations** to end the military stalemate.
- From May 1951, Communist accusations that the United States was using biological warfare in Korea were damaging America's international reputation. Historians disagree over the truth of the accusation. Some, for example, Cumings, have shown that the use of chemical warfare was seriously considered: huge stockpiles of sarin nerve gas were being prepared for use in the war. In 1976, the head of the CIA admitted that the Army Bacteriological Warfare Laboratories at Fort Detrick in Maryland had been commissioned in early 1952 to develop bacteriological agents and delivery systems.
- Some feared that if the conflict continued, the USSR might join in the fighting and the Korean War could escalate into a third world war.
- In May 1951, General Omar Bradley, chairman of the JCS, told Congress that China was not the greatest threat faced by the United States and that an escalated clash with China would be 'the wrong war, at the wrong place, at the wrong time, and with the wrong enemy'. He did not want the United States to be pinned down by the Korean conflict: if trouble erupted in Europe, American forces would be overstretched and unable to meet the Communist threat there.

The other combatants wanted peace because:

- China needed to concentrate on its domestic problems. Its economy was suffering, hundreds of thousands of soldiers were dying, and China feared the conflict might escalate.
- The Soviet Union wanted to decrease the risk of general war and hoped to create tensions between the United States and its less belligerent allies.
- Kim Il Sung was increasingly anxious to end the conflict because North Korea was suffering food shortages and it was clear that he was not going to attain reunification.

Difficulties in reaching a settlement

Although China proposed an armistice in June 1951, it was not finally signed until July 1953. Why did it take so long?

- All the negotiators (Chinese, North Korean and UN) were military men rather than experienced diplomats.

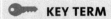

KEY TERM

Non-aligned nations
Countries that remained neutral in the Cold War.

- From the first, each side was anxious not to give the other any advantage. For example, in June 1951, both the Americans and the Chinese issued public statements about the desirability of ending the conflict, but the Chinese suggested laying down arms and then talking, while the Americans feared that China would use such a pause to prepare for another offensive and said agreement on armistice terms had to precede the cessation of hostilities.

- Much time was taken up by a preoccupation with saving face. When the UN negotiator, US Vice Admiral C. Turner Joy, put a UN flag on the table on the first day (10 July 1951) of the negotiations, the North Korean representative quickly put up a larger North Korean flag. The talks were initially located in North Korean/Chinese-held territory, at Kaesong, and the Chinese made sure that while they sat on high, upholstered chairs, the UN negotiators were given smaller, wooden seats. After a few weeks, the talks were moved to Panmunjom, midway between the front lines.

- The bitterness engendered by the war made it difficult for the participants to agree on peace. Ridgway worked hard to ensure that Chinese 'face' was satisfied, but he found the process repugnant and cabled the JCS:

  To sit down with these men and deal with them as representatives of an enlightened and civilised people is to deride one's own dignity and to invite the disaster their treachery will inevitably bring upon us … [Our delegates should] employ such language and methods as these treacherous savages cannot fail to understand, and understanding, respect.

- The historian Peter Lowe said negotiations were slowed down because the Americans were simplistic, the Communists inflexible and Syngman Rhee ('Our goal is unification') obstructive. Rhee's behaviour was such that the US considered replacing him.

- The American position hardened as the negotiations wore on. First, the NSC (see page 52) hoped to continue to inflict heavy losses upon the Chinese that would stop them causing trouble elsewhere. Second, Republicans such as Senator Knowland pressed Truman to adopt MacArthur-style policies. Third, Acheson wanted to build up the South Korean Army to assist in America's global containment of Communism and did not want to alienate Rhee (infuriated by US/UN negotiations with the Communists, Rhee complained that he was surrounded by 'political nincompoops').

- Truman played a major part in delaying the peace, because he wanted Chinese Communist POWs to be given a free choice as to whether they returned to China. The Chinese pointed out that POWs had to be repatriated under international law. Some historians attribute Truman's inflexibility to principle and humanitarian motives. Others say he sought a propaganda victory in the Cold War. It seems unlikely that he expected domestic political advantage from his stubborn stance, as Americans were impatient to end the war (more than half of Americans were willing to use the atomic bomb to do so).

- In summer 1952, the United States greatly escalated its air attacks on North Korea, hoping to make the Chinese more amenable in the negotiations. However, the bombing of a dam and power station and multiple bombings of Pyongyang made Mao less inclined to co-operate.
- Some historians have suggested that Stalin prolonged the war by pressuring Mao and Kim to continue so as to distract the United States from Europe.

Defectors

It has been estimated that there were 21,805 Chinese and North Korean POWs who did not want to be repatriated, and 23 Americans and one Briton who defected to Communism.

How peace was finally achieved

The change in personnel in both the USSR (with the death of Stalin in March 1953) and the United States (with the accession of Eisenhower to the presidency in January 1953) made it easier to achieve peace:

- The new leaders of the USA and the USSR had neither started nor sustained their nation's involvement in the war, so their prestige was not at stake in the way that their predecessors' prestige had been.
- Soviet politicians wanted to focus on the succession to Stalin.
- The Chinese conceded that POWs unwilling to be repatriated could be handed over to a neutral state that would decide their fate.
- The American public trusted General Eisenhower's judgement in matters of war.
- Eisenhower effectively 'bought off' Syngman Rhee by offering him financial aid and a promise to defend South Korea if attacked (the President was careful to make it clear that there would be no US aid if South Korea attacked North Korea).
- The Eisenhower administration and some historians believed that Eisenhower repeatedly saying that he was prepared to use atomic weapons helped persuade the Chinese to sign the armistice.
- Much credit was due to the backroom talks at the UN between George Kennan (see page 12) and the Soviet ambassador to the UN, Jacob Malik. Their talks, away from the public posturings characteristic of many peace negotiations, did important groundwork for the eventual armistice.

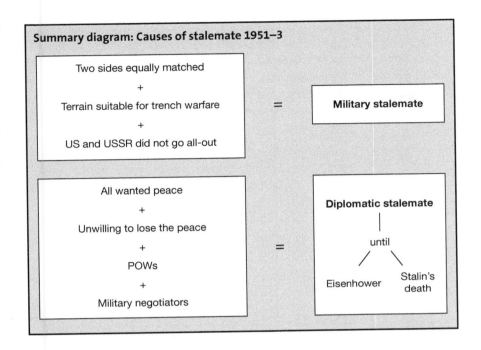

Summary diagram: Causes of stalemate 1951–3

Two sides equally matched
+
Terrain suitable for trench warfare   =   **Military stalemate**
+
US and USSR did not go all-out

All wanted peace
+
Unwilling to lose the peace
+   =   **Diplomatic stalemate**
POWs |
+   until
Military negotiators   /   \
                          Eisenhower   Stalin's
                                          death

5 The outcome for the participants

▶ *How did the Korean War affect the combatants?*

The Korean War had a great impact upon many of the participants, but most of all upon the two Koreas.

The outcome for Korea

The war had a devastating effect on many Koreans. Millions of Korean civilians had their lives disrupted by the war and became refugees. Although estimates vary, it seems likely that South Korea had around 250,000 military casualties and a million civilian casualties, while North Korea had roughly 400,000 military casualties and 600,000 civilian casualties. During the fighting, Koreans, Chinese and Americans committed atrocities that were sometimes directed against civilians. While South Korean and North Korean troops killed and harmed far more civilians, the Americans also killed some. For example, in No Gun Ri village, near Taejon, American soldiers fired on and killed several hundred civilian refugees, while American soldiers blew up a bridge after the refugees on it had ignored warnings not to cross (the United States persuaded the United Nations to keep such things quiet).

Korean troops suffered greatly. Communist troops were poorly fed and clothed; South Korean soldiers were poorly paid and their casualty rate was around 40 per cent. When Matt Clark replaced Ridgway as UN Commander in May 1952, he put South Korean troops on the front line in order to save American lives (troops of all nationalities were likely to suffer from malaria, dysentery, encephalitis or yellow fever in the summer, and frostbite in the winter).

Predominantly agricultural South Korea suffered great economic problems during and immediately after the war. However, the post-war American build-up of the South Korean armed forces led to the injection of $1.5 billion per annum (Washington reasoned that as a South Korean soldier cost $8 per month and an American cost $1650, this was a cheaper way to fight the Cold War). American aid helped ensure that South Korea was increasingly prosperous from the 1960s onwards. The North Korean economy also suffered greatly from the war, primarily due to American aerial bombing.

Politically, the bitterness of the war confirmed the division of the peninsula and helped the two authoritarian leaders to consolidate their power. At the 1954 Geneva conference, negotiations on Korean reunification failed because each participant rejected reunification if 'their' Korea could not dominate the peninsula. Rhee became a reliable American ally and many Americans considered South Korea a model state in the context of US containment policies in Asia. Rhee held on to power until 1960, when he was driven out by a combination of nationwide student demonstrations and US exasperation with his rigged elections. Kim retained power until his death in 1994, his control and propaganda such that he remains greatly revered by North Koreans. As of today, the two Koreas remain divided, there is still no peace treaty that has ended the Korean War, and while South Korea is prosperous and democratic, Communist North Korea is a secretive and impoverished nation.

The outcome for the United Nations

Views on the outcome of the Korean War for the United Nations depend upon one's interpretation of the war (see Table 2.2).

Table 2.2 Viewpoints on the outcome for the United Nations

Viewpoint on the Korean War		Impact of viewpoint on the UN and the Korean War
The Korean War was a genuine UN war and a just war against North Korean aggression	→	The Korean War was a UN triumph. The UN saved South Korea from North Korean aggression
The UN got involved in what was essentially a Korean civil war	→	The UN had no right to intervene in a civil war, and in doing so perpetuated the division of Korea
The Korean War was a US war	→	The UN was an American tool

The outcome for the United States

Over 30,000 Americans died in Korea: for contemporaries, this now 'forgotten war' was immensely important and significant for US foreign policy and in domestic politics.

A US foreign policy triumph?

Containment (see page 10) could be said to have worked. The United States went to war to save South Korea from Communism and to restore the *status quo* in the Korean peninsula. In that it succeeded. The United States showed itself willing and able to halt Communist expansion, 'saved' South Korea and ensured Japanese security. The war could be said to have helped American prestige and credibility in that the United States held the line against the Communists and restored the *status quo*, but the United States had failed in its attempt to reunify the peninsula. General Matt Clark said, 'I gained the unenviable distinction of being the first United States Army Commander in history to sign an armistice without victory.'

A Cold War turning point?

In many ways, the Korean War was a great turning point in the Cold War.

- Although the Truman administration was dominated by Europe-firsters, it can be argued that the Korean War had shifted the storm centre of the Cold War from Europe to Asia, which made the Soviets feel more secure. Truman had dramatically expanded and militarised US policy in Asia.
- The Korean War poisoned Sino-American relations. It would be nearly two decades before the two nations finally exchanged ambassadors.
- Although the United States believed and claimed that it fought for democracy in the Cold War, the Korean War left it wedded to undemocratic regimes in Taiwan (see page 54) and South Korea.
- The Korean War escalated the Soviet–American arms race. US defence expenditure quadrupled between 1950 and 1953, and when Truman ordered a speeding up of the US hydrogen bomb programme, the Soviets did likewise.
- The Korean War inspired the United States to strengthen **NATO**, the new defensive Western military alliance established in 1949. Building up NATO led the US to initiate the remilitarisation of West Germany.
- The Korean War helped transform the US relationship with Germany and Japan, who had been America's great enemies, but now became America's close allies.
- The historian James Matray (2002) saw the 'main legacy' as being that the 'United States thereafter pursued a foreign policy of global intervention and paid an enormous price in death, destruction, and damaged reputation'. This was particularly the case in relation to Vietnam, US interest in which was fatally increased by the Korean War (see page 100).

KEY TERM

NATO The North Atlantic Treaty Organisation was an anti-Communist Western military alliance established by the United States in 1949.

The impact of the Korean War on Japan

The Korean War speeded up Japan's development into a reliable and invaluable US ally (see page 21) and greatly benefited the Japanese economy. The US relied heavily upon Japanese products and facilities: for example, Nissan and Toyota produced and repaired trucks for the Americans during the Korean War, and soon grew into industrial giants on the world stage. Japanese prosperity also owed much to internal factors (such as the hard work ethos) and the United States bearing the financial burden of Japan's defence. By 1965, Japan was the second most prosperous nation in the world (the United States was the first). By the 1970s, Japanese nationalist antipathy towards the United States was often quite strong, while the perceived economic threat from Japan aroused American antagonism. However, it was not until the 1980s that Japanese–American relations deteriorated dramatically. Significantly, that deterioration paralleled the winding down of the Cold War.

The impact upon US domestic politics

The Korean War:

- exacerbated the anti-Communist hysteria that Senator McCarthy had generated since February 1950 (see page 52). Sales of backyard bomb shelters increased and schools had atomic attack drills in which children were trained to hide under desks in the event of a Soviet bomb being dropped on them. Communists were banned from employment as teachers or civil servants. Free speech was badly affected as left-wingers and suspected Communists were persecuted.
- cost the United States $67 billion (billions more were subsequently spent on rebuilding South Korea). The increased defence expenditure boosted the gross national product, but also generated inflation.
- greatly damaged Truman's presidency. His failure to obtain a congressional declaration of war helped to saddle him with all the blame for 'Truman's war', and, according to the historian James Patterson (1996), rendered him 'virtually powerless' either to control Congress or to lead the country effectively. He decided against standing for re-election in 1952 because his popularity ratings had plummeted. The war helped to ensure the 1952 victory of the Republican Dwight D. Eisenhower, because voters hoped he would bring peace. American people were tired of Truman and felt that General Eisenhower could be trusted to bring an acceptable peace in Korea, where his son was fighting.
- hastened the desegregation of the army ordered by President Truman in 1948. Under the pressure of war, the army top brass integrated black and white American soldiers in Korea.

The outcome for China and the USSR

As far as the Chinese and the Soviets were concerned, the Korean War had mixed results:

- China's military performance in Korea impressed the world. In the military stalemate from 1951 to 1953, Chinese troops effectively held the Americans to a draw. On the other hand, these triumphs came at the cost of around a million Chinese casualties.
- The war strengthened the relationship between China and North Korea and, in some ways, strengthened the Sino-Soviet alliance. It encouraged the Soviets to set China on the road to becoming a nuclear power from 1955, but the Chinese nursed resentment that the Soviets had left them to do all the fighting, and this played a part in the subsequent Sino-Soviet split (see page 177).
- The war poisoned Sino-American relations and contributed greatly to Western opposition to Chinese membership of the UN.
- The war consolidated the power of Mao's government, which promoted national unity through the 'Resist America' campaign and used the war as an excuse to introduce greater repression.
- The Korean War was in some ways a triumph for the USSR: it demonstrated Communist military effectiveness, tied down the Western powers in Asia, and caused tensions within the Western alliance. On the other hand, it led to the remilitarisation of two Soviet rivals, Japan and Germany, and to their integration into the Western defensive system.

The situation in Asia in 1953

At the end of the Korean War, North Korea and South Korea were devastated and remained divided, Cold War tensions remained high, and Asia was clearly the new centre of those tensions. The United States and its allies still faced what they perceived as Communist aggression: although the Communist insurgencies in the Philippines and Malaya neared defeat, the Vietnamese Communists were doing well (see Chapter 3).

While the Korean War increased US interest and aid in Asian countries such as French Indochina, the Philippines and Pakistan, it also encouraged several states to distance themselves from the Cold War. Amongst the neutralist or non-aligned nations were Egypt, India and Indonesia. Indian Prime Minister **Jawaharlal Nehru** had criticised not only North Korean aggression in 1950, but also American policy towards Taiwan and French Indochina. He supported the entry of Communist China into the United Nations and opposed the crossing of the 38th parallel. Nehru had proclaimed Cold War neutrality as early as December 1947, but the Korean War intensified his belief in non-alignment and encouraged others to agree with him, as demonstrated at the Bandung conference (see page 89).

 KEY FIGURE

Jawaharlal Nehru (1889–1964)

A leading figure in the Indian campaign for independence from Britain, he was the first Prime Minister of an independent India (1947–64). He encouraged the Non-Aligned Movement of nations that sought to keep out of the Cold War conflict.

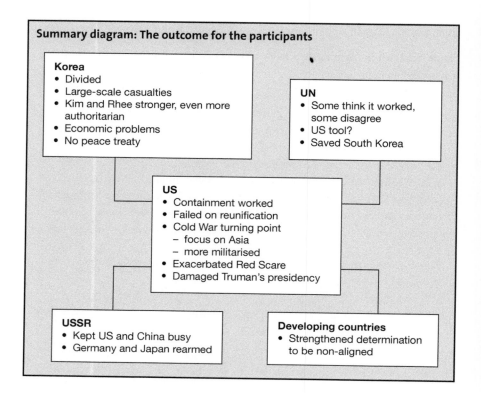

Summary diagram: The outcome for the participants

Korea
- Divided
- Large-scale casualties
- Kim and Rhee stronger, even more authoritarian
- Economic problems
- No peace treaty

UN
- Some think it worked, some disagree
- US tool?
- Saved South Korea

US
- Containment worked
- Failed on reunification
- Cold War turning point
  - focus on Asia
  - more militarised
- Exacerbated Red Scare
- Damaged Truman's presidency

USSR
- Kept US and China busy
- Germany and Japan rearmed

Developing countries
- Strengthened determination to be non-aligned

The impact of the Korean War to 1977

▶ *How did the Korean War affect international relations from 1954 to 1977?*

Even after the Korean War ended in July 1953, the conflict continued to impact upon international relations, contributing to:

- US involvement in Vietnam until 1975 (see Chapters 3–5)
- the rearmament of Japan and West Germany
- the Sino-American hostility that kept Communist China out of the United Nations for two decades
- the Soviet–American arms race
- the strengthening of the Sino-Soviet alliance
- the development of the non-aligned movement.

Non-alignment

An old Korean proverb said, 'When whales collide, the shrimp suffer'. In the Cold War struggle between the USA and the USSR and China, some Koreans considered themselves the shrimp. The Korean War encouraged many other nations emerging from colonialism to avoid a similar fate.

The relationship between the newly emerging independent Asian and African nations and the Cold War was complex. In some ways, the Cold War hastened decolonisation: imperialist powers such as Britain, France and the Netherlands, already weakened by the Second World War, faced great and successful American pressure to increase their defence expenditure (which further drained their strength) and to grant their colonies independence. In other ways, the Cold War perpetuated Western attempts to dominate Asia, as with US involvement in Vietnam (see page 112). The very process of decolonisation tempted each side in the Cold War to try to win friends and allies amongst the new nations.

Some of those struggling to free themselves from Western colonialist masters and their capitalism found the Communist ideology more appealing, but many did not want to have to choose Cold War sides. Some **Third World** leaders aimed at non-alignment and a good relationship with both West and East. They sought economic and technological aid from as many countries as possible and felt that Cold War divisions would hamper their progress. The first international indication of this mindset came at Bandung.

KEY TERM

Third World Cold War-era name for developing nations.

The Bandung conference, 1955

In April 1955, many of the newly independent countries and nationalist movements in Africa and Asia sent representatives to a conference at Bandung in Indonesia. The moving force behind the organisation of the conference was nations such as Burma (Myanmar), Sri Lanka, India, Indonesia and Pakistan. The 29 countries represented at Bandung constituted nearly half of the world's population.

The conference aimed to promote five guiding principles in international relations:

- sovereignty
- independence
- equality
- non-aggression
- non-interference in the affairs of other nations.

These principles were promoted by Nehru (see page 87) and were clearly aimed against the interventionism of the Cold War protagonists, particularly the United States.

The participants at Bandung declared their opposition to:

- racism (Asians and Africans resented the 'politics of pigmentation' under which arrogant whites lorded it over 'lesser peoples')
- colonialism
- Soviet–American expenditure on nuclear weapons while much of the rest of the world suffered from poverty and needed aid

and said they hoped that increased Afro-Asian economic co-operation would decrease Third World economic dependence upon the great powers.

Nehru thought dialogue with China would be more helpful than isolation and, at his insistence and despite the reservations of the many participants who faced Communist insurgencies, China was invited to Bandung. The Chinese had already declared their acceptance of Nehru's five principles in an April 1954 Sino-Indian trade agreement and Chinese Foreign Minister **Zhou Enlai** made a favourable impression at Bandung. He seemed moderate and accommodating, as when he signed the declaration that Chinese living overseas owed their first loyalty to the nation where they lived and not to Mao's China.

The significance of Bandung

The Bandung conference was the first major meeting of the developing nations, more commonly known during the Cold War as the Third World. It demonstrated the resentment that many newly emerging nations felt about Western and Soviet policies in areas such as Asia, especially as those policies were invariably formulated and acted upon without consultation with Asian nations. It also demonstrated fear and resentment of Cold War antagonisms.

Bandung demonstrated the difficulty of a large number of countries attempting to gain agreement:

- Countries such as North Korea and South Korea were considered potentially divisive and were not invited.
- After much debate as to whether the Soviet Union should be criticised for its colonialism in Eastern Europe and Central Asia (the Americans and British coached their Pakistani, Thai and Filipino friends on what to say on this issue), the conference implicitly criticised the Soviets when it denounced 'colonialism in all of its manifestations'.
- It proved difficult to reconcile the conflicting feelings of participants about the West and the Cold War. Some of those attending were very close to the two great Cold War antagonists – for example, Thailand and the Philippines resented Nehru's criticism of their involvement in the US-initiated Southeast Asia Treaty Organisation (SEATO) (see page 109). While US Secretary of State John Foster Dulles (see page 105) said SEATO was 'of first importance' as a way to 'demonstrate that free Asian countries and Western countries could deal together with profit and harmony', Nehru said such military alliances were tools of great power domination. Thailand and Philippines responded that they were grateful for the American guarantee of their security.

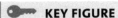

KEY FIGURE

Zhou Enlai (1898–1976)

Well educated and middle class, he joined the Chinese Communist Party in its early years. He was Prime Minister of the People's Republic of China from 1949 to 1976. He was also Foreign Minister from 1949 to 1958. He played a leading role in Chinese intervention in the Korean War, in the Geneva Conference of 1954, at Bandung in 1955, and in the detente with America in 1971–2.

The United States had feared that the Bandung conference would demonstrate and increase antagonism towards the West, but the presence of pro-Western nations such as Japan and the Philippines helped modify the anti-Western sentiments of some of those who attended. The difficulties in gaining agreement meant that, from the Soviet and American viewpoints, Bandung had no adverse impact on the Cold War.

The Cold War protagonists naturally responded to Bandung – and quite positively:

- Within weeks of the conference, Nehru visited the USSR and obtained Soviet acceptance of his five principles. This was quickly followed up by a visit to India by the new Soviet leader Nikita Khrushchev (see page 119).
- Like the Soviets, the Americans were inspired to take greater interest in, and provide more aid for, developing nations.

Bandung is generally seen as a forerunner of the **Non-Aligned Movement** (NAM), which like Bandung itself was hampered by divisions amongst participants.

The development of non-alignment after Bandung

In September 1961, Yugoslavia, India and Egypt led a meeting of non-aligned leaders in Belgrade. Although their Non-Aligned Movement was troubled by disagreements (for example, Yugoslavia and Egypt were uneasy about the strong anti-Western positions of China and Indonesia), non-alignment helped the development of the idea of a Third World independent of the Soviet and American blocs. The movement grew more popular in the 1970s, by which time the post-war **bipolar world order** had declined, but even then, nations such as Korea, Vietnam and Cambodia (see Chapter 6) still suffered as a result of Cold War rivalries.

 **KEY TERMS**

Non-Aligned Movement
Loose association of Third World nations anxious to distance themselves from Cold War antagonisms.

Bipolar world order In the first decades after the Second World War, the Soviet Union and the United States were by far the most powerful countries in the world and international relations were dominated by their antagonism. From the 1960s, the Soviets and Americans were increasingly unable to dominate other nations in a newly multipolar world.

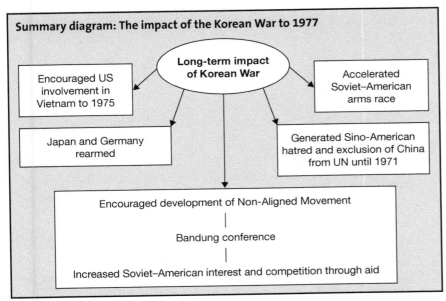

Summary diagram: The impact of the Korean War to 1977

Chapter summary

The origins of the Korean War lay in the division of Korea in 1945, the Soviet and American establishment of Korean states in their own image, and the conflicting ambitions of Kim Il Sung and Syngman Rhee for the leadership of a reunified Korea. The United States joined in the Korean War because of anti-Communism, national security and domestic politics. The Truman administration ensured it had UN support for its intervention.

The unprepared US/ROK troops did badly at first, but then broke out from the Pusan Perimeter thanks to MacArthur's brilliance at Inchon. US/UN/ROK troops then drove northward, and amidst rather unclear orders, crossed the 38th parallel and reached the Yalu River and the border with China. When the US/UN/ROK war aim changed from the restoration of the *status quo* to total reunification of the peninsula, China joined in the war.

China drove US/UN/ROK troops back into South Korea and took Seoul. MacArthur was now tainted by failure, his shortcomings shown up by the superb performance of General Matt Ridgway, who soon stabilised the lines of battle at the 38th parallel.

MacArthur publicly rejected Truman's strategy and demanded an all-out effort against mainland China. Truman therefore dismissed him. Military setbacks had already turned many Americans against the war, and the dismissal of MacArthur made Truman even more unpopular. American public opinion had a massive impact upon US policy in Korea prior to the dismissal of MacArthur.

By summer 1951, the war and the peace talks were stalemated. The participants sought peace with varying degrees of enthusiasm, and coupled with the desire not to lose out, prolonged the peace negotiations by two years.

When an armistice was finally signed in summer 1953, Korea was devastated. It remains divided today. Once again, Western policies in Asia had a dramatic and adverse effect upon Asian peoples. US foreign and defence policies were transformed. Whether or not the United States had become a security state as some argue, its Cold War focus was now indisputably Asia. China had impressed many with its military performance and was in some ways the greatest beneficiary of the war, which was not Stalin's intent. The Korean War encouraged some Third World nations to commit to non-alignment.

Refresher questions

Use these questions to remind yourself of the key
material covered in this chapter.

1 Why did North Korea attack South Korea in June
   1950?

2 To what extent was the United States to blame for
   the outbreak and continuation of the Korean War?

3 How much did Stalin help Kim Il Sung?

4 How and why did Inchon add to MacArthur's
   reputation?

5 List the arguments that the Korean War a) was and
   b) was not a UN war.

6 When and why did the United States change its
   war aims in Korea?

7 How did Ridgway restore the US/UN/ROK
   position?

8 Why did Truman dismiss MacArthur?

9 Why did the nature of the war change from
   mid-1951?

10 Why did the participants find it difficult to agree on
   a peace settlement?

11 What was the outcome of the war for a) North
   Korea, b) South Korea, c) the USA, d) the USSR,
   e) China, f) the United Nations and g) the
   non-aligned nations?

 Question practice

ESSAY QUESTIONS

1 To what extent did US public opinion affect the outbreak, course and consequences of the Korean War?

2 Who was more important in the outbreak of the Korean War? i) Syngman Rhee. ii) Stalin. Explain your
   answer with reference to both i) and ii).

3 In what ways was China significant in the Korean War?

INTERPRETATION QUESTION

1 'The war in Korea was the lever through which Washington finally found a reliable method that would pay
   the bills for hot and cold wars on a global scale.' (From Bruce Cumings, *Still the American Century*, 1999.)
   Evaluate the strengths and limitations of the interpretation, making reference to other interpretations that
   you have studied.

CHAPTER 3

Indochina 1945–63

Between 1945 and 1954, Indochina (Cambodia, Laos and Vietnam) remained a French colony. Unable to defeat the Vietnamese Communists and nationalists led by Ho Chi Minh, the French agreed to withdraw from Indochina at the Geneva conference (1954). The United States ignored the Geneva settlement and Presidents Eisenhower and Kennedy perpetuated a divided Vietnam by sponsoring the anti-Communist 'state' of South Vietnam. Although Kennedy rejected suggestions that he send in troops to combat Communism in Laos and Vietnam, he significantly escalated the American commitment to Vietnam by sending over 16,000 'advisers'.

These developments are covered in sections on:

★ French Indochina

★ The Geneva conference and the division of Vietnam

★ Two Vietnams and two leaders

★ Eisenhower's policies toward Indochina

★ Kennedy's policies toward Indochina

Key dates

1887		Vietnam, Cambodia and Laos became part of French Indochina	1955		US increased aid to South Vietnam
1941–5		Japanese dominated Vietnam	1960		National Liberation Front (NLF) increasingly disrupted South Vietnam
1945–6		Franco-Viet Minh war began			
1950		Truman began aiding French in Vietnam	1961	Spring	Kennedy humiliated by Bay of Pigs; anxious about Laos
1954	May	French defeated at Dien Bien Phu			Strategic hamlets programme
	July	Geneva Accords temporarily divided Vietnam	1963	Jan.	Battle of Ap Bac
	Sept.	US established Southeast Asia Treaty Organisation (SEATO)		Nov.	Assassinations of Diem and Kennedy

French Indochina

▶ *Why did the French leave Indochina in 1954?*

The vast majority of nineteenth-century Vietnamese people were peasant farmers producing rice on fertile river deltas: the growing of rice was a communal activity carried out by the people of each village. Such community spirit, along with nationalism, had helped fend off centuries of Chinese attempts to conquer Vietnam. During those frequently successful struggles against their giant neighbour, the Vietnamese had perfected guerrilla warfare techniques and harassed the Chinese into confusion and exhaustion.

During the late nineteenth century, the French attacked Indochina and by 1887 the countries subsequently known as Vietnam, Cambodia and Laos were under the control of the French and collectively referred to as French Indochina.

French colonial government in Indochina

By 1900, French Indochina was governed by a French-appointed Governor-General and administratively divided into the colony of Cochin China (southern Vietnam) and four protectorates:

- Annam (central Vietnam)
- Tonkin (northern Vietnam)
- Cambodia
- Laos.

Although the French talked a great deal of their 'civilising mission', their main concern was to exploit Indochinese resources. The French discouraged Indochinese manufacturing industries because they wanted Indochina to be a market for French goods. Cochin China was rich in natural resources and as a result French attention was focused there. While the French governed through local administrators in other regions, Cochin China had direct French rule and French governmental and legal traditions imposed upon it. Furthermore, French emigrants tended to settle in Cochin China, in the fertile Mekong Delta. As a result, southern Vietnam experienced greater French economic exploitation and cultural influence. The most important south Vietnamese city was Saigon (now called Ho Chi Minh City), which became known as the 'Paris of the Orient'. A wealthy Vietnamese middle class developed in Saigon. Its members were educated in French schools and many of them admired French culture, but many harboured nationalist resentment at French economic domination.

In the first half of the twentieth century, a Vietnamese nationalist movement emerged. Nationalists in Cochin China, such as the Constitutionalist Party, favoured non-violent reform and hoped to change French colonial policy while nevertheless remaining within the French Indochinese Union. However, the

Figure 3.1 French Indochina in the early twentieth century.

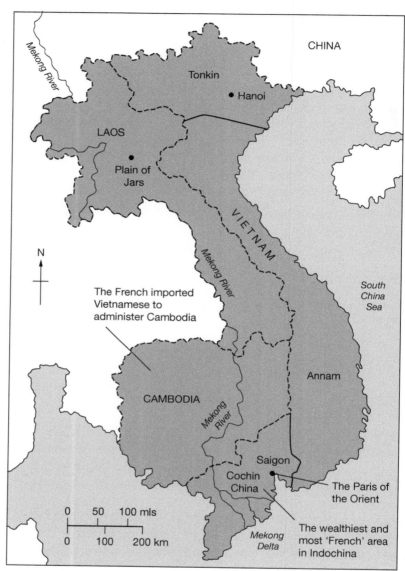

French ignored their pleas for economic and political reform during the 1920s and the party declined. This inspired more militant anti-colonialism, notably the Indochinese Communist Party (ICP).

Ho Chi Minh and the rise of the Viet Minh

The son of a Vietnamese nationalist, Ho Chi Minh opposed French colonialism. Although impressed by many Communist beliefs, especially opposition to the colonialist nations that dominated Asians and Africans, Ho subsequently said, 'It was patriotism and not Communism that originally inspired me.' By 1930,

Ho Chi Minh

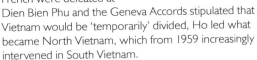

1890	Born in central Vietnam
1911–41	Travelled to observe other countries
1941	Returned to Vietnam and established League for the Independence of Vietnam (Viet Minh)
1945	Declared independent Democratic Republic of Vietnam (DRV)
1945–6	Franco-Viet Minh War began
1950	Soviets and Chinese recognised DRV
1950–3	Viet Minh controlled most of the countryside
1954	French defeated at Dien Bien Phu; Geneva Accords recognised Communist domination of northern Vietnam
1960s	Increasingly in the background but greatly revered
1969	Died

Background

Ho Chi Minh was born to a Vietnamese nationalist of the **mandarin** class in central Vietnam. During 30 years of travel to observe and learn from the strengths and weaknesses of other countries, Ho became a Communist and established the Indochinese Communist Party. He returned to Vietnam and led the Viet Minh during the Second World War. The French ignored his 1945 declaration of the independence of the Democratic Republic of Vietnam and the Franco-Viet Minh war began. After the French were defeated at Dien Bien Phu and the Geneva Accords stipulated that Vietnam would be 'temporarily' divided, Ho led what became North Vietnam, which from 1959 increasingly intervened in South Vietnam.

Achievements

One of the most influential Communist leaders of the twentieth century, Ho Chi Minh led the Vietnamese people to victory over the Japanese and the French, and then towards victory over the United States.

Significance

Ho was a nationalist first and a Communist second. He was willing to dilute or even ignore Communist ideology in order to maximise support. He was a genuinely popular leader, who successfully cultivated the 'common touch'. In the 1950s, American observers reported that the bulk of the population supported 'Uncle Ho', as he called himself. He was to be seen everywhere – villages, rice fields, meetings and the battlefront. Ho never married and paid little attention to his blood relations, so he really seemed like 'Uncle' Ho to many of his fellow countrymen.

Vietnamese nationalists were repeatedly clashing with their French colonialist oppressors, so Ho decided the time would soon be ripe for a Vietnamese revolution and established the Vietnamese Communist Party in Hong Kong in 1930. Throughout the 1930s, Ho's writings were smuggled into Vietnam while he studied Communism in China and the Soviet Union, in preparation for the struggle for Vietnamese independence. His great opportunity came in the Second World War.

The impact of the Second World War

A major reason why Ho Chi Minh was a popular leader was because of the dearth of appealing alternatives. One such unappealing alternative was the Vietnamese Emperor **Bao Dai**, whose association with the French compared unfavourably with Ho's patriotism. During the Second World War (1939–45) Bao Dai exchanged French domination for Japanese domination. Exasperated by Bao Dai's collaboration with foreign imperialists, many Vietnamese nationalists looked to Ho Chi Minh to provide effective leadership.

 KEY TERM

Mandarin A high-ranking civil servant.

 KEY FIGURE

Bao Dai (1913–97)

The last reigning Emperor of Vietnam (1926–55), Bao Dai was dominated in turn by the French, the Japanese, the French again, and then Diem. He never exercised any real power or gained any real popularity.

In early 1941, Ho and the other ICP leaders met in a cave on the Sino-Vietnamese border. There, they established the Revolutionary League for the Independence of Vietnam, using the word 'Vietnam' rather than 'Indochina' for greater emotional appeal to the Vietnamese. This League became commonly known as the **Viet Minh**. Ho's Viet Minh had two great aims:

- independence from foreign domination
- social reform.

Ho encouraged other nationalist groups and sympathisers to unite to fight both the Japanese and their French collaborators in Indochina. The Viet Minh were both nationalists and Communists, and their programme of more equal distribution of wealth and power, and freedom from the repressive Japanese and their French puppets had considerable popular appeal.

The Second World War was thus a major turning point in French colonial rule in Indochina because:

- the fall of France to the Germans in 1940 destroyed the illusion of French power
- Viet Minh opposition to the Japanese demonstrated their nationalist credentials
- the war discredited the Emperor Bao Dai
- the war brought Vietnam to US attention.

Roosevelt, Truman and Vietnam

The United States first paid attention to Indochina during the Second World War. State Department experts offered President Roosevelt (see page 2) conflicting advice: the Department's Far East division criticised French rule and claimed that unless France allowed self-government in Indochina there would be years of bloodshed and unrest; the pro-French European specialists valued France as an ally in Europe and urged Roosevelt to refrain from alienating the French over Indochina.

Ho's early relationship with the Americans was promising: Americans valued Viet Minh co-operation in the fight against the Japanese and Ho hoped to gain US support for Vietnamese independence. However, although President Truman (see page 5) encouraged the French to grant more self-government to the Vietnamese, he sided with the European specialists in the State Department and assured the French that America recognised their pre-eminent position in Indochina.

Ho's declaration of independence

After the Japanese surrendered, Ho declared the independence of the Democratic Republic of Vietnam in a speech before hundreds of thousands of his fellow countrymen on 2 September 1945. He enlisted the aid of some Americans in drafting the speech, in which he quoted the American Declaration

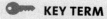

KEY TERM

Viet Minh Ho's Vietnamese nationalist followers were known as the Viet Minh after 1941.

of Independence and President Roosevelt, who had repeatedly said that he wanted 'to see sovereign rights and self-government restored to those who have been forcibly deprived of them'.

Anxious to compensate for their wartime humiliation, the French ignored Ho's declaration of independence. Within days of Ho's declaration, there were clashes between the Viet Minh and French soldiers. Some consider this the outbreak of the first Vietnam War (others date it to 1946). The clashes escalated as increasing numbers of French troops were transported to Indochina by the British, who sympathised with France's desire to retain its empire. Truman went along with this, reluctant to alienate the French as Soviet–American relations deteriorated.

Between October 1945 and February 1946, eight friendly messages from Ho to Washington went unanswered. By late 1945, Ho was cynical about Americans:

> *They are only interested in replacing the French … They want to reorganise our economy in order to control it. They are capitalists to the core. All that counts for them is business.*

Reasons for Truman's involvement in Vietnam

By 1947, the developing Cold War had led the Truman administration to conclude that Ho was probably Stalin's puppet, even though:

- the USSR still recognised French rule over Vietnam
- some State Department specialists pointed out in 1948 that Ho had made friendly gestures to America and that the Vietnamese Communists were *not* subservient to Moscow.

Unfortunately, the United States saw Vietnam as a Cold War battleground, and failed to see that Ho Chi Minh's supporters sought social justice and national sovereignty rather than participation in any worldwide struggle to promote Communism.

Events in the winter of 1949–50 propelled Truman towards aid to the French in Indochina. The Communist threat had greatly increased when China became Communist in October 1949 and Truman was

- under attack from the Republicans for 'losing' China and from Senator McCarthy for supposedly harbouring Communists in the State Department
- informed by the JCS that the world balance of power was at stake in Southeast Asia, where there were strategically vital materials such as rubber and American allies such as Japan and Australia that might be vulnerable to Communist attack
- anxious when Ho, having failed to obtain American recognition in exchange for a promise of neutrality in the Cold War, persuaded China and the Soviets to recognise his Democratic Republic of Vietnam in January 1950
- greatly influenced by NSC-68 (see page 52).

Firmly convinced that the Communists were now on the march in Asia, the United States finally recognised the supposedly independent Associated State of Vietnam set up by the French under the nominal leadership of the Emperor Bao Dai in 1949. Washington put intense diplomatic pressure on the newly independent countries in South and Southeast Asia to recognise the Bao Dai regime, but those countries generally viewed the conflict in Vietnam as a nationalist struggle against colonialism rather than part of the Cold War. Even the Philippines and Thailand were unimpressed by Bao Dai and were convinced that the United States was supporting French colonialism.

The US support for French colonialism owed much to repeated French reassurances that Ho was part of a worldwide Communist conspiracy orchestrated by Moscow and likely to lead to Soviet domination everywhere. The Truman administration considered the French invaluable allies against Communism in both Indochina and Europe. Acheson (see page 39) and Truman adjudged France important to the stability of the Western alliance in Europe and to NATO (see page 85). When France linked Franco-American co-operation in Europe with American aid in Indochina, it served to confirm the US belief that they must become more involved there. As State Department official **Dean Rusk** said, Vietnam 'is part of an international war'.

American aid for Vietnam

By early 1950, China was supplying arms, equipment and sanctuary when necessary to the Viet Minh. In May 1950, Truman offered $10 million to support the French military effort and established a fifteen-strong US Military Assistance Advisory Group (MAAG) in Saigon. The North Korean attack on South Korea (June 1950) and the entry of Chinese troops into the Korean War (October 1950) confirmed American fears of Communist expansionism and the Truman administration decided Indochina must not be allowed to fall into Communist hands.

By December 1950, the US had given France $100 million, along with aircraft, patrol boats, napalm bombs and ground combat machinery. By the end of Truman's presidency (January 1953), the Americans were more convinced than the French of the importance of Vietnam in the global struggle against Communism and were paying nearly 80 per cent of the French bill for Indochina. Between 1950 and 1953, in an early and ominous indication of how the United States saw Vietnam as a military rather than a political problem, Truman gave over $2 billion to the French war effort, compared to $50 million for economic and technical aid to the Vietnamese people.

Franco-American relations were not always smooth: French unwillingness to grant any real independence to Vietnam made Washington anxious, while some feared that Indochina distracted France and America from the more important

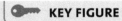

KEY FIGURE

Dean Rusk (1909–97)

An academic in the 1930s, he worked for War Department, Defence Department and State Department before President Kennedy made him Secretary of State. He continued in that post under President Johnson. While Secretary of State (1961–9), he was a keen supporter of the Vietnam War.

issue of European defence against Communism. One State Department Far East specialist admitted that 'the trouble is that none of us knows enough about Indochina' and a Defence Department official warned in November 1950 that:

we are gradually increasing our stake in the outcome of the struggle … we are dangerously close to the point of being so deeply committed that we may find ourselves completely committed even to direct intervention. These situations, unfortunately, have a way of snowballing.

Reasons for the French failure in Indochina

President Eisenhower inherited Truman's commitment to the French and continued to finance their military effort, but the French still lost ground, because of:

- Ho's popularity
- Viet Minh General Giap's brilliance
- the strength and ingenuity of the Viet Minh
- French arrogance.

KEY TERM

Rollback The Eisenhower administration verbally rejected President Truman's containment of Communism and advocated pushing back Communism in places where it was already established.

Dwight D. Eisenhower

1890	Born in Texas
1942–5	Supreme Commander of US troops in Europe in Second World War
1950	Supreme Commander of NATO
1953–61	President of the United States
1953	Ended Korean War
1954	Rejected Geneva Accords; established South Vietnam and SEATO
1960	Anxious about Laos
1969	Died

Background

Born to a staunchly Republican family in Texas, Eisenhower was a career soldier. Roosevelt appointed him to lead US troops in Europe in the Second World War and Truman appointed him Supreme Commander of NATO in 1950. He was elected President in 1952 on a platform that included ending the Korean War and

'**rollback**'. Re-elected in 1956, he was one of America's most popular Presidents.

Achievements

President Eisenhower ended the Korean War and forced the Chinese to back down when they threatened the islands of Quemoy and Matsu in the Taiwan Strait. Initially, he continued Truman's policy of helping the French to fight Communism in Vietnam, then after the French withdrew, he set up a South Vietnamese state in defiance of the Geneva Accords (see page 107). He sent military advisers to help South Vietnam, but decided against sending American combat troops.

Significance

Eisenhower's defiance of the Geneva Accords and his establishment of SEATO constituted a great commitment of US prestige to the maintenance of South Vietnam. It could be argued that Vietnam was 'Eisenhower's war'.

Ho's popularity

In late 1951, a US official pointed out the unpopularity of the French puppet emperor, Bao Dai (see page 97), whose government 'has no appeal whatsoever to the masses'. In sharp contrast, Ho was seen by many Vietnamese as a patriot who cared about the ordinary people of Vietnam. His fairer redistribution of land and educational and health-care programmes helped to win over the Vietnamese peasantry.

Viet Minh strengths

Although the French had more men and materials, Ho's Viet Minh proved elusive and determined. 'You can kill ten of my men for every one I kill of yours', Ho told one Frenchman, 'but even at those odds, you will lose and I will win'. Viet Minh guerrilla tactics utilised the physical geography of the country. The Viet Minh would make surprise attacks then retreat to western Vietnam's jungle and mountains, which were enveloped by monsoon mist for half the year. In contrast to the Viet Minh's mobile guerrilla units, the road-bound French armoured columns struggled on Vietnam's frequently flooded dirt tracks. 'If only the Vietnamese would face us in a set battle', lamented one French officer, 'how we should crush them'. The Chinese supplied Ho with weapons and most important of all, the Viet Minh fought for an inspiring cause, Vietnamese freedom and social justice.

Giap

The brilliant Viet Minh General **Vo Nguyen Giap** contributed greatly to the French defeat. Giap's father and sister were 'subversives', killed by the French, and from the age of thirteen, Giap was on the French list of revolutionary nationalists. He joined the Indochinese Communist Party in 1937, believing that the Communist emphasis on co-operation and sharing fitted well with Vietnamese traditions.

Giap trained and commanded the Viet Minh forces from 1944. Initially numbering around 5000, they declared war on the French in November 1946. Giap's strategy was to start with guerrilla warfare to wear down the enemy, then move to set-piece battles as his army grew stronger. Like Ho, Giap paid great attention to winning over the ordinary people. Mao's 1949 triumph (see page 30) transformed the situation. Mao gave the Democratic Republic of Vietnam diplomatic recognition, armaments, advice, and sanctuary in China if Vietnamese soldiers were in trouble. By 1952, Giap commanded over 250,000 regular soldiers and a militia nearing 2 million. Each army division was supported by 40,000 porters carrying rice or ammunition along jungle trails and over mountain passes. Many porters were unmarried women, the so-called 'long-haired army', whom the Viet Minh found more effective than the male porters because they were easier to train, had no family responsibilities, and were perceived as less threatening by the enemy. Giap's soldiers willingly

---

KEY FIGURE

Vo Nguyen Giap (c.1911–2013)

Minister of the Interior in Ho Chi Minh's new Democratic Republic of Vietnam in 1945, Giap defeated the French at Dien Bien Phu (1954), then became Deputy Prime Minister of North Vietnam. He helped defeat America and its anti-Communist regime in South Vietnam. Giap was Defence Minister in the newly united Communist Vietnam (1976–80).

suffered for their country and their freedom, marching over mountains and through jungles, often with insufficient food. Units held self-criticism sessions, during which errors were admitted and forgiven. Giap paid great attention to winning over the ordinary people and his soldiers followed his rules when dealing with civilians:

- be polite and fair
- do not bully
- do not fraternise with women
- try not to cause damage and if you do, pay for it.

The battle of Dien Bien Phu, 1954

While Ho and Giap went from strength to strength, the French had problems. They tried what they called 'yellowing' their army (enlisting native Vietnamese) but did not trust these new recruits and gave them little responsibility. In France itself, many people were beginning to lose heart and interest in Indochina. This made the great military struggle between the French and the Viet Minh at Dien Bien Phu particularly important.

In 1954, the French built a fortress at Dien Bien Phu in an attempt to prevent Ho invading nearby Laos and to draw the Viet Minh into a set-piece battle. Both the French and the Americans thought Dien Bien Phu could be held indefinitely. They failed to anticipate that thousands of peasant volunteers would dismantle heavy, long-range guns, take them piece by piece up into the surrounding hills, successfully camouflage them until they were ready to be fired, and bombard the fortress from the surrounding high ground.

SOURCE A

What does Source A suggest about Ho's role in the planning? **?**

Vo Nguyen Giap (standing, right) and Ho Chi Minh (second left) plan the attack on Dien Bien Phu.

Eisenhower's policies toward Indochina during Dien Bien Phu

Although Eisenhower had given the French $385 million worth of armaments for an offensive against the Viet Minh not long before the showdown at Dien Bien Phu, many questions were being asked within the Eisenhower administration about the extent to which America should be involved in Vietnam:

- Was Southeast Asia vital to US security?
- If it was, should America get involved in Indochina?
- If America got involved, should involvement take the form of financial aid to the French, US military advisers assisting the French, US air and/or sea support for the French, or the sending of US ground troops to Indochina?
- Was victory possible in Indochina in conjunction with the French or if America were there alone?
- Was America willing to risk a Sino-American clash over intervention in Indochina?
- How much was America willing to do without allied (including UN) support?

Like most people in his administration, Eisenhower considered Southeast Asia vital to US security. As Communism threatened America and the French were fighting Communism, it was easier and cheaper to pay the French to fight Communism than to send American boys to do it. However, early in 1954 Eisenhower responded to French pleas for extra help by sending US bombers accompanied by 200 American technicians. He told Congress he disliked putting them in danger but that 'we must not lose Asia'.

By March, the situation at Dien Bien Phu was beginning to look hopeless, so France requested a US air strike against the Viet Minh in order to strengthen the French negotiating position at the forthcoming Geneva conference (see page 107). Eisenhower gave the request serious consideration, while many Americans schools led pupils in prayer for the French to defeat the atheist Communists.

Arguments for American intervention at Dien Bien Phu

Eisenhower worried about Vietnam and Dien Bien Phu for several reasons:

- Eisenhower wanted France to be a strong NATO member to help defend Western Europe against the Soviet threat, and French strength was being drained in Vietnam.
- The French threatened to exit Indochina without American aid.
- During the 1952 presidential election campaign, Eisenhower rejected Truman's policy of containment of Communism and advocated liberation of Communist countries ('rollback'), but by 1954 had not 'liberated' a single soul from Communism.
- Eisenhower did not want the Democrats to say he had 'lost' Vietnam.

- In a March 1954 speech, Eisenhower's Secretary of State **John Foster Dulles** said the administration feared Chinese influence and aggression in Indochina.
- Most important of all, Eisenhower feared that if the US allowed Vietnam to fall to Communism, other Southeast Asian countries would follow. At a press conference in April 1954, Eisenhower articulated his '**domino theory**'. He said Vietnam was vitally important to America, because if it fell to Communism neighbouring countries might follow like dominoes, which would mean the loss of raw materials and millions of people to the Communist world.

Eisenhower privately said that 'in certain areas at least we cannot afford to let Moscow gain another bit of territory' and briefly toyed with the idea of a lightning American air strike at Dien Bien Phu – in unmarked planes because 'we would have to deny it for ever'.

SOURCE B

From President Eisenhower's April 1954 press conference (available at http://coursesa.matrix.msu.edu/~hst306/documents/domino.html).

You have the specific value of a locality in its production of materials [rice, rubber, coal, iron ore] that the world needs. You have the possibility that many human beings pass under a dictatorship that is inimical to the free world. You have the broader considerations that might follow what you would call the 'falling domino' principle … You have a row of dominoes set up, you knock over the first one, and what will happen to the last one is the certainty that it will go over very quickly. So you could have the beginning of a disintegration that would have the most profound influences … You are talking about millions and millions of people … So, the possible consequences of the loss are just incalculable to the free world.

Arguments against American intervention

Some influential Americans opposed US intervention at Dien Bien Phu:

- Some questioned Eisenhower's domino theory.
- Some of the military and the Secretary of Defence considered Indochina 'devoid of decisive military objectives' and felt any US intervention there would be 'a serious diversion of limited US capabilities'.
- Some feared the intervention would lead to greater involvement.
- Many considered it unwise to be too closely entangled with the French, whom Eisenhower privately described as 'a hopeless, helpless mass of protoplasm' (the French resented American suggestions that they grant total independence to Vietnam and then carry on fighting there under a US commander).
- Eisenhower considered military victory in the Vietnamese jungle was impossible for either French or American troops, feared the United States could find itself fighting Communists everywhere, and felt he could not put

What reasons does Source B give to explain the importance of Vietnam?

 **KEY TERMS**

Cold Warrior One who wanted the US to wage the Cold War with even more vigour.

Domino theory President Eisenhower's belief that if one nation fell to Communism, neighbouring nations were likely to follow.

US troops on the Asian mainland again one year after he had gained massive popularity by getting them out of Korea.

- Eisenhower subsequently wrote that 'the strongest reason of all' for America to stay out was that America's unique tradition of anti-colonialism enhanced its reputation in the Cold War world and would be jeopardised if he seemed to be replacing French colonialism with American colonialism.
- Perhaps most importantly, Eisenhower tried but failed to get the British support that Congress required before approving American military intervention. Prime Minister Churchill (see page 4) said the struggle was not winnable and might trigger the third world war, and he rejected the domino theory, unconvinced that what happened in Vietnam would impact upon British Malaya. Senator Lyndon Johnson said, 'We want no more Koreas, with the United States furnishing more than 90 per cent of the manpower.'

Eisenhower finally decided against direct American intervention in Vietnam, which doomed the French to defeat at Dien Bien Phu and ensured that the French government and people were ready to give up Indochina.

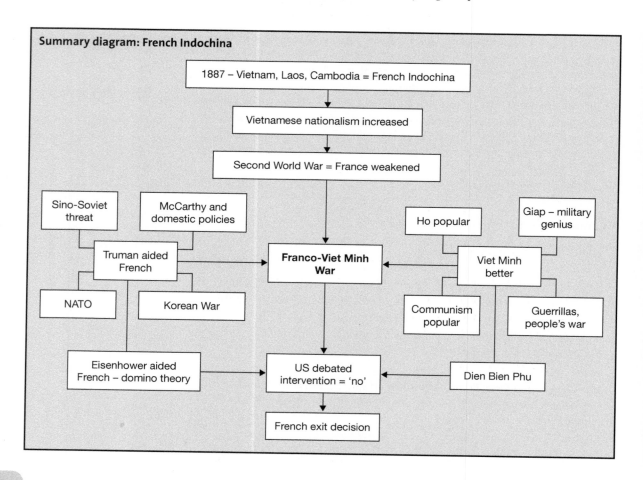

Summary diagram: French Indochina

1887 – Vietnam, Laos, Cambodia = French Indochina

Vietnamese nationalism increased

Second World War = France weakened

Sino-Soviet threat

McCarthy and domestic policies

Truman aided French

NATO

Korean War

Franco-Viet Minh War

Ho popular

Giap – military genius

Viet Minh better

Communism popular

Guerrillas, people's war

Eisenhower aided French – domino theory

US debated intervention = 'no'

Dien Bien Phu

French exit decision

The Geneva conference and the division of Vietnam

▶ *What was the significance of the Geneva conference?*

While the French and Viet Minh battled at Dien Bien Phu, preparations were underway for an international conference to discuss Indochina. The participants had different agendas (see Table 3.1).

Table 3.1 The differing agendas at the 1954 Geneva conference

France	Many in France were tiring of the struggle and aware of worldwide expectation that the war ought to be brought to an end
USSR	After Stalin died in 1953, the new Soviet leaders sought to demonstrate their interest in a Cold War thaw, to play upon Franco-American tensions over possible French concessions at Geneva, and to keep the Americans out of Vietnam
China	Communist China favoured negotiations because it wanted to forestall American involvement in Indochina and judged that participation in the peace talks would gain it increased international recognition and respectability
USA	America hoped to avoid Communist participation in the government of Vietnam, but recognised that a united non-Communist Vietnam was unlikely
Ngo Dinh Diem	Bao Dai's new Prime Minister Ngo Dinh Diem feared and distrusted the French and Ho, and did not want to negotiate with them. Diem hoped against hope for a united and independent Vietnam
The Viet Minh	The Vietnamese Communists were clearly winning the struggle for Vietnam and saw little to be gained from talking. They sought a united and independent Vietnam and felt they were well on the way to achieving it

On 7 May 1954 the victorious Viet Minh raised their red flag over Dien Bien Phu. The next day delegations representing France, Bao Dai, the Viet Minh, Cambodia, Laos, the United States, the Soviet Union, the People's Republic of China and Britain assembled in Geneva to discuss ending the war in Indochina.

The Geneva Accords, 1954

In the **Geneva Accords**, France, China, the USSR, Britain and the Viet Minh agreed that:

- The Communists would govern northern Vietnam, and Bao Dai and his new Prime Minister, Ngo Dinh Diem (see page 111), would govern the south. Ho's Viet Minh would have to give up the territory they occupied south of the 17th

Figure 3.2 French Indochina consisted of what Americans would come to know as Vietnam, Laos and Cambodia. At Geneva, Vietnam was temporarily (supposedly) divided along the 17th parallel into a Communist North (under Ho) and a non-Communist South (under Bao Dai and Diem). Elections would (supposedly) be held in 1956 to reunite the country. Laos and Cambodia gained independence.

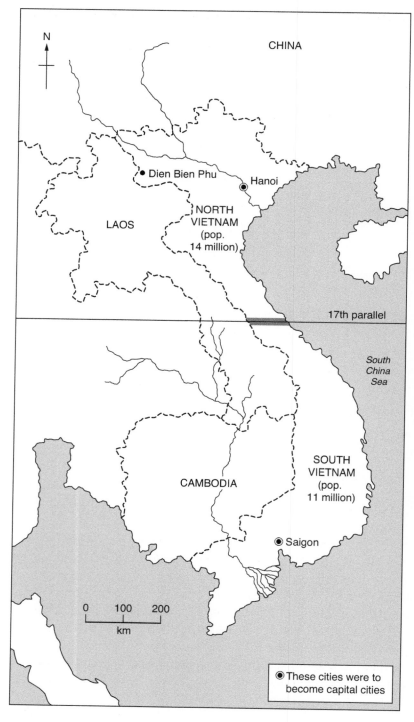

parallel (see Figure 3.2). There would be a 10-km Demilitarised Zone (DMZ) above that parallel.

- There would be a truce between the French and Viet Minh.
- Nationwide democratic elections would be held in 1956 and Vietnam would be reunified.
- Neither the northern nor the southern Vietnamese were to make any military alliances with foreign powers or to allow foreign military bases in their territories.

The significance of the Geneva Accords

The Accords were significant in several ways. The negotiations showed Ho Chi Minh that Chinese and Soviet support was limited: in order to gain the ceasefire they deemed best for their own interests, they made him accept a settlement that forced the Viet Minh to retreat behind the 17th parallel. Ho reluctantly agreed, because he believed there would be nationwide elections in 1956 (Eisenhower wrote in his 1963 memoirs that Ho would have won 80 per cent of the vote in a fair election) and because he needed Chinese and Soviet aid and time to consolidate the new regime in North Vietnam. The United States was significantly slow to pick up and/or exploit those divisions within the Communist world. Although Dulles knew there were Sino-Soviet tensions, he did not use them to advantage at Geneva.

The ceasefire was between the French and the Viet Minh – not between the Viet Minh and any South Vietnamese government. New Premier Diem of South Vietnam rejected the Accords because they put half of Vietnam under Communist control. He rightly predicted that 'another more deadly war' lay ahead. Unwilling to recognise Communist control of the northern half of Vietnam, the Eisenhower administration agreed to respect but not to sign the Geneva agreements, saying 'the United States has not itself been a party to or bound by the decisions taken', and warning that America would view 'any renewal of aggression' with 'grave concern'. America chose to misinterpret the temporary ceasefire line of the 17th parallel as a permanent division between a northern Communist state and a southern anti-Communist state. The Geneva settlement and Vietnam had become victims of the Cold War.

The creation of SEATO in September 1954

Eisenhower considered the Geneva Accords to be a Communist triumph and felt that the United States had to do something to 'restore its prestige in the Far East'. Dulles therefore quickly masterminded the **Southeast Asia Treaty Organisation (SEATO)** in the hope that it would become a Southeast Asian equivalent of NATO. Significantly, most of the newly independent nations in the region refused to take part (apart from the Philippines and Thailand), so most SEATO members were Western states (America, Britain, France, Australia and New Zealand). Each member pledged that in the event of an attack on a

 **KEY TERM**

Southeast Asia Treaty Organisation (SEATO)
Defensive alliance between USA, Britain, France, Australia, New Zealand, Pakistan, the Philippines and Thailand, 1954.

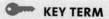

KEY TERM

Protocol In this context, an agreement between signatory nations.

Southeast Asian nation it would respond 'in accordance with its constitutional processes' – an elastic phrase that represented a rather ill-defined commitment. Under a separate **protocol**, SEATO members agreed to protect South Vietnam, Cambodia and Laos – a transparent American device to circumvent the Geneva stipulation that the Vietnamese must not enter into foreign alliances or allow foreign troops on their soil. The British diplomat and naval strategist James Cable memorably described SEATO as 'a fig leaf for the nakedness of American policy' and a 'zoo of paper tigers'.

SEATO and its failure to 1977

With its central headquarters in Bangkok, SEATO conducted joint military exercises and anti-Communist intelligence activities. However, SEATO military forces were never deployed, the organisation was generally despised by non-members, and its creation antagonised China (see page 182). While SEATO allies sent forces to assist the United States in Vietnam after 1965, they were few in number – Australia 5000, Thailand 2000, the Philippines 2000 (non-combatants) and New Zealand under 500. SEATO effected some admirable social and economic work in Southeast Asia, but Pakistan left the organisation in 1972, the French withdrew financial support in 1975, and SEATO was formally dissolved in 1977.

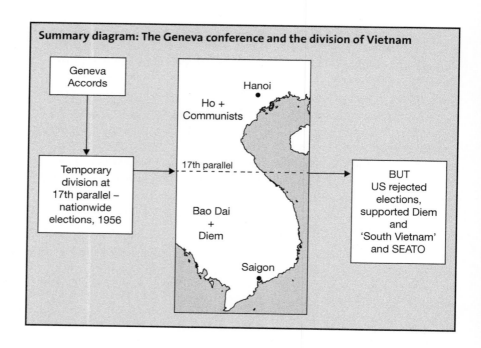

Summary diagram: The Geneva conference and the division of Vietnam

3 Two Vietnams and two leaders

▶ *Had Ho or Diem the skill and support to reunify Vietnam?*

After the Geneva conference, Ho and the Communists governed North Vietnam (from Hanoi) while Diem governed South Vietnam (from Saigon). Both would have preferred a united Vietnam.

Ngo Dinh Diem and South Vietnam

In 1954, Bao Dai thought that the American contacts of the exiled Vietnamese nationalist Ngo Dinh Diem might make him useful, so he made Diem his Prime Minister. By that time most potential Vietnamese nationalist leaders were Viet Minh. Most of the other non-Communists with leadership qualities had been killed by the French or the Viet Minh, or had given up political activities, so Diem slid into a leadership vacuum.

Ngo Dinh Diem

1901	Born in central Vietnam
1933	Resigned in protest against French domination
1933–45	Lived quietly in Hue but in touch with other nationalists
1945	Rejected participation in Ho Chi Minh's government
1950–4	Exile in the USA
1954	Prime Minister of US-backed South Vietnam
1955	Defeated Bao Dai in government-controlled referendum; made himself President of newly declared Republic of South Vietnam
1956	Refused to carry out nationwide elections; increasingly autocratic
1963	Persecution of Buddhist majority led United States to withdraw support and collude in his assassination by his army generals

Background

Diem was born into a Catholic mandarin Vietnamese family in central Vietnam. Minister of the Interior under the Emperor Bao Dai, he resigned in 1933 in protest against French domination. Captured by Communist forces in 1945, he declined offers to join Ho Chi Minh's government and went into exile in the United States, where he won support from prominent Catholic senators such as John Kennedy and Mike Mansfield. In 1954, the Emperor Bao Dai asked Diem to return to Vietnam to become Prime Minister of the US-backed government in South Vietnam. Diem agreed and soon marginalised Bao Dai and established control of the government in Saigon.

Achievements

Remaining in power in South Vietnam from 1955 to 1963 was a considerable achievement on the part of a member of the Catholic minority who had no empathy with the peasant population. An authoritarian ruler, Diem had considerable success in ridding himself of potential opponents in Saigon but failed to halt the ever-increasing Communist threat.

Significance

Diem was important in that many influential Americans perceived him as the only non-Communist anywhere near capable of running Vietnam. While he frequently showed considerable political cunning, his US-supported South Vietnamese government was always unpopular. The fact that there was no clear alternative non-Communist leader suggests South Vietnam was not a viable state.

Diem (whom the French Prime Minister described as incapable and mad) rejected nationwide elections stipulated by the Geneva Accords because he knew Ho would win. He looked to the Americans for aid and they quickly and enthusiastically pledged him their support (in April 1956, Dulles described Dien Bien Phu as 'a blessing in disguise' because it got rid of the French: 'We have a clean base there now, without the taint of [French] colonialism').

Diem's government of South Vietnam, 1955–61

Diem and his American patrons agreed that the Communist menace must be halted and that one way to do this was to build a stable, non-Communist South Vietnamese state. Although the Eisenhower administration urged Diem to implement **land reform**, it was MAAG (see page 100) and its emphasis on military solutions rather than social and economic reform that dominated US assistance to Diem.

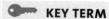

KEY TERM

Land reform Even anti-Communist Americans saw the need for a more equal distribution of land in Vietnam: an estimated 1 per cent of the population owned all the cultivable land in the south.

The Americans were not entirely happy with Diem. Vice President Richard Nixon said the problem was that 'the [South] Vietnamese lacked the ability to conduct a war by themselves or govern themselves', while Dulles admitted that America supported Diem because he was the best of a bad bunch. Indeed, at one point, Dulles guessed that the chances of success for the creation of the South Vietnamese state were only 10 per cent. American officials variously referred to Diem as a 'yogi-like mystic' or a 'Messiah without a message', while the JCS considered Diem's regime unstable, even hopeless. The Eisenhower administration nearly withdrew their support, but were encouraged by Diem's demonstration of political skill in outmanoeuvring and defeating Bao Dai and other non-Communist opponents in spring 1955.

Increased American aid

In October 1955, Diem held an election in South Vietnam, now clearly a separate state. Those voting for Bao Dai were punished: some were held down to have pepper sauce poured into their nostrils. Diem claimed 98.2 per cent of the vote, rejecting an American adviser's proposals that 60 or 70 per cent was a more credible figure. Out of 450,000 registered voters in Saigon, Diem claimed that 605,025 had voted for him. Through a combination of force, fraud and friendship with America, Diem appeared to have made himself undisputed leader of the new state of South Vietnam. Impressed by Diem's ruthlessness in dealing with opponents, the Eisenhower administration increased aid to his regime.

American aid took several forms. Diem was given:

- hundreds of millions of dollars
- advice on politics, land reform and covert operations against the Viet Minh

- American aid in the transportation of approximately a million mostly middle-class, educated and Catholic Vietnamese from the north to the south. They were (initially) supportive of Diem, but their arrival made Diem even less popular among the predominantly Buddhist southerners, who had always resented Catholic Vietnamese collaboration with the French.

Miracle man of Asia?

When Diem visited America in 1957, Eisenhower praised him as the 'miracle man' of Asia. Unfortunately, Diem's belief in his own infallibility and rectitude was so strengthened by such words that when Americans advised him that his repressive and unpopular administration needed to reform to ensure long-term survival, Diem dug his heels in and did nothing. His family dominated the government, with his brother **Ngo Dinh Nhu** and his wife Madame Nhu wielding considerable power and influence, and while Diem himself lived frugally, his family squabbled amongst themselves in their struggle to get rich.

Diem favoured his fellow Catholics from the wealthy landowner class and never appealed to the ordinary people. Like his American patrons, Diem failed to comprehend how Viet Minh advocacy of greater economic equality could win so many peasant hearts. Diem promised a land reform programme, but proved uncommitted to it: for example, in Long An province, near Saigon, fewer than 1000 out of 35,000 tenants received property. Indeed, Diem infuriated peasants by demanding payment for land they had been given for free by the Viet Minh in the war against the French. Diem disliked meeting his people and only reluctantly toured South Vietnam at the behest of his American patrons who rightly feared that unlike 'Uncle Ho' he lacked the common touch.

Support for Ho and Communism

In many ways, the Communist regime in the North was as unpleasant as that of Diem in the South. Ho's Communists liquidated thousands of landlords and opponents and even loyal Viet Minh by mistake. When Ho's **People's Army of Vietnam (PAVN)** had to put down a revolt in 1956, 6000 peasants were killed or deported. Subsequently, Ho and Giap admitted having wrongfully resorted to terror.

On the other hand, egalitarian and free from apparent foreign domination, Ho's regime often won the hearts of the people in a way that Diem's never did. Joseph Alsop, one of the few Americans who had toured rural South Vietnam when it was still occupied by the Viet Minh, reluctantly admitted that he had seen a great deal of evidence of their support amongst the peasantry in August 1954. Many southerners remained quietly loyal to Ho after Vietnam was divided in 1954, although others disliked both Diem and the Communists.

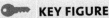 **KEY FIGURE**

Ngo Dinh Nhu (1910–63)
Diem's younger brother and chief political adviser, Nhu had special responsibility for the South Vietnamese Army and the strategic hamlets programme.

 KEY TERM

People's Army of Vietnam (PAVN) Formal name of Ho's North Vietnamese Army (NVA) by 1956.

? How useful is Source C for a historian studying Vietnam after the Geneva Accords?

SOURCE C

Columnist Joseph Alsop on his 1954 visit to Vietnam, published in the 31 August 1954 issue of the *New York Herald Tribune*, quoted in Ngo Vinh Long, 'From Polarisation to Integration in Vietnam', *Journal of Contemporary Asia*, volume 39, number 2, Routledge, 2009, pp. 295–304.

In the area I visited, the Communists have scored a whole series of political, organisational, military – and one has to say it – moral triumphs … What impressed me most, alas, was the moral fervor they had inspired among the non-Communist cadres and the strong support they had obtained from the peasantry.

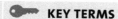

KEY TERMS

Hanoi and Saigon Nations are often referred to by the name of their capital, where the government resides, so 'Hanoi' can be used instead of North Vietnam, and 'Saigon' instead of South Vietnam.

Ho Chi Minh Trail North Vietnamese Communist supply route going south from North Vietnam through Cambodia and Laos to South Vietnam.

National Liberation Front (NLF) From 1960, Ho's southern supporters gave themselves this name.

Viet Cong After 1960, Diem called the National Liberation Front 'Viet Cong' (Vietnamese Communists or VC).

People's Liberation Armed Forces (PLAF) The name which Ho's southern supporters called their forces after 1960.

Agrovilles New and well-defended villages set up by Diem's regime to keep Communists out.

Relations between Diem and Hanoi

Relations between **Hanoi and Saigon** were uneasy between 1955 and 1959, even though Ho discouraged supporters in the South from attacking Diem's regime. Hanoi wanted to be seen to be abiding by the Geneva agreements and was bitterly divided about whether consolidation in the North should take priority over liberation of the South. Hanoi's conservatism gave Diem the opportunity to arrest and execute many southern Communist activists, whose numbers dropped from around 10,000 in 1955 to nearer 2000 by 1959. That forced the South's Communists into open revolt and by 1960 Hanoi had decided to give liberation equal priority with consolidation. Hanoi created what would soon become known as the **Ho Chi Minh Trail** (see page 137), over which men and supplies would be moved from North Vietnam to South Vietnam via Laos. Many of the Viet Minh who had come to the North after Geneva were now sent back to South Vietnam with instructions to work to undermine the Saigon government.

The formation of the NLF

From 1960, Ho's southern supporters called themselves the **National Liberation Front (NLF)**, but Diem called them **Viet Cong** (Vietnamese Communists or **VC**). Like the Viet Minh in 1945, the NLF emphasised national independence rather than social revolution and contained non-Communists. The NLF organised itself into the **People's Liberation Armed Forces (PLAF)**. The second Indochina War or Vietnam War had begun.

The impact of the NLF

Diem responded to the rising levels of violence and disruption caused by the NLF by relocating peasants to army-protected villages called **agrovilles**. The peasants hated forced, expensive removals from their homes, lands and sacred ancestral tombs, and dissatisfaction with the regime of 'American Diem' increased. In 1960, eighteen prominent Vietnamese nationalists petitioned Diem for moderate reform, but he responded with greater repression. The US ambassador recommended that Diem introduce political and social reform rather than concentrate on the use of military force, but MAAG (see page 100) disagreed.

By 1961, Diem had received around $7 billion from the Eisenhower administration. 'We bet pretty heavily on him', said Eisenhower. Senator Kennedy described Diem as 'our offspring', while one exasperated US official in Saigon described Diem as 'a puppet who pulled his own strings – and ours as well'. Many knowledgeable Americans warned that the struggle could not be won with Diem in power, but others saw the conflict in Vietnam in simple military terms and believed that Diem's battles were against unpopular Communists and could be won by pouring in more military aid and money. The problem was that the Communists had considerable popular support in South Vietnam and that Diem had to deal with so much non-Communist opposition. Even his army (the **Army of the Republic of Vietnam** or **ARVN**) contained opponents, some of whom unsuccessfully rebelled against him in 1960. By 1961 America was supporting a very unpopular regime in South Vietnam.

 **KEY TERM**

Army of the Republic of Vietnam (ARVN) South Vietnamese forces – the Army of the Republic of Vietnam.

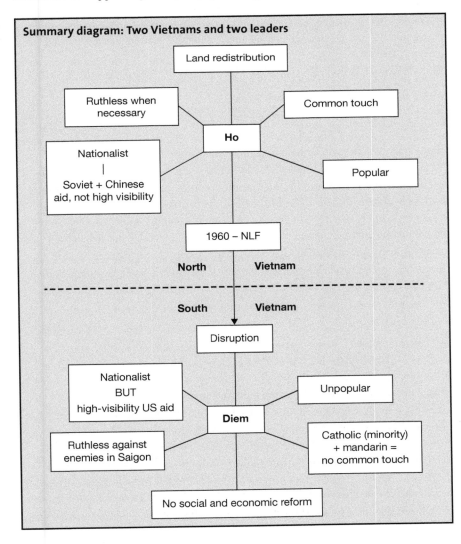

Summary diagram: Two Vietnams and two leaders

- Land redistribution
- Ruthless when necessary
- Common touch
- **Ho**
- Nationalist | Soviet + Chinese aid, not high visibility
- Popular
- 1960 – NLF

North **Vietnam**

- -

South **Vietnam**

- Disruption
- Nationalist BUT high-visibility US aid
- Unpopular
- **Diem**
- Ruthless against enemies in Saigon
- Catholic (minority) + mandarin = no common touch
- No social and economic reform

Eisenhower's policies toward Indochina

 ▶ *Was Vietnam 'Eisenhower's war'?*

Eisenhower's policies toward Indochina can be divided into two phases. In the first phase, Eisenhower's policy in Vietnam was to continue Truman's financial and advisory support for the French colonial regime in its struggle against the Communists. The second phase was the establishment of the anti-Communist state of South Vietnam. Eisenhower knew that if the elections prescribed by the Geneva Accords were held in 1956, the whole of Vietnam would have become Communist, so it could be argued that his nation-building in South Vietnam constituted rollback. However, his nation-building was not very successful. By the end of Eisenhower's presidency in January 1961, Diem's regime was greatly threatened by the Communist opposition.

Eisenhower's role in the Vietnam War

Eisenhower's successors greatly escalated the US involvement in Vietnam, which raises the question as to the extent of Eisenhower's responsibility for the Vietnam War.

Historians generally consider Eisenhower's Vietnam policy to have been a success. First, he rejected the atomic option at Dien Bien Phu. Some members of the administration, including Vice President Nixon, were willing to use atomic weapons to help the French there, but Eisenhower recognised that it would probably lead to conflict with the Soviets and China and said, 'You boys must be crazy. We can't use those awful things against Asians for the second time in less than 10 years. My God.' Second, Eisenhower did not send thousands of American troops to Vietnam as Johnson did. When Eisenhower left the White House in January 1961, there were just under 700 military advisers in South Vietnam – in line with the maximum mandated by the Geneva Accords.

On the other hand, it was perhaps only congressional leaders and the reluctance of his British allies that stopped him increasing direct American involvement during the struggle for Dien Bien Phu. In defiance of the Geneva Accords, Eisenhower effectively made the United States the guarantor of an independent state of South Vietnam and committed it to the defence of a particularly unpopular leader in Diem. Ambassador Eldridge Durbrow advocated political reforms to make South Vietnam a genuine democracy, but the State Department and Dulles favoured concentration upon a strong government in Saigon to combat Communism. Eisenhower gave Diem large-scale financial aid and 1500 American advisers, nearly half of whom were military. Once such a commitment was undertaken, it was arguable that America had incurred an obligation to see it through. It would prove to be but a short step to putting American soldiers into

Vietnam. The Eisenhower administration made Vietnam far more important to the United States than it had been under Truman and in some ways Vietnam could justly be called 'Eisenhower's war'.

In order to come to conclusions about Eisenhower's responsibility for the American involvement in Vietnam, several questions need to be answered:

- Could any American President be seen to ignore any 'threat' from Communism in the Cold War era?
- After one President had committed American foreign policy in a certain direction, could another feasibly reverse it?
- Once America had greatly aided the South Vietnamese anti-Communists, could it then legitimately abandon them?

Those who would answer 'no' to any of these questions would seem to suggest that Eisenhower was right, and that what was right would inevitably lead to American involvement in Vietnam.

However, much depends on the sort of questions one asks:

- Was Communism really such a threat to America?
- Would Vietnam turning Communist really affect the course of the Cold War?
- Did America have any right to intervene in what was in effect an internal debate about what kind of government Vietnam should have?

Negative answers to these questions would suggest that Eisenhower was mistaken in his policies. On the other hand, many Americans agreed with him, raising final questions. Can any President transcend the prejudices and preoccupations of his time? And if he does, will he and his party get re-elected?

Eisenhower and Laos

Eisenhower was anxious about Laos as well as Vietnam. Unlike Vietnam, Laos had no nationalist (let alone Communist) pre-war independence movement, so the French returned with minimal opposition in 1945. One small opposition group developed during the war under Prince Souphanouvong. The group took refuge in the jungle and maintained close contact with the Viet Minh. During the Franco-Viet Minh war, the Viet Minh sought sanctuary in northeastern Laos, where they worked closely with the Laotian Communists – the **Pathet Lao**. By the time of the Geneva conference, the Viet Minh-supported Pathet Lao independence movement controlled roughly half of Laos. After Laotian independence was confirmed under the Geneva Accords, the Pathet Lao, who controlled the northern provinces adjoining North Vietnam, rejected suggestions that they integrate with the Royal Lao Army.

After Geneva (see page 107), the Eisenhower administration incorporated Laos in SEATO, then sent in billions of dollars in military aid and advisers to assist pro-Western Laotian politicians and generals. For example, in the winter of 1959–60, the United States gave considerable aid to General Phoumi Nosavan.

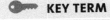

KEY TERM

Pathet Lao Laotian Communists.

By that time, three factions were engaged in the Laotian civil war:

- General Phoumi's pro-Western group
- the Communist Pathet Lao
- neutralists who sought to keep out of the Cold War.

The Soviets and Chinese assisted the Pathet Lao and neutralist forces against General Phoumi's US-supplied troops, and by early 1961, the Pathet Lao seemed on the verge of victory. Advised that the situation was desperate, Eisenhower said, 'We cannot let Laos fall to the Communists, even if we have to fight … with our allies or without them.'

Eisenhower's advice to Kennedy on Laos

When President-elect Kennedy met outgoing President Eisenhower in January 1961, Kennedy said Laos topped his list of eight areas of foreign and defence policy importance. Eisenhower told Kennedy that Laos was 'the cork in the bottle' – a vital domino, whose independence the United States had to preserve in the face of attempted Chinese, North Vietnamese and Soviet domination. Eisenhower advised Kennedy not to opt for neutralisation: 'It would be fatal for us to permit Communists to insert themselves into the Laotian government.' He said if America failed to persuade its SEATO allies to help defend the freedom of Laos, it would simply have to act alone. Eisenhower's emphasis upon the importance of Laos greatly impressed Kennedy and greatly impacted upon Kennedy's policies in Vietnam.

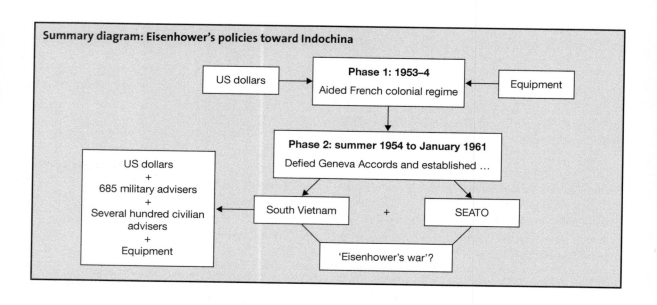

Summary diagram: Eisenhower's policies toward Indochina

5 Kennedy's policies toward Indochina

 ▶ *Was Vietnam 'Kennedy's war'?*

In early 1961, President Kennedy considered tiny, impoverished, mountainous Laos and its 3 million population a greater problem than Vietnam. His belief that the Laotian civil war was part of the Cold War struggle was strengthened by **Khrushchev**'s January 1961 speech in support of wars of national liberation in the Third World (it was designed to show the USSR led world Communism and more likely to have been aimed at China than at the United States). The new President weighed up whether or not the United States should intervene in Laos.

Decisions over intervention in Laos

The State Department, the CIA, the JCS and close advisers such as Kennedy's friend General Maxwell Taylor and his national security adviser Walt Rostow urged military intervention, but Kennedy knew it would be hard to explain to the American public why he was sending American troops to Laos – 'I don't think there are probably 25 people [in the United States] other than us in the room who know where it is.' Furthermore, the US ambassador to Laos, Winthrop Brown, declared it unrealistic to expect 'any satisfactory solution of the problem in the country could be found by purely military means … Laos was hopeless … a classic example of a political and economic vacuum. It had no national identity. It was just a series of lines drawn on a map.' Brown said the Laotians were 'charming, indolent, enchanting … but they are just not very vigorous, nor are they very numerous, nor are they very well organized.' Kennedy's ambassador to India, the famous economist John Kenneth Galbraith, and British Prime Minister Harold Macmillan (1957–63) made similar arguments. Macmillan told Kennedy Laos was militarily indefensible and not vital to Western security. Like Macmillan, France's leader General **Charles de Gaulle** refused to support any US military intervention in Laos. De Gaulle suggested neutralisation: 'For you, intervention in this region will be an entanglement without end.'

Initially, it seemed that Kennedy might send American troops to Laos. In a 23 March 1961 news conference he said, 'Laos is far away from America, but the world is small … The security of all Southeast Asia will be endangered if Laos loses its neutral independence.' He told a *Washington Post* reporter that military intervention was a realistic option and he was willing to go in if necessary – even if that meant that he would only be a one-term President. In late March, he sent 500 Marines to the border between Thailand and Laos. On 26 April, with American 'advisers' in Laos involved in combat operations and the CIA's **'Air America'** on alert and ready to bomb Communists on the Plain of Jars (see Figure 3.1 on page 96), Ambassador Brown reported that the Communists

 KEY FIGURES

Nikita Khrushchev (1894–1971)

Leader of the USSR from 1955 to 1964, Khrushchev was unpredictable. His 1956 anti-Stalin speech destabilised Eastern Europe and infuriated China. He declared **'peaceful coexistence'** with the West desirable, but triggered crises over Berlin (1960–1) and Cuba (1962), after which Soviet–American relations improved. Sino-Soviet relations deteriorated under Khrushchev, who was ousted from power in 1964.

Charles de Gaulle (1890–1970)

President of France from 1959 to 1969, he rejected American Cold War leadership and withdrew France from NATO in 1966. He was highly critical of America's Vietnam policies.

KEY TERMS

Peaceful coexistence
Policy of Soviet Premier Nikita Khrushchev, who said that as nuclear weapons made a US–Soviet war undesirable, there should be attempts to get along with the West.

Air America A supposedly civilian air carrier that the CIA used, for example in Laos during the Vietnam War.

would win control of Laos unless Kennedy authorised the use of US air and ground forces. Keen to keep the Communists away from its own borders, Thailand urged SEATO intervention in Laos, but Britain and France rejected the idea. Supported by Congress, Kennedy never sent American ground troops to fight in Laos, but he increased covert intervention there in collaboration with Thailand.

Why Kennedy did not send troops to Laos

Kennedy did not send Americans to fight in Laos because:

- US involvement in an unsuccessful attempt to overthrow the left-wing Fidel Castro in Cuba in spring 1961 made him more cautious
- the number of available soldiers and aircraft was limited
- Congress feared intervention might lead to a clash with China
- landlocked Laos was relatively inaccessible
- he knew the American people and important allies opposed the idea
- the leader of the pro-American faction, General Nosavan Phoumi, was unpopular and even less competent than Diem (Kennedy described him as a 'total shit').

In May 1961, the Soviets suggested a ceasefire then agreed with the Americans that Laos should be neutralised in the Cold War. However, the different Laotian factions continued to fight. By October 1961, Kennedy had sent 300 US military advisers to assist Nosavan Phoumi, which emboldened the general to provoke a battle with the Pathet Lao at Nam Tha in May 1962, in the belief that the Americans would send support. His forces did badly, but one of his US military advisers saw cause for hope:

> The morale of my [Laotian] battalion is substantially better than in our last engagement. The last time, they dropped their weapons and ran. This time, they took their weapons with them.

Kennedy moved 3000 US troops to Thailand, which prompted the Soviets to quickly reaffirm their support for a neutral Laos.

In July 1962, the Laotians finally agreed to a coalition government under **Souvanna Phouma**. Sixteen nations, including the USA and the USSR, signed the declaration on the neutrality of Laos, but that was not the end of the story for Kennedy. First, although Kennedy withdrew around 600 members of the US armed forces from Laos after the Geneva conference of 1962, the 7000 or so North Vietnamese forces there did not leave, and so the United States quickly initiated another military assistance programme to Prime Minister Souvanna Phouma, now opposed by both the Pathet Lao and neutralists. In contrast, the Soviets really had got out of Laos. In July 1963, Khrushchev said, 'I have no interest in Laos.' Second, although the neutralisation of Laos did not cause the great Cold Warrior outcry in the United States that many in the Kennedy administration had feared, it nevertheless impacted greatly upon Kennedy's Vietnam policies.

Vietnam – Kennedy's war?

While Vietnam was a minor Cold War sideshow under Truman and Eisenhower, it became far more important during the Kennedy presidency. The considerable debate over Kennedy's Vietnam policy has been affected by the knowledge that the Vietnam War became controversial and unpopular under his successor, President Lyndon Johnson (see page 136). Kennedy's supporters often argue that the Vietnam War was 'Johnson's war' and that Kennedy was planning to get America out. The Johnson administration was much criticised for its apparent lack of understanding of Vietnam and for reliance on military solutions to the problems there. However, the study of the Kennedy administration's policies reveals similar failures of perception as well as a massive increase in the American military commitment in Vietnam. These issues are sometimes forgotten by those who concentrate upon Johnson's presidency in isolation.

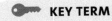

KEY TERM

Cuban Missile Crisis
In 1962, President Kennedy's pressure forced Soviet leader Khrushchev to remove Soviet nuclear missiles from Cuba.

John Fitzgerald Kennedy

1917	Born in Boston, Massachusetts
1940	*Why England Slept* published
1941–3	Second World War hero
1947–53	Congressman
1953–60	Senator
1961–3	President of the United States
1961	Cuban invasion fiasco (April)
	Vienna summit (June)
1962	Cuban Missile Crisis (October)
1963	Nuclear Test Ban Treaty (August)
	Assassinated (November)

Background
Born to a wealthy Irish Catholic Democrat family in Boston, Massachusetts, Kennedy wrote the bestselling *Why England Slept* after graduation from Harvard University. Kennedy's book criticised British unpreparedness for war, but recognised the difficulty of gaining popular support for a war in a democracy. He received acclaim for heroism during the Second World War, which helped his political career. A relatively insignificant Congressman (1947–53) and Senator (1953–60), with a poor attendance record, Kennedy's great interest was foreign policy. His foreign policy pronouncements were always militantly anti-Communist and critical of colonialism. While on the Senate Foreign Relations Committee, he advocated massive aid to emerging Third World nations. His presidential election campaign in 1960 was characterised by Cold War rhetoric and Kennedy family glamour and money. It won him a very narrow victory over Republican candidate Richard Nixon.

Achievements
Kennedy managed little of note in terms of domestic legislation, but many have praised his foreign policy achievements, especially his handling of the **Cuban Missile Crisis** and his refusal to put American troops in Vietnam.

Significance
Kennedy is important in the Cold War context in that his presidency was full of crises, for which he and/or Soviet leader Khrushchev clearly bore some blame. Despite his Cold Warrior rhetoric, he seemed to be advocating a Cold War thaw in the last year of his presidency. He is important in the Indochinese context in that he opted against military intervention in Laos but dramatically increased US involvement in Vietnam.

Kennedy's early ideas about Vietnam

As a young Democrat Congressman, Kennedy agreed with the Democrat President Truman that the expansion of Communism must be 'contained' by America, but attacked him for 'losing' China in 1949 (see page 36). Like most Americans, Kennedy believed in Eisenhower's domino theory, but he criticised Eisenhower for allowing the rise of Communism in the newly emergent nations of the Third World, which Kennedy considered to be the new Cold War battleground. In a 1956 speech to the American Friends of Vietnam, Kennedy said South Vietnam was:

- an important domino, the fall of which would threaten countries such as India, Japan, the Philippines, Laos and Cambodia
- the 'cornerstone of the free world in Southeast Asia … a proving ground for democracy in Asia … a test of American responsibility and determination in Asia', where the 'relentless' Chinese had to be stopped, for the sake of US security.

During his 1960 presidential election campaign, Kennedy said that the country needed a President 'to get America moving again', especially against Communism, which he described as 'unceasing in its drive for world domination'.

Clearly, Kennedy's background suggested that he might be even more interested in and committed to Vietnam than his predecessors.

SOURCE D

? Looking at the map in Source D, why did it make more sense for the United States to intervene in Vietnam rather than in Laos?

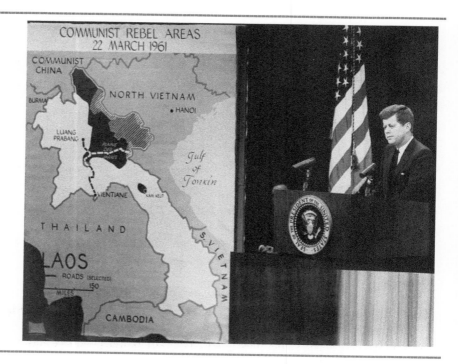

President Kennedy explaining the situation in Vietnam.

The President and his advisers

The interests, emphases and characters of President Kennedy and his chosen advisers shaped US policy towards Vietnam. Kennedy's sensitivity about his youth (at 43, he was the youngest President voted into office) and inexperience made him keen to be assertive in foreign affairs. At a 1961 White House luncheon, a newspaper editor challenged Kennedy:

> *We can annihilate Russia and should make that clear to the Soviet government ... you and your Administration are weak sisters ...* [America needs] *a man on horseback ... Many people in Texas and the Southwest think that you are riding* [your daughter] *Caroline's tricycle.*

A red-faced Kennedy, who retorted 'I'm just as tough as you are' was clearly a President who thought he had much to prove. Furthermore, Kennedy was something of a prisoner of his own Cold War campaign rhetoric. Having made much of the need for a more dynamic foreign policy, he felt bound to increase defence expenditure and foreign involvement.

Just before Kennedy's inauguration, Khrushchev had forecast the ultimate triumph of Communism through wars of national liberation in Third World countries such as Vietnam, for which he promised Soviet aid. Kennedy also believed that the Third World was likely to be the main future arena of the Cold War. Kennedy's character and beliefs, in combination with Eisenhower's warning that the Republican Party would attack 'any retreat in Southeast Asia', suggested Kennedy was likely to make a stand somewhere in Southeast Asia, be it Laos or Vietnam.

McNamara and Rusk

Kennedy's eagerness to 'get America moving again' made him impatient with the State Department, so he frequently looked to Secretary of Defence **Robert McNamara** for advice on Vietnam. McNamara and the Defence Department were naturally more inclined than the State Department and its diplomatic experts to see problems in terms of military solutions. McNamara's friendship with the President and powerful personality, coupled with Secretary of State Dean Rusk's deliberately colourless public persona (see page 100), made the Secretary of Defence a formidable figure within the cabinet.

Enormous influence and judgemental lapses on the part of McNamara proved unfortunate in Vietnam. McNamara firmly believed in the US commitment to Vietnam, but his solutions to problems there were always military – an emphasis which proved unhelpful. A *New York Times* reporter commended McNamara's efficiency but worried about McNamara's total conviction that he was always right, lack of historical knowledge, and tendency to try to reduce problems to statistics by eliminating the human factor. Trained in the importance of statistics, McNamara tended to look at numbers of weapons and men and to forget that poorly armed people will sometimes fight to the death for independence and

 KEY FIGURE

Robert McNamara (1916–2009)

Secretary of Defence under Kennedy (1961–3) then Johnson (1963–8). He encouraged them to send US ground troops to Vietnam and advocated large-scale bombing. He had changed his mind about Vietnam by late 1967, and declared that the US had got it all wrong.

social justice. McNamara subsequently admitted that his weaknesses proved disastrous in Vietnam. 'We were kidding ourselves into thinking that we were making well-informed decisions', said one McNamara deputy years later. Unfortunately, President Lyndon Johnson retained McNamara as Secretary of Defence until early 1968.

This was an explosive situation: a crusading President keen to be assertive and to make a name for himself, who was convinced that the Third World and probably Southeast Asia was the next great Cold War arena, and who listened to those more likely to put the emphasis on military battles than on the battles for the hearts and minds of the people. All this, in combination with Kennedy's frustration over events in Cuba and Laos, contributed to increasing US military involvement in Vietnam.

Cuba, Laos and Vietnam

In his first week in office Kennedy privately declared that the major problem areas of the Third World included Cuba, Laos and Vietnam, the last being 'the worst we've got'. Events in Cuba and Laos greatly impacted upon Kennedy's Vietnam policies.

Despite a few warning voices within the administration, Kennedy sponsored an ill-conceived and unsuccessful anti-Communist invasion by Cuban exiles at the Bay of Pigs in Cuba in 1961. The failure of the Bay of Pigs, coupled with the 'draw' consequent on the supposed neutralisation of Laos, convinced Kennedy that he needed outright victories elsewhere. 'There are just so many concessions that one can make to the Communists in one year and survive politically', Kennedy told a friend after the Bay of Pigs. 'We just can't have another defeat in Vietnam.' He confided to a *New York Times* reporter, 'Now we have a problem in making our power credible, and Vietnam is the place.' One insider has suggested that **hawks** within the administration would only accept neutrality in Laos in return for an activist policy in Vietnam, which was more suitable for US intervention than Laos in that it had a long coastline where US naval supremacy could be brought to bear. Furthermore, many Americans thought Diem had South Vietnam under control and democracy seemed to have a good chance of working there.

Kennedy and Diem's government, 1961–3

President Kennedy had several options in relation to Vietnam.

Option 1 – exit

In October 1954, Eisenhower told Diem that US aid was dependent upon Diem 'undertaking needed reforms'. In 1961, the US ambassador to South Vietnam, Elbridge Durbrow, informed Kennedy that these conditions had not been met. Kennedy could have cited this as a reason for US withdrawal but his administration never seemed to give the exit option serious consideration.

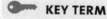

KEY TERM

Hawks Militant Cold Warriors in the USA; those at the other end of the spectrum were known as doves.

The JCS warned Kennedy that, 'any reversal of US policy could have disastrous effects, not only on our relationship with South Vietnam, but with the rest of our Asian and other allies as well'. Rusk and McNamara told Kennedy that because of Eisenhower's commitment to South Vietnam, a US departure would result in a loss of face, 'undermine the credibility of American commitments everywhere', and give the Republicans a chance to attack the administration. Painfully aware of the furore over Truman's 'loss' of China, Kennedy scarcely needed that reminder.

Option 2 – peace

Kennedy sanctioned unofficial peace talks in the summer of 1962, but Hanoi's position was that America must exit before any meaningful negotiations could take place, while the Americans opposed any meaningful negotiations unless the Saigon regime was clearly winning the war – and it never was.

Option 3 – military solutions

At Kennedy's accession, there were around 700 American military advisers in South Vietnam. When Diem's 250,000 soldiers still could not wipe out the Viet Cong, McNamara, General Maxwell Taylor (whom Kennedy had sent to evaluate the situation in October 1961), the JCS and the National Security Council recommended putting US ground troops in. McNamara said it should be done even if it meant Chinese and Soviet intervention. However, Kennedy preferred to increase the number of military advisers – there were 12,000 by 1962. Increasing quantities of American weaponry flooded into South Vietnam and although Kennedy publicly denied it, American helicopters and pilots were actively involved in the war. They transported troops, undertook reconnaissance missions, provided fire support for Army of the Republic of Vietnam (ARVN) units, and sprayed defoliants to strip the trees and enable better aerial observation. Meanwhile, on the ground, more and more American advisers accompanied ARVN units. This increased US military involvement was orchestrated by the **Military Assistance Command, Vietnam** (MACV), which replaced MAAG (see page 100) in February 1962.

In late 1961, the massive increase in American aid seemed to be paying off: the unprecedented mobility provided by the helicopters proved particularly useful to Diem's troops. When McNamara visited Vietnam in May 1962, he declared that 'every quantitative measurement we have shows we are winning the war', but this was a dubious assertion and there were warning voices. De Gaulle (see page 119) counselled Kennedy:

> … the more you become involved out there against Communism, the more the Communists will appear as the champions of national independence … You will sink step by step into a bottomless military and political quagmire, however much you spend in men and money.

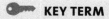 **KEY TERM**

Military Assistance Command, Vietnam
MACV was created by Kennedy to co-ordinate US efforts in South Vietnam in February 1962.

In November 1961, Kennedy sent his trusted friend Kenneth Galbraith to Saigon to assess the situation. Galbraith said:

- Vietnam was a political not military problem
- Diem was a loser
- the Americans looked like the French colonialists
- Vietnam was not strategically important
- increased US involvement could only end in defeat and humiliation.

Under-Secretary of State George Ball warned that 'we'll have 300,000 men in the paddies and jungles' within five years, but Kennedy responded, 'George, you're crazier than hell. That just isn't going to happen.' In November 1962, Kennedy sent Senator Mike Mansfield to report on Vietnam. When Mansfield criticised Diem and the increasing American involvement, Kennedy was displeased. 'You expect me to believe this?' 'Yes. You sent me', replied Mansfield. 'This isn't what my people are telling me', said Kennedy. Subsequent reports were a mixture of pessimistic references to Diem and the optimistic belief that American firepower must win eventually and that the VC could not afford to continue the struggle in the face of it.

Meanwhile, Diem's forces continued to lose ground. Their weakness and the role of the US military under Kennedy was demonstrated in the battle of Ap Bac in January 1963.

The battle of Ap Bac (January 1963)

In January 1963, a Viet Cong force was located in Ap Bac, near Saigon. Around 2000 ARVN troops, accompanied by 113 American armoured personnel carriers, American-operated helicopters and bombers, and American advisers surrounded Ap Bac, unaware that there were as many as 350 guerrillas there.

The ARVN troops refused to attack the Viet Cong at Ap Bac, five US helicopters and three pilots were lost, and the ARVN troops refused to mount a rescue mission. The US/ARVN effort had failed because:

- The VC were unexpectedly strong and prepared.
- The Americans claimed ARVN General Cao was unwilling to fight.
- Diem refused to listen to American advice on the deployment of his troops, preferring to use his best CIA-trained soldiers to keep himself in power.
- The Americans had delayed the attack by a day to enable their pilots to sleep off the excesses of New Year's Eve.

Ap Bac was highly significant. First, it drew unprecedented attention in the US, where the South Vietnamese performance was unfavourably reviewed. Second, it showed that, despite ever-increasing American aid, Diem was probably militarily incapable of winning the war against the Communists. Indeed, in early 1963 American officials estimated that while Saigon controlled only 49 per cent of the population, the Viet Cong controlled 9 per cent and the rest was still in dispute. Nevertheless, Kennedy still resisted the American ground troops option. He feared American power might become overextended and he doubted that Congress and America's SEATO allies (see page 109) would be tempted to intervene in Vietnam, which was not a clear-cut case of Communist aggression as Korea had supposedly been (see page 50). Furthermore, millions had been spent there for nearly a decade without success, and he was convinced that once American troops were there, there would soon be demands for more.

Option 4 – the reform option

Neither the Eisenhower nor the Kennedy administration managed to persuade Diem to introduce meaningful reforms. The Kennedy administration frequently advised Diem that one of the best ways to defeat the Communists was to introduce greater political, social and economic equality to South Vietnam, but Diem ignored the advice. In November 1961, Kennedy's negotiator over Laos, Averell Harriman, told the President that Diem's regime was 'repressive, dictatorial and unpopular' and advised that the United States should not 'stake its prestige in Vietnam'.

In 1962, Diem introduced '**strategic hamlets**', fortified villages in which the Vietnamese peasants would hopefully be isolated from the Viet Cong. Unfortunately, the Viet Cong frequently joined the other residents and played on their discontent at having to pay for and build the stockades. This prompted an American observer to note that the Saigon regime's urbanite officials 'haven't the faintest idea what makes peasants tick'. The strategic hamlets scheme was run by Diem's highly unpopular brother Ngo Dinh Nhu (see page 113), whom the American journalist Stanley Karnow felt was 'approaching madness' by this time. Nhu ignored US advice about introducing social, economic and political reforms within the hamlets and about where to establish them, so that within a year, the Viet Cong captured thousands of US weapons from hamlets foolishly set up too far from Saigon. Years later it was revealed that Nhu's deputy in this business was a Communist who did his best to sabotage the scheme.

The American press increased coverage of Diem's political and military ineptitude during 1962 despite Kennedy administration pressure to avoid such criticism. As yet though, the press was not questioning the wisdom of involvement in Vietnam, just the tactics pursued and the results attained. By spring 1963, relations between Diem and the US were very tense. Diem resented US 'advice' and seemed to be considering a settlement with Hanoi which would get the Americans out, while Kennedy told a journalist friend that:

> we don't have a prayer of staying in Vietnam … These people hate us. They are going to throw our asses out … But I can't give up a piece of territory like that to the Communists and then get the American people to reelect me.

Their shared Catholicism probably played a part in Kennedy's support of Diem, but Catholics were a minority in South Vietnam and in spring 1963 there was trouble.

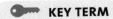

KEY TERM

Strategic hamlets
Policy used in Malaya and Vietnam to cut off villages from Communist guerrillas by surrounding them with stockades and monitoring ingress and egress.

Catholics versus Buddhists

In spring 1963, Diem allowed the flying of Catholic flags to honour his brother (an archbishop in the Catholic Church), but banned flags to celebrate Buddha's birthday. When 10,000 Buddhists protested, Diem sent in soldiers. Seven Buddhists were killed. In June, a 73-year-old Buddhist priest set himself alight in protest. His flesh burned away leaving only his heart, which became an object of worship to the Buddhist majority. This dramatic protest made headlines in America. Other such deaths followed and Nhu's unpopular wife ('No Nhus is good news', joked one American reporter) made things worse by flippant references to barbecues.

Kennedy was shocked at the front-page newspaper pictures of the Buddhist martyrs. 'How could this have happened?' he asked. 'Who are these people? Why didn't we know about them before?' Possibly Kennedy was simply trying to deflect blame from himself here, but if he really did not know of the Catholic–Buddhist tension, he had not done his homework on a country to which he had sent several thousand Americans.

? Suggest reasons why Source E was headline news in America at a time when the public were not particularly interested in or knowledgeable about Vietnam.

SOURCE E

A Buddhist priest burns himself to death in protest against Diem's religious policies, 11 June 1963.

By August, Diem appeared to be waging religious war on the Buddhist majority. With neither the military option nor the reform option working, Kennedy thought it time to replace Ambassador Frederick Nolting, who knew little about Asia, with Henry Cabot Lodge II, who knew a little more. Under Lodge, the US chose a third and more ruthless option, getting rid of Diem.

Option 5 – replace Diem

A January 1963 State Department report had said the US lacked vision and planning in its Vietnam policy, and recommended the appointment of a 'strong' ambassador to Vietnam to co-ordinate the military and 'nation-building' efforts there. Rusk told the newly appointed Ambassador Lodge that Vietnam had become a great burden to the President, taking up more of his time than any other issue. Rusk urged Lodge to be 'tough', to 'act as a catalyst' and not to 'refer many detailed questions to Washington'. Lodge obliged.

Lodge arrived in August 1963, convinced that the United States had to help South Vietnam and that effective help required the removal of Diem. An anti-Diem group in the Kennedy administration got a preoccupied President (he was focused on the forthcoming civil rights March on Washington) to agree that Diem must go unless he instituted dramatic changes. There had been no real discussion of getting rid of Diem, to the anger of McNamara and other influential men: 'My God', said the President, 'my government's coming apart'.

In what was primarily a signal to Diem that he should reform, Kennedy criticised the Saigon regime in September interviews, saying that the US could send advisers, 'but they have to win it – the people of Vietnam – against the Communists', and that Diem was 'out of touch' with his people and needed to change his policies and personnel. However, Kennedy said it would be a mistake for the United States to get out of Vietnam, reiterated the domino theory, and warned of the influence of expansionist China in Vietnam.

In September, Kennedy sent more observers, including McNamara and Taylor, to Vietnam: they reported optimistically on US military efforts but pessimistically on Diem's regime. By this time, Nhu was negotiating with Hanoi and Diem resisted American pressure to remove him. Kennedy was now convinced that the new Saigon government was necessary because of the 'harm which Diem's political actions are causing to the effort against Viet Cong'. Bobby Kennedy, the President's brother, floated the idea that perhaps 'now was the time to get out of Vietnam entirely', but no one in the administration was willing to take up the challenge to look at the problem afresh.

Diem's assassination

In the absence of firm leadership from Washington, Ambassador Lodge acquired considerable control over US policy in Vietnam. He turned Congress and American public opinion against Diem and Nhu through press 'leaks' on their activities, and was happy to learn of an ARVN plot against Nhu. The ARVN plotters were assured that they would have America's tacit support in their coup, which occurred on 2 November 1963. Lodge gave vital encouragement but publicly denied any US involvement.

It was perhaps naive to think there could be a coup without assassinations. When Diem and Nhu were found dead, Lodge said triumphantly, 'Every Vietnamese has a grin on his face today', but Kennedy heard the news 'with a look of shock and dismay'. We might never know for certain whether Kennedy tacitly approved the idea of assassinating his Vietnamese ally Diem (or his Cuban enemy Castro, against whom the CIA frequently plotted). It seems possible that he did. Ironically, Kennedy himself would meet the same fate as Diem within three weeks. 'The chickens have come home to roost', said Madame Nhu with grim satisfaction.

The historian Fredrik Logevall (2001) emphasised that 'public outrage' in the US at Diem's refusal to reform and mistreatment of Buddhists gave Kennedy 'a plausible excuse for disengaging the United States from Vietnam' – had he wanted to do so. Vice President Lyndon Johnson and General William Westmoreland (see page 145) believed that American complicity in the coup 'morally locked us in Vietnam'. Having got rid of Diem, the United States was obliged to assist any successor.

Diem was not so bad

Mao Zedong said he and Ho Chi Minh were surprised the Americans got rid of Diem – they thought Diem 'was not so bad' and guessed that the problem might have been that he 'had not wanted to take orders'. A few historians have attempted to rehabilitate Diem.

The situation at Kennedy's death

When Kennedy died in November 1963, there were over 16,000 American 'advisers' in Vietnam The greatly increased number of American advisers is the most convincing argument that Kennedy would not have 'got the United States out of Vietnam', although he was talking of a thorough review of America's Vietnam policy just before he died and some of his intimates insist he would have got out. Kennedy told one senator friend, 'I can't [get out] until 1965 – after I'm reelected.' However, Rusk, Johnson and Bobby Kennedy were among those who said he had no plans to get out. Indeed, Bobby, who knew him best, said his brother had no plans at all. Kennedy's biographer James Giglio (1991) described Kennedy's Vietnam policy as a shambles at the time of his death.

Many historians have defended Kennedy's Vietnam policy, arguing that as Truman and Eisenhower had committed the US to involvement in Vietnam,

Kennedy was caught in a '**commitment trap**'. Kennedy himself told President de Gaulle that he had inherited the possibly unwisely created SEATO from Eisenhower and that it would look bad if the United States abandoned SEATO. The United States could not be seen to lack the will to stop dominoes falling.

Kennedy's conviction that Vietnam was so important might seem ludicrous to us, but many other Cold War Americans agreed with him. Like his predecessors, Kennedy had interpreted events in Vietnam within a Cold War context, but Ho Chi Minh was not a puppet of Moscow or of Beijing. In the mistaken belief that he was, Kennedy invested Vietnam with a Cold War importance it did not really merit. Despite his frequent uncertainty about the wisdom of US involvement, Kennedy had increased his country's commitment to an unpopular regime and then overthrown it, thereby greatly increasing American's obligation to subsequent Saigon governments, as Kennedy himself recognised in a message to Lodge on 6 November. The Kennedy administration claimed to be promoting democracy in South Vietnam but had supported a dictator and then a military clique. Kennedy had passed a poisoned chalice to his successor.

KEY TERM

Commitment trap
The theory that each President after Truman was bound to continue the US involvement in Vietnam because the preceding president(s) had made Vietnam seem of increasing importance to the United States.

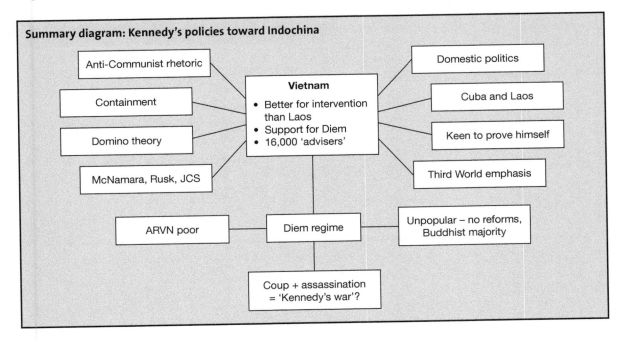

Summary diagram: Kennedy's policies toward Indochina

Anti-Communist rhetoric

Containment

Domino theory

McNamara, Rusk, JCS

Vietnam
- Better for intervention than Laos
- Support for Diem
- 16,000 'advisers'

Domestic politics

Cuba and Laos

Keen to prove himself

Third World emphasis

ARVN poor

Diem regime

Unpopular – no reforms, Buddhist majority

Coup + assassination = 'Kennedy's war'?

Chapter summary

By 1954, the Viet Minh had effectively driven the French out of Vietnam because of the popular appeal of their social and economic reforms, Vietnamese nationalism, the leadership of Ho Chi Minh, the military genius of General Giap, and French war-weariness and miscalculation over Dien Bien Phu.

Truman and Eisenhower initiated the American involvement in Vietnam when they gave financial aid and advice to the French. Both were motivated by fears that Asian Communism was dangerously expansionist and by the desire to support France, an important NATO ally. Domestic politics also played a part: Truman was stung by Republican accusations that he had 'lost' China, and he and Eisenhower feared McCarthyite attacks if they were not seen to be militant Cold Warriors.

At the Geneva conference in 1954, the French agreed to exit Indochina. Vietnam was temporarily divided into a northern part under Communist rule and a southern part under an anti-Communist regime. Eisenhower ignored the Geneva Accords and made the division permanent when he established the 'state' of South Vietnam under Diem.

While Diem proved good at dealing with other opponents to his regime, he could not defeat the Communists after Hanoi's 1960 decision to give liberation of the South equal priority with consolidation in the North. The Communists always had far greater popular support than 'American Diem', who was upper class and Catholic in a country where most of the population was peasant and Buddhist.

Eisenhower feared Communism in Laos, but Kennedy eventually decided against US military intervention there. However, the neutrality of Laos and the Bay of Pigs fiasco convinced Kennedy he had to make an anti-Communist stand somewhere – and 'Vietnam is the place'. Kennedy greatly escalated the US involvement there (the number of 'advisers' rose from 685 to over 16,000), motivated by events in Cuba and Laos, his belief in containment and the domino theory, his militant Cold War rhetoric and domestic considerations (he felt he needed to be seen as tough on Communism). The Kennedy administration's collusion in the assassination of Diem further increased the US moral obligation to support a new regime in Saigon. Although Vietnam is most frequently referred to as 'Johnson's war', there is a good case to be made for calling it 'Kennedy's war'.

Refresher questions

Use these questions to remind yourself of the key material covered in this chapter.

1 Which countries comprised French Indochina?

2 Why could the French not defeat the Viet Minh?

3 Why did Truman and Eisenhower aid the French colonial regime in Indochina?

4 Why did Eisenhower not intervene at Dien Bien Phu?

5 What was the significance of the Geneva conference?

6 Why was 1960 a turning point in the history of South Vietnam?

7 Give arguments in support of Eisenhower's policies in Vietnam.

8 Argue that Vietnam was 'Eisenhower's war'.

9 Why did Eisenhower consider Laos important?

10 Why did Kennedy not send American troops to Laos?

11 Why did Kennedy send over 16,000 American 'advisers' to Vietnam?

12 Why do some people talk of 'McNamara's war'?

13 What options did President Kennedy have in Vietnam?

14 Which option(s) did he favour and why?

15 Argue for and against the contention that if Kennedy had lived he would have taken the United States out of Vietnam.

 Question practice

ESSAY QUESTIONS

1 Which did more to bring about the French exit from Indochina? i) Ho Chi Minh. ii) Dien Bien Phu. Explain your answer with reference to both i) and ii).

2 Assess the reasons for the French exit from Vietnam in 1954.

3 How important was Truman's doctrine of containment in Kennedy's policies toward Indochina?

CHAPTER 4

Johnson's Vietnam policy

President Lyndon Baines Johnson (1963–9) massively increased the American involvement in Vietnam. By 1968, he had sent in over 500,000 US ground troops and Vietnam had been bombed more than Germany in the Second World War. 'Johnson's war' made him unpopular at the time and ever since. Despite his efforts, it was clear by spring 1968 that the war as fought by Washington and Saigon was unwinnable. The Saigon regime, an artificial American creation, was never viable in the face of determined, popular and effective Communist opposition. Johnson finally recognised this and halted the escalation. These developments are covered in sections on:

★ Why Johnson continued the US involvement in the war

★ The Gulf of Tonkin resolution (1964)

★ The start of the US escalation of forces in Vietnam (1965)

★ The reasons why the United States failed to win the war

★ Interpretations

Key dates

1963	Nov.	Kennedy assassinated, Johnson became President	1965	Oct.–Nov.	Battle of Ia Drang
1964	Aug.	Gulf of Tonkin resolution	1967	Jan.	Martin Luther King Jr publicly criticised the war
	Nov.	Johnson elected President; Working Group recommended escalation		Aug.	Unpopular tax rises
				Nov.	McNamara resigned
1965	Feb.	Viet Cong attacked US base near Pleiku; Johnson authorised Rolling Thunder	1968	Jan.	Tet Offensive and battle of Khe Sanh
	March	First American ground troops in Vietnam; first anti-war protests in American universities		March	My Lai massacre; 'Wise Men' advised against further escalation

1 Why Johnson continued the US involvement in the war

▶ *Did Kennedy's assassination make Johnson's continuation of the war inevitable?*

Vice President Lyndon Baines Johnson (LBJ) supported President Kennedy's dramatically increased involvement in the Vietnam War because, like many of his contemporaries, Johnson

- was intensely patriotic: America had always been victorious in wars and defeat by what he called 'that damn little pissant country', 'that raggedy-ass little fourth-rate' Vietnam was inconceivable
- genuinely believed his country fought for world freedom as well as American security in two world wars, in Korea, and in Vietnam
- looked back at the appeasement of Hitler in the 1930s and consequently abhorred the idea of appeasing an enemy: 'If you let a bully come into your front yard one day, the next day he'll be up on your porch, and the day after that he'll rape your wife in your own bed'
- believed that Vietnam was a 'domino': if it fell to Communism the countries around it would rapidly follow suit
- found it quite difficult to understand foreign affairs and foreigners. 'The trouble with foreigners is that they're not like the folks you were reared with', he said, only half jokingly. He felt that Ho Chi Minh was another Hitler and should be treated accordingly.

Did Johnson's patriotism, anti-Communism and misunderstanding of foreigners make it inevitable that he would continue American involvement in Vietnam? Perhaps not. He knew a long war would probably lose the support of Congress and the public. He knew the weaknesses of the Saigon government: in 1961 he said that Diem must reform and fight his own war. He knew that only China and the USSR would benefit if America got 'bogged down chasing guerrillas' over Asiatic rice fields and jungles. Nevertheless, he continued the American involvement. The main reason for this was what historians have called the 'commitment trap': Eisenhower had created 'South Vietnam' and established SEATO (see page 109), and Kennedy had continued to support both, so Johnson considered it was a question of national honour for the United States to continue its commitment to them.

The impact of Kennedy's assassination

Johnson resented the younger and less experienced Kennedy being President and amidst the sorrow he felt at Kennedy's assassination in November 1963, there was joy at attaining the presidency. Feelings of guilt and the constitutional propriety of continuing Kennedy's policies as he finished Kennedy's term

Lyndon Baines Johnson

1908	Born in Texas
1937–49	Congressman
1949–61	Senator
1961–3	Vice President
1963	Kennedy assassinated, Johnson became President
1964	Elected President
1965	First US ground troops and Rolling Thunder in Vietnam
1968	Tet Offensive (January)
	Decided against standing for re-election, initiated peace talks (March)
1969	Retired to Texas
1973	Died

Background

Born in Texas, Johnson spent his life in public service – teacher, head of a Texas New Deal agency (1935–7),

Congressman (1937–49), Senator (1949–61), Vice President (1961–3) and President (1963–9). His great ambition was domestic reform and an American Great Society without poverty or racism.

Achievements

Johnson persuaded Congress to pass an unprecedented quantity of domestic reforming legislation designed to help the disadvantaged, but his most criticised and best-remembered achievement was his escalation of the Vietnam War. Despite his introduction of American ground troops and large-scale bombing, it was clear by early 1968 that the war was unwinnable and he halted the escalation.

Significance

In the Cold War context, Johnson's great significance was 'Johnson's war' in Vietnam, although it can be persuasively argued that he was the victim of the commitment trap set by his predecessors.

contributed to Johnson's determination to stand by all Kennedy had done and those who had helped Kennedy do it. 'I swore to myself that I would carry on', Johnson subsequently explained. 'I would continue for my partner who had gone down ahead of me … When I took over, I often felt as if President Kennedy were sitting there in the room looking at me.' Two days after Kennedy's assassination, the new President told Ambassador Lodge he was not going to 'lose Vietnam … Tell those generals in Saigon that Lyndon Johnson intends to stand by our word'. 'My first major decision on Vietnam had been to reaffirm President Kennedy's policies', Johnson said later.

The tragic circumstances of Johnson's accession to power thus caused him to make a vital decision with little apparent debate and discussion. Emotionally and constitutionally, he felt he had to continue the policies of his properly elected predecessor. Knowing he had no real **popular mandate**, Johnson hesitated to abandon any Kennedy commitment or Kennedy officials. The retention of Kennedy's advisers helped to ensure continued involvement in Vietnam.

Johnson and Kennedy's advisers

Johnson's freedom of action and thought were circumscribed by the circumstances of his accession to power. Johnson's retention of Kennedy men such as Robert McNamara and Dean Rusk meant no fresh ideas emerged on the Vietnam problem. Secretary of State Rusk was totally committed to the

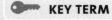 **KEY TERM**

Popular mandate Clear evidence that a political leader has the majority of the people behind him and his policies.

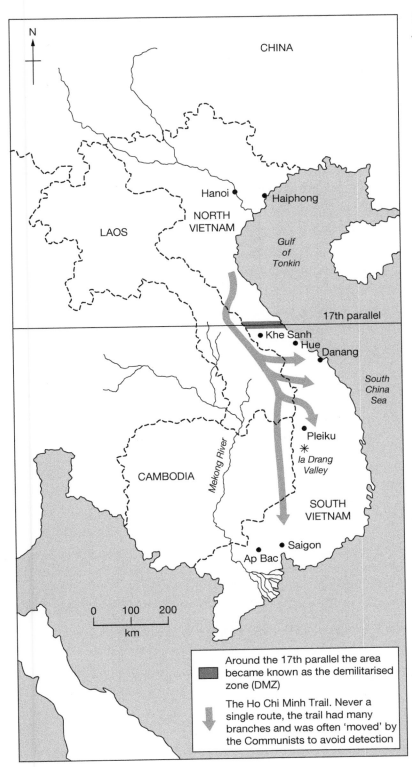

Figure 4.1 Important places in the American era in Vietnam (*c.*1956–73).

struggle in Southeast Asia, convinced that withdrawal would cause loss of faith in America's commitment to oppose Communist aggression and lead to a third world war. Secretary of Defence McNamara was so important in making policy that some called Vietnam 'McNamara's war'. In his memoirs (1995), McNamara criticised both himself and Johnson's other civilian and military advisers for an inability to ask the searching and relevant questions that needed to be asked at every stage of US involvement in Vietnam. He also lamented the administration's lack of historical knowledge and understanding of matters such as Sino-Vietnamese rivalry (due to McCarthyism, experts on China were sacked from the State Department because their praise of Mao's military achievements was perceived as pro-Communism).

Warnings from individuals such as Mike Mansfield (see page 111) continued. Mansfield repeatedly asked Johnson:

- Why support undemocratic military governments in Saigon?
- Did the South Vietnamese really want an anti-Communist crusade?
- What US interest was at stake in Vietnam?

Johnson did not want this kind of discussion. 'The president expects that all senior officers of the government will move energetically to insure the full unity of support for … US policy in Vietnam', said a secret memorandum of November 1963. Despite CIA pessimism about the situation in Vietnam, many in the administration believed America would somehow triumph. The Kennedy men remaining in the State and Defence Departments and the White House wanted to save face. No one wanted to admit past errors. No one seemed to want real debate.

Johnson was frequently alarmed by the beliefs of the military, especially air force chief Curtis LeMay, who wanted to 'bomb Vietnam back into the Stone Age'. However, Johnson inherited involvement in a war and as Commander-in-Chief felt duty-bound to listen to the generals. As Vietnam was the only war the generals had, they wanted to continue and indeed intensify it in order to win. Johnson's personal political ambition reinforced what the generals were advising. He repeatedly said he did not want to be the first President to lose a war, especially to the Communists. Johnson's military and civilian advisers and his own beliefs and ambitions thus guided him towards the continuation of the commitment to Vietnam, especially as the situation there was deteriorating.

'South Vietnam wants our support'

From December 1963, Hanoi sent increasing numbers of People's Army of North Vietnam (PAVN) regulars south, which greatly strengthened the Viet Cong (VC). Diem's successor, General 'Big' Minh (November 1963 to January

1964), was soon deposed. Minh's successors were even less impressive. The strategic hamlets programme (see page 127) was clearly a failure and the VC impressively countered US air power with ever-increasing supplies of Soviet and Chinese weaponry. It was estimated that the Communists controlled around half of South Vietnam. General Maxwell Taylor and McNamara visited Saigon in March 1964 and described the situation as 'very disturbing': the South Vietnamese were generally apathetic and unwilling to fight, and new Prime Minister Khanh (January 1964 to February 1965) begged for more American aid.

Taylor, McNamara, Rusk and the JCS favoured escalation and direct action against North Vietnam. LeMay said 'swatting flies' in South Vietnam was insufficient – 'we should be going after the manure pile and bombing North Vietnam itself'. Johnson felt the war needed to be won quickly before Congress demanded American withdrawal and on 20 April, he publicly declared that America was 'in this battle as long as South Vietnam wants our support' in its fight for freedom. However, his private doubts were revealed in May 1964 conversations (Source A).

SOURCE A

From transcripts of Johnson's telephone conversations with Senator Richard Russell and National Security adviser McGeorge Bundy, 27 May 1964 (available at http://americanradioworks.publicradio.org/features/prestapes/lbj_rr_052764.html and www.mtholyoke.edu/acad/intrel/vietnam/lbjbundy.htm).

[Johnson to Russell] *I don't think the people of the country know much about Vietnam, and I think they care a hell of a lot less. We tell* [Moscow, Beijing and Hanoi] *… that we'll get out of there* [Vietnam] *… if they will just quit raiding their neighbors. And they say 'Screw you'. All the senators are all saying 'Let's move, let's go into the North.' They'd impeach a president that would run out, wouldn't they? …*

[Johnson to Bundy] *I stayed awake last night thinking of this thing … It looks to me like we're getting into another Korea … I don't think that we can fight them 10,000 miles away from home … I don't think it's worth fighting for. And I don't think that we can get out. It's just the biggest damned mess … What the hell is Vietnam worth to me? … What is it worth to this country? … Of course if you start running from the Communists, they may just chase you into your own kitchen … This is a terrible thing we're getting ready to do.*

What arguments does Source A give for and against the involvement in Vietnam? **?**

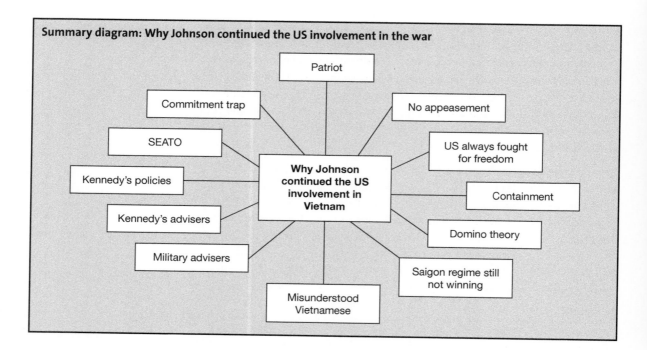

Summary diagram: Why Johnson continued the US involvement in the war

- Patriot
- Commitment trap
- No appeasement
- SEATO
- US always fought for freedom
- Kennedy's policies
- **Why Johnson continued the US involvement in Vietnam**
- Containment
- Kennedy's advisers
- Domino theory
- Military advisers
- Saigon regime still not winning
- Misunderstood Vietnamese

2 The Gulf of Tonkin resolution (1964)

▶ *Did Johnson mislead Congress and voters over escalation?*

By July 1964, 200 Americans had died in Vietnam, and Johnson had added 2500 'advisers', but South Vietnam's war against the Communists was still not going well. Johnson thought that if the time came to increase the American involvement in Vietnam, he would need congressional and public support. He believed that he obtained the former with the Gulf of Tonkin resolution, and the latter in the presidential election of November 1964.

The Gulf of Tonkin incident

The CIA had been sending South Vietnamese teams on secret sabotage missions to the North for a decade. In the first half of 1964, South Vietnamese gunboats raided North Vietnam's coast and American ships such as the *Maddox* went on espionage missions in the North's coastal waters.

In early August, Johnson announced that the North Vietnamese had made two unprovoked attacks on the *Maddox* and the *Turner Joy* in the Gulf of Tonkin. He asked for congressional support for avenging the attacks. Believing that the lives of innocent American sailors had been jeopardised by the North Vietnamese, Congress willingly passed the Gulf of Tonkin resolution. The resolution gave the President the power to wage war in Vietnam: Johnson said it was 'like grandma's night-shirt – it covered everything'. The resolution said North Vietnamese naval units had violated international law, so for the sake of world peace and American security, and because of SEATO obligations, the President was authorised to 'take all necessary steps' to help South Vietnam defend its freedom. The resolution would expire when the President believed that 'peace and security' reigned in Southeast Asia or when Congress decided to terminate it.

Led by Mansfield, a few senators were sceptical. One bitterly pointed out that they had no choice but to support the President when he said there was a crisis. Another said 'all Vietnam is not worth the life of a single American boy'. No one listened. The Senate had been two-thirds empty for the debate on the resolution, which it passed 88 to 2.

Was Congress misled?

Should Congress be blamed for giving Johnson the power to escalate the war? Critics claim Johnson and McNamara were not totally open with them

- over the covert raids (American naval missions were provocative)
- about the incident (there was definitely a first North Vietnamese attack, but there are many doubts surrounding the second North Vietnamese 'attack' – 'Hell', the President admitted years later, 'for all I know, our navy was shooting at whales out there')
- about the implementation of the resolution (it has been claimed that the administration waited for and even created the incident in order to ensure the passage of the resolution that they had prepared back in June 1964 and to enable Johnson to escalate the involvement).

In Johnson's defence:

- it was difficult to know exactly what had happened in the Gulf of Tonkin
- the navy told him there had been attacks and Americans would expect their Commander-in-Chief to respond
- it would have been irresponsible not to have had a resolution ready for an emergency
- when he escalated, it was because he considered it necessary rather than desirable.

Many believe that political calculations played a big part in Johnson's actions. During the summer of 1964, the Republican presidential candidate Barry Goldwater was accusing Johnson of being 'soft on Communism', so the President wanted to appear firm. Did Johnson exploit events to win over the American public in an election year? In his defence, he was under great pressure: while he was trying to decide whether there had been a second attack, the press reported the supposed incident and he felt trapped, fearing that if he did nothing his Republican opponent in the presidential election would call him a coward.

With this vitally important resolution, Johnson appeared to have the nation behind him and he could take retaliatory action against the North. American aircraft bombed North Vietnam for the first time. That made Johnson look tough, raised his public approval rating from 42 to 72 per cent, and helped him to win the presidential election. Ominously, American prestige was even more firmly committed to defending South Vietnam and further escalatory steps would be even easier, especially when the presidential election result suggested a nation united behind its President in his Vietnam policy.

The 1964 presidential election

During the election campaign voters asked many questions about Vietnam:

- Why are we still there?
- Why are we there at all?
- Why haven't we trained the Vietnamese to do their own fighting?
- Why can't we win?
- Why can't it be a UN effort like Korea?

Foreign policy issues were probably more important than usual in the 1964 presidential election. When the Republican candidate Barry Goldwater said America ought to use all its strength to win in Vietnam, he was seen as a trigger-happy hawk. He was widely if wrongly perceived as recommending the use of atomic weapons on Hanoi, while Johnson was perceived as the peace candidate. To Johnson's relief, Goldwater privately said that as Vietnam was 'a national burden' and the people were divided over both the legitimacy of US involvement and the conduct of the war, it was not in America's best interests to make the war a campaign issue. As a result, there was no great open debate on Vietnam.

Johnson knew that if left-wingers accused him of being a warmonger or if right-wingers accused him of being 'soft on Communism' he might not get re-elected. Like most politicians, he told everyone what they wanted to hear. He reassured the left by saying he did not intend to do anything rash or have a major war. He made a promise that might have been crucial to his re-election: 'We are not going to send American boys away from home to do what Asian boys ought to be doing for themselves.' On the other hand, he reassured the right by saying 'America keeps her word'. At Christmas 1963, he had told the JCS that he did not want to lose South Vietnam or get America into a war before the election: 'Just let me get elected and then you can have your war.' He also gained votes by appearing tough over the Gulf of Tonkin incident.

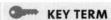 **KEY TERM**

Ground troops In March 1965, President Johnson sent the first few thousand regular soldiers (rather than just 'advisers') to Vietnam.

Johnson won the election by a landslide. Did he plan to escalate once elected? Johnson hoped Saigon would be able to win its own war. Neither he nor his advisers knew for sure exactly what to do about Vietnam, but most were reluctantly concluding that sending US **ground troops** was the only answer. Having won the election, he believed that he had a popular mandate to do as he saw fit.

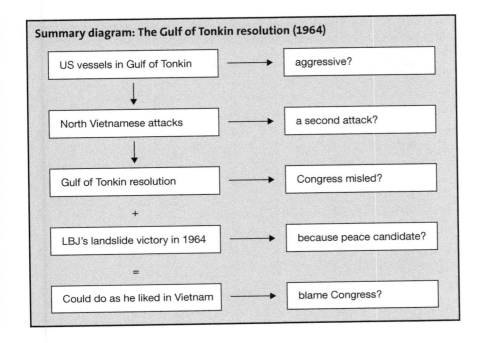

Summary diagram: The Gulf of Tonkin resolution (1964)

US vessels in Gulf of Tonkin	→	aggressive?
North Vietnamese attacks	→	a second attack?
Gulf of Tonkin resolution	→	Congress misled?
+		
LBJ's landslide victory in 1964	→	because peace candidate?
=		
Could do as he liked in Vietnam	→	blame Congress?

3 The start of the US escalation of forces in Vietnam (1965)

▶ *Why did Johnson escalate the US involvement?*

Although some people considered that Johnson's frequently combative, arrogant and overconfident personality made escalation inevitable, generalisations about Johnson's character are probably unhelpful. There was fear and uncertainty behind his confident bluster. Privately and frequently he admitted that he did not know what to do about Vietnam. More often than not, he responded to advice and the pressure of events.

Why Johnson escalated the US involvement

The underlying cause of Johnson's increased involvement was that the Saigon regime was obviously not winning the war. Ambassador Lodge (see page 129) had had enough by late 1964. All he could suggest was that America should be prepared to run South Vietnam. Hoping to please the JCS, Johnson replaced him with General Maxwell Taylor. Taylor was no diplomat: in December 1964 he lambasted the Saigon generals: 'Do all of you understand English? I told you all clearly at General Westmoreland's dinner that we Americans were tired of coups. Apparently I wasted my words … Now you have made a real mess. We cannot carry you forever if you do things like this.' Meanwhile, back in

Washington, Dean Rusk said, 'Somehow we must change the pace at which these people move, and I suspect that this can only be done with a pervasive intrusion of Americans into their affairs.'

The consensus among Johnson's advisers was that something must be done, especially when the Viet Cong seemed able to strike at will at Americans in South Vietnam. In November 1964, 100 VC had attacked and greatly damaged a US airbase near Saigon and the JCS demanded retaliatory air strikes on North Vietnam. These VC attacks, which the Saigon regime seemed powerless to halt, nudged the Johnson administration towards increased involvement. It seemed necessary for the safety of Americans in Vietnam.

The Working Group recommendations

KEY TERM

Working Group A group of experts brought together by President Johnson to study Vietnam and make suggestions for future policies in autumn 1964.

In autumn 1964, Johnson ordered a **Working Group** from the Defence Department, the State Department, the CIA and the JCS to study Vietnam and suggest policy options. The Working Group:

- reiterated the domino theory
- said an independent and anti-Communist South Vietnam was vital to US 'national prestige, credibility, and honor'
- emphasised that escalation was necessary as the Saigon government was 'close to a standstill' and 'plagued by confusion, apathy, and poor morale'
- suggested heavier bombing, to be halted only if North Vietnam would agree to the continued existence of a non-Communist South Vietnamese government.

Dissenting voices

An influential minority regretted how Vietnam had taken on such disproportionate significance. George Ball (see page 126) wanted to focus on containment in Europe. He warned Johnson that the more America got involved in Vietnam, the harder it would be to get out, and that the American public would not continue to support the war for long. Ball saw no point in bombing a country with a primarily agricultural economy, with industrial needs served by China and the USSR. Bombing the jungle in search of Viet Cong would be like seeking needles in a haystack. He felt that American soldiers were ineffective in Asiatic jungles and an increasing American presence was no substitute for good government in Saigon. He feared that while perseverance proved America's reliability as an ally, it also suggested lack of judgement. He worried about worldwide reaction to a superpower's bombing of a tiny Asiatic country. Ambassador Taylor warned that once American forces were committed, more would have to be sent in to protect them. He rightly forecast that Americans would fight no better than the French had in Asian jungles and would be unable to distinguish between a Viet Cong and a friendly Vietnamese farmer. He feared Americans would look like colonialists and conquerors and discredit any nationalist credentials of the Saigon regime. Senator Mike Mansfield (see page 111) foresaw thousands of US soldiers going to Vietnam, thereby alienating Congress and world opinion. He rightly pointed out that sending in American ground troops was the way to keep Moscow and Beijing involved. Soviet-designed anti-aircraft defences were already bringing down many American planes. Like Ball, Mansfield feared Chinese involvement.

Clearly, although Johnson is blamed for the greatly increased involvement, most of those whom American journalist and historian David Halberstam bitterly called 'the best and the brightest' were behind him. Johnson was Commander-in-Chief and his military and civilian experts were urging escalation in the interests of national security. Congress and the public seemed to be supportive.

The start of Operation Rolling Thunder

In early 1965 Johnson took the first great escalatory step, when he began large-scale and continuous bombing in Vietnam.

The immediate trigger for the escalation was concern over the security of US bomber bases and personnel. On Christmas Eve 1964, Viet Cong in South Vietnamese Army uniforms bought on the black market, planted a bomb in a bar frequented by American officers. Not wanting any dramatic change at Christmas, Johnson did nothing. Then the VC attacked a huge American camp near Pleiku in February 1965. Eight Americans were killed and 100 were wounded. Johnson was furious: 'I've had enough of this'. The pressure from his advisers was great. Even Ball urged retaliation.

Johnson ordered massively increased air attacks on North Vietnam. America now moved beyond occasional air-raid reprisals to a limited air war against carefully selected parts of North Vietnam. Such was the intensity of the air strikes that by March they were known as '**Rolling Thunder**'. Polls revealed that 67 per cent of Americans approved. Bombing the routes taking men and materials to the South would hopefully:

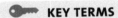

KEY TERMS

'Rolling Thunder' Heavy, often non-stop US bombing of Vietnam.

Great Society Johnson programme aimed at decreasing American economic and racial inequality.

- secure the position of Americans in South Vietnam
- decrease infiltration from the North
- demoralise Hanoi
- revitalise Saigon in the face of some strong middle- and upper-class pressure for negotiations with Hanoi and an end to the bombing.

In February 1965, the *New York Times* said, 'It is time to call a spade a bloody shovel. This country is in an undeclared and unexplained war in Vietnam.' However, Johnson refused to declare war, because he feared extreme Cold Warriors would want an all-out effort. That would jeopardise the financing of the **Great Society** and lead to increased Soviet or Chinese involvement. 'Think about 200 million Chinese coming down those trails', said Johnson. 'No sir! I don't want to fight them.'

In March 1965, Johnson took his second great escalatory step: in response to a request from General William Westmoreland, he sent large numbers of American ground troops to Vietnam. Westmoreland had commanded the 'advisers' in Vietnam since June 1964. In spring 1965 he requested US Marines be brought in to protect the vital US bomber base at Danang. Rolling Thunder triggered Westmoreland's request and the escalation, but as has been seen (pages 135–45), there were many other reasons that help to explain Johnson's action.

The first ground troops in Vietnam

The first 3500 Marines landed at Danang beach on 8 March 1965, cheered by pretty Vietnamese girls in a welcome arranged by the US Navy. Four weeks later, Johnson approved an increase of over 18,000 American support forces to keep his soldiers supplied and sent in more Marines. Privately, he said he wanted to avoid 'publicity' and 'minimize any appearance of sudden changes in policy'. In a speech on 7 April, Johnson summed up the reasons why the United States had to escalate its commitment to Vietnam:

- The US needed to fight if it wanted to live securely in a free world.
- Moscow and Beijing sought to conquer all of Asia and their North Vietnamese puppet must be opposed.
- Eisenhower and Kennedy had helped to build and defend South Vietnam: abandonment would be dishonourable and cause other US allies to doubt America's word and credibility.
- Appeasement could lead to a third world war.

Many accuse Johnson of waging war without a declaration of war, but he had considerable support. When Congress granted $700 million for military operations in Vietnam in May 1965, Johnson told them that this was no routine grant: it was a vote to continue opposing Communism in Vietnam. The House of Representatives voted 408 to 7 in favour, the Senate 88 to 3. As yet, the majority of American journalists were also hawks, even those like Halberstam who later became bitterly anti-war. When Vietnam is called 'Johnson's war', this support from Congress and the press at the time of massive escalation should be remembered.

'Where are we going?'

Johnson had hoped the arrival of American troops in Vietnam would help protect the bomber bases and improve the position of the Saigon regime, but the situation continued to deteriorate. In June 1965 the civilian government of Phan Huy Quat (February 1965 to June 1965) was overthrown by the military. General **Nguyen Van Thieu** became head of state and Air Vice-Marshal **Nguyen Cao Ky** became Prime Minister – 'absolutely the bottom of the barrel', said one Johnson adviser. A former commander of the South Vietnamese air force, Ky was a flamboyant figure, fond of purple jumpsuits, pearl-handled revolvers and dark sunglasses. He demonstrated particular stamina in relation to alcohol, gambling and women, and repeatedly asserted that Vietnam needed men like Hitler. Under the incompetent, corrupt and unpopular Ky and Thieu, the Saigon government controlled less of South Vietnam and with decreasing effectiveness.

 KEY FIGURES

Nguyen Van Thieu (1923–2001)

Fought for the Viet Minh, the French and Diem. He participated in Diem's overthrow (1963), in Ky's military government (1965–7), then became President of South Vietnam (1967–75). After American troops left South Vietnam in 1973, his regime soon fell to the Communists (1975) and he went into exile.

Nguyen Cao Ky (1930–2011)

Commanded the South Vietnamese air force from 1963 to 1965, then joined Thieu and 'Big' Minh in the military coup against Premier Quat. His authoritarianism made him an unpopular Prime Minister (1965–7). As Vice President from 1967 to 1971, he was powerless and insignificant. When South Vietnam fell to Communism, he fled to America.

Johnson, Laos and Cambodia

Hanoi sent men and materials to South Vietnam down the Ho Chi Minh Trail, which went through Laos and Cambodia, and in June 1966, Johnson told British Prime Minister Harold Wilson of his concerns about 'the expansion of the illegal corridor through Laos' and 'the growing abuse of Cambodian neutrality.'

At Kennedy's death, there were around 5000 PAVN (see page 113) troops protecting the Ho Chi Minh Trail (see page 137) and the support system through which the Soviets and the North Vietnamese gave military aid to the Pathet Lao (see page 117). In spring 1964, Souvanna Phouma's neutralist Laotian government was under attack from the Pathet Lao (see page 120) and from right-wingers and appeared near disintegration. The Johnson administration responded by training and supplying Souvanna's air force and by putting both the 7th Fleet and American troops in Okinawa on alert.

Even before the Gulf of Tonkin resolution, the United States conducted low-level photo reconnaissance missions over Laos, accompanied by US fighter escorts. In May 1964, the United States began using American civilian pilots and the CIA-backed Air America on combat missions over Laos. They attacked Communist targets on the Plain of Jars. Thai pilots also conducted air strikes, some of which were not authorised by their American allies. China had engaged in military activity in Laos since 1962: for example, between 3000 and 10,000 Chinese soldiers were involved in road building in order to assist the Pathet Lao.

In spring 1967, Westmoreland and the JCS urged Johnson to expand the Vietnam War to Laos in order to counter infiltration via the Ho Chi Minh Trail, but the administration focused upon the air war in Laos, because US Ambassador Leonard Unger recommended 'that US prestige not, repeat not be publicly linked with such an inept and uninspired army' as that of Souvanna. The United States also funded anti-Communist operations by Thai soldiers, and **Hmong** guerrillas.

It is difficult to know for certain just how many Americans served in Laos under Johnson, as the administration did its best to keep this a 'secret war'. However, a good idea of the numbers involved can be gleaned from a March 1968 incident at the radar installation at Pha Thi, 20 miles from the North Vietnamese border. There were 100 Hmong and 200 Thais stationed there, along with eighteen Americans (sixteen air force technicians, one air force air controller, and one CIA officer). When 100 Pathet Lao and over 200 North Vietnamese overran the site on 11 March 1968, US Air Force and Air America helicopters arrived to rescue the seven surviving Americans and a few of the Hmong and Thais.

Despite the American air war in Laos, a June 1968 report said the bombing there (and in North Vietnam) was not disrupting the Communist ability to get troops and supplies to South Vietnam. US intervention in Cambodia was similarly unproductive (see Chapter 6).

More American troops

Thieu estimated that the VC controlled 75 per cent of the countryside by 1965. As Taylor had feared, the more American troops poured in, the less the ARVN wanted to fight. As usual, Westmoreland demanded more American troops to prevent South Vietnam's collapse and to protect the American troops already there. In cabinet meetings throughout July, Johnson expressed doubts about the usefulness of sending more American troops. However, on 28 July 1965 (at noon, when TV audiences were minimal), he announced that Westmoreland had asked for more men. He said the 75,000 troops in Vietnam would be increased to 125,000 and that 'We will stand in Vietnam'. Congressional leaders had given their assent the day before.

 KEY TERM

Hmong Mountain people residing in Laos, Vietnam, Thailand and China.

During 1965, polls and White House mail showed that:

- 70 per cent of the nation backed Johnson
- 80 per cent believed in the domino theory
- 80 per cent favoured sending American soldiers to stop South Vietnam falling
- 47 per cent wanted Johnson to send in even more troops.

Clearly, Johnson's Vietnam policy was supported by the majority of Americans. By December 1965, nearly 200,000 American soldiers were in Vietnam. On the rare occasions that these American troops faced regular Communist soldiers (rather than guerrillas), they gave a very good account of themselves. In October 1965, for example, American troops defeated North Vietnamese regulars at the battle of Ia Drang (see page 155).

Doubts and further escalation

Not everyone was sure further escalation was the right answer. Protests began in the universities in March 1965 (see page 162). On hearing that a plane had been shot down, Johnson himself cried, 'Where are we going?' He confessed that hawkish General Curtis LeMay 'scares the hell out of me'. A December 1965 cabinet meeting showed the doubts within the administration. George Ball thought the situation hopeless, Taylor and the CIA opposed sending more US troops, McNamara considered military victory unlikely, and the JCS disagreed over tactics. 'Tell me this', said Johnson to the JCS chairman, 'what will happen if we put in 100,000 more men and then two, three years later, you tell me we need 500,000 more? … And what makes you think that Ho Chi Minh won't put in another 100, and match us every bit of the way?' Johnson knew all the dangers. He was doubtful America could win, but certain it could not get out without irreparable damage to his own and his country's position.

Despite their doubts about the competence of the Ky/Thieu regime, General Westmoreland, the JCS and McNamara all agreed that the number of American troops in South Vietnam should be increased to 200,000 in the second half of 1965. McNamara did not claim that this would bring victory, but it would 'stave off defeat in the short run and offer a good chance of producing a favourable settlement in the longer run'. There were 385,000 American troops in Vietnam by December 1966, and 535,000 by early 1968, while US planes bombed both North Vietnam and South Vietnam from 1965 onwards. Westmoreland had initially believed that he could end the Communist insurgency within six months, but his strategy of a **war of attrition**, using technology and firepower, failed to wear down the enemy (see page 159).

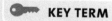 **KEY TERM**

War of attrition
Westmoreland believed that US numerical and technological superiority would wear down the Viet Cong who must, after losing a certain number of men, finally decide to give up.

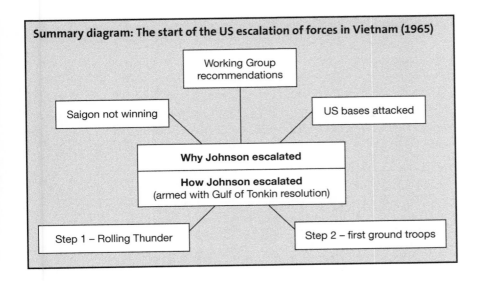

Summary diagram: The start of the US escalation of forces in Vietnam (1965)

Working Group recommendations

Saigon not winning

US bases attacked

Why Johnson escalated

How Johnson escalated
(armed with Gulf of Tonkin resolution)

Step 1 – Rolling Thunder

Step 2 – first ground troops

The reasons why the United States failed to win the war

▶ *Why could the United States not defeat the Vietnamese Communists?*

The United States failed to win the war because of:

- the inability of Washington and Saigon to win the hearts and minds of the South Vietnamese people
- the Communist performance
- the role of the US military in Vietnam
- problems on the home front.

Winning the hearts and minds of the South Vietnamese

The main reason the Americans could not defeat the Communists was because they and the Saigon regime were unable to win the hearts and minds of the Vietnamese. General Giap said that Hanoi won because it waged a people's war, a total war in which every man, woman and even child was mobilised, whether militarily or emotionally. He maintained that human beings were the decisive factor.

There were thousands of American civilian 'experts' in Vietnam during the war. These doctors, schoolteachers and agricultural advisers thought too little was done to win the hearts and minds of the people. Understandably, the military men thought in terms of force. 'Grab 'em by the balls and their hearts and minds will follow', said the American military.

Understanding the Vietnamese

Most Vietnamese were rice-growing peasants, who lived in small villages in mud and bamboo houses with dirt or wooden floors. The dirt paths between their houses were piled with stinking human and animal excrement for fertilising the fields. There was neither running water nor electricity. American soldiers could not conceive of 'real' people living like this, which goes a little way towards explaining why Americans sometimes treated the Vietnamese peasants as sub-human (see page 151) and were consequently unable to win many of them over to their side.

Maxwell Taylor admitted years later that Americans never really knew or understood any of the Vietnamese. When Thieu told Johnson that the Communists would win any South Vietnamese elections, Johnson's response was significant: 'I don't believe that. Does anyone believe that?' Johnson never really understood what motivated Ho and his armies. In April 1965 he promised Ho economic aid if he would stop the war: 'Old Ho can't turn that down'. Johnson did not seem to understand that Ho was fighting for a united Communist Vietnam and would not compromise. The North Vietnamese knew why they fought and were willing to wait, suffer and persevere to achieve their aims in a way that many Americans and South Vietnamese were not.

The Vietnamese Communists understood their fellow countrymen better. Peasants who struggled to provide sufficient food for their families had long relied upon collective discipline and endeavour. Harvesting was best approached communally, so many villages adapted with relative ease to the principles of Communism. The Communists worked hard and successfully to win over the peasantry, offering them land and urging Communist soldiers to avoid the rape and pillage characteristic of the ARVN.

Although the Communists were generally better at winning the hearts and minds of the peasantry, they were ruthless when necessary. For example, during the 1968 Tet Offensive (see page 164), the Viet Cong dragged 'unfriendly' people out of their houses in Hue and shot them, clubbed them to death or buried them alive. Over 3000 bodies were found in the river or jungle. A judicious mixture of ruthlessness and frequent good behaviour gained the VC the sullen acquiescence or support of the peasants that was vital in guerrilla warfare.

The Viet Cong, guerrilla warfare and villagers

Giap's strategy was to use the Viet Cong for incessant guerrilla warfare to wear down Saigon and its American allies, while the PAVN would fight conventional set-piece battles at times and places when it was sufficiently strong.

The Americans were frustrated by guerrilla warfare. Westmoreland would have preferred meeting the Communist forces in more traditional set-piece battles, while his men found it difficult to know whether someone was a guerrilla, a guerrilla sympathiser, neutral or pro-Saigon. Villagers often gave guerrillas the food, shelter and hiding places necessary for survival, which turned many American soldiers against the people they were supposed to be helping and made it difficult to win the war. In 1965, some Marines were supposed to search hamlets for VC and dispense food and medical care. However, one of those Marines recalled how they thought the villages were probably VC and treated the villagers badly, 'and if they weren't pro-Viet Cong before we got there, they sure as hell were by the time we left'. Another Marine recalled, 'Our emotions were very low because we'd lost a lot of friends', so when his unit entered a village suspecting of supporting the VC, 'we gave it to them … whatever was moving was going to move no more'.

The most famous example of American hatred of the Vietnamese was the massacre at apparently pro-Communist My Lai on 16 March 1968. American soldiers and their officers beat and killed 347 unarmed civilians: old men, women, teenagers and even babies. Women were beaten with rifle butts, raped and shot. Water buffalo, pigs and chickens were shot then dropped in wells to poison the water. Such American actions, a result of VC guerrilla warfare, made the Americans even less popular and contributed greatly to their inability to win the war.

The American high-tech war

American technology created formidable new fighting weapons, such as the cluster bombs the Vietnamese called 'mother bombs' because after exploding in mid-air they released 350–600 baby bombs. Each one exploded on impact into thousands of metal pellets. When fibreglass was substituted for metal, X-rays could not detect it, so it was harder and more painful to remove from casualties.

Ironically, American firepower was concentrated more on South Vietnam than North Vietnam, because the Americans wanted to destroy the Ho Chi Minh Trail and drive the Viet Cong guerrillas out of the South and the dependent Saigon regime was unlikely to complain. In the search for VC, Americans dropped bombs that forced many peasants to move away from the homes, crops and ancestral graves which meant so much to them, and that killed and wounded tens of thousands of civilians who might or might not have been Communist sympathisers. When asked about civilian casualties Westmoreland agreed it was a problem, 'but it does deprive the enemy of the population, doesn't it? They are Asians who don't think about death the way we do.' Neither the US Army nor the ARVN would take responsibility for wounded civilians, who were left to get what (if any) primitive medical care was available. Bombing obliterated five towns with populations over 10,000, and many villages. Some civilians lived like moles in caves and tunnels, emerging to work but ready to go back down when planes appeared. Children were kept below ground for days at a time.

From 1962, **Agent Orange** was used to defoliate South Vietnam's jungles in order to make the enemy more visible and to kill the rice crops that were partly

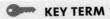

KEY TERM

Agent Orange Herbicide used by the USA in Vietnam to defoliate the trees and destroy enemy cover. It can cause illness and deformities in the descendants of those exposed.

SOURCE B

One of the most famous photos of the war: ten-year-old Kim Phuc (centre) ran away from her village, badly burned by napalm dropped from American bombers in 1972.

? Why do you suppose Source B is one of the most famous photos of the Vietnam War?

used for feeding the VC. Chemicals and bombs fitted well with American technological superiority, wealth and reluctance to lose American lives, but they were not the way to win this war: these methods alienated friendly and neutral Vietnamese and Americans themselves. It was not surprising that the Communists controlled most of the countryside, as the JCS admitted in February 1968. McNamara subsequently wrote that the administration was wrong to allow an arrogant American military to attempt a high-tech war of attrition against a primarily guerrilla force willing to absorb massive casualties, in a state like South Vietnam which lacked the political stability and popularity necessary to conduct effective military and pacification operations.

Life in Saigon

Incessant fighting and bombing drove roughly one-third of South Vietnam's peasant population out of the countryside into the towns and cities. Many were housed in camps where primitive sanitation bred disease. Many lived off Americans, particularly in Saigon.

Mid-twentieth-century Saigon was a strange and lovely mixture of Southeast Asia and provincial France, with tree-shaded streets lined with quiet shops and sleepy pavement cafés and beautiful villas with lush tropical gardens of scented jasmine and purple and red bougainvillaea. Saigon became an unsavoury city in the American war years. Drugs were sold in its bars. Many hotels were brothels. The streets were awash with black-market goods, American soldiers, orphans, cripples, beggars and 56,000 registered prostitutes. The beggars targeted 'rich' Americans, tugging at them and making crying sounds. Limbless Vietnamese victims of the war crawled along crab-like, seeking handouts from GIs.

The war had destroyed the social fabric of South Vietnam, uprooting peasants to the cities and dividing families. Poor peasant girls who turned to prostitution dismayed their families, despite earning more in a week than the whole family did in a year. American dollars distorted the economy. The salary of the lowest ranking American was gigantic by Vietnamese standards. Taxi drivers would not stop for other Vietnamese if it was possible to be hailed by an American. Vietnamese professionals lost status and influence in this new dollar-dominated world. Doctors earned less than waiters who served big-tipping Americans. Garbage and sewage disposal suffered as municipal workers sought higher wages working for Americans. On one pavement pile of rat-covered garbage was a sign: THIS IS THE FRUIT OF AMERICAN AID. One Vietnamese nun told an American relief worker that Vietnam was a beautiful country 'until *you* arrived'.

Saigon was full of Vietnamese and American officials. There was much talk but little real communication. The Americans would put forward plans designed to help win the war and, so long as America financed them, the Vietnamese would agree, although not necessarily co-operate. One jaundiced American official said, 'We report progress to Washington because Washington demands progress.'

The Saigon regime

Washington talked of bringing democracy to Vietnam but the concept was meaningless to the Vietnamese who had no tradition of American-style politics. The strongest Vietnamese political tradition was the hatred of foreigners, and although the Communists had Soviet and Chinese aid, that aid lacked the high visibility of the American presence in the South. While the Communists seemed to be anti-American patriots, successive South Vietnamese governments were all too clearly bound up with and dependent on the foreigners.

Ky's government, corrupt and averse to political or economic reform, faced many calls for negotiations with Hanoi and many protests during 1966–7. A Buddhist nun sat cross-legged, her hands clasped in prayer, in a temple in Hue. A friend doused her with petrol. The nun lit a match to set herself alight while the friend poured peppermint oil on her to disguise the smell of burning flesh. The dead nun's letters were widely circulated; they blamed Johnson for her death because he helped the repressive Saigon regime. 'What are we doing here?' asked one American official when American Marines helped Ky to attack Buddhist strongholds. 'We are fighting to save these people and they are fighting each other.' At Johnson's insistence, Ky held democratic elections, observed by American politicians (one repeatedly called the country 'South Viet Cong'). Although Ky ran the election, his candidate for President, Thieu, still managed only 37 per cent of the vote.

American aid rarely reached the peasants for whom it was primarily intended. Much of that aid found its way into the pockets of the military and urban elites. An investigation revealed that the amount of cement supposedly needed by and given to Vietnamese officials in one year could have paved over the whole country. When President Thieu fled Vietnam in April 1975, he carried away millions of dollars in gold. The endemic corruption owed much to the Vietnamese emphasis on family duty. Poorly paid officials and even the highly paid President wanted to provide well for their relations. Thieu's cousin ran a wealthy province: for a fee he would let VC out of jail or keep ARVN men out of battle.

The ARVN

The corruption and mismanagement that characterised South Vietnam's government naturally permeated its armed forces. ARVN performed badly for several reasons:

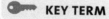

KEY TERM

Search and destroy
General Westmoreland's tactics included finding and killing groups of Viet Cong guerrillas.

- Saigon wanted to avoid losses. For example, in February 1971, 30,000 ARVN invaded Laos with orders to retreat if over 3000 died. They retreated, halfway to their objective (see page 192). The Americans described their own tactics as **'search and destroy'** but those of the ARVN as 'search and avoid'. Poor results damaged morale and led to further failure.
- Many military leaders were appointed for political rather than military reasons. The high command spent more time fighting among themselves than against the enemy. The urban middle-class officers did not get on well with the peasants in the lower ranks (Buddhists constituted 80 per cent of the South Vietnamese Army, but only 5 per cent of its leadership).
- ARVN wages were so low that some ARVN officers pocketed the pay of thousands of deserters and sick or dead men. Lower ranks bullied and robbed the population. Some deserted to the Communists.
- The ARVN were compromised in the eyes of the Vietnamese people by their association with the Americans, while Americans such as Westmoreland were frequently unwilling to use ARVN assistance because they despised them and preferred to use Americans. In Westmoreland's headquarters in Saigon there were hidden nozzles to spray his 'elite' ARVN guards with tear gas if they defected.

While the ARVN were often remarkably tenacious when cornered (many ARVN fought frequently and bravely, and tens of thousands of them died), ARVN morale and performance was a major factor in the defeat of the Washington–Saigon alliance.

Communist determination, ingenuity and organisation

Inspired by Communism and nationalism, the PAVN and VC won admiration from their American foes for their determination. The Vietnamese had always struggled for their existence against both nature and hostile peoples such as the Chinese. Continuous struggle ensured unusual patience in the face of adversity, which helps to explain Hanoi's refusal to be beaten. As Giap said:

> We were not strong enough to drive out a half million American troops, but that was not our aim. Our intention was to break the will of the American government to continue the war.

In 1965, a PAVN regiment clashed with the US Army in the 34-day battle of Ia Drang: 305 Americans and 3561 North Vietnamese died. Both sides thought they had won, that the other would not be able to sustain such losses. It was the North Vietnamese who were eventually proved right. Ia Drang is a good illustration of the Communist determination which helped to ensure their eventual victory. Americans did not understand such determination: their strategy never took it into account, and this was an important factor in their inability to win.

Communist ingenuity and preparedness was vitally important. For example, the Communists had a network of tunnels in which VC could hide, shelter and regroup. In January 1967 the Americans found a maze of such tunnels north of Saigon. These were like an underground city, full of stoves, furniture, clothing and paperwork. An exploring American officer was killed by a **booby trap** so the Americans just pumped in tear gas, set off explosives, then got out. They had just missed the VC headquarters, several miles of tunnels away.

Communist preparedness was particularly well illustrated by the Ho Chi Minh Trail. First constructed in 1959, the trail (see Figure 4.1, page 137) came southward via Cambodia and Laos. Both sides knew keeping the trail open was vital to the Communist war effort because men and materials came south upon it. Giap's porters carried most of the war materiel down the trail from 1959 to 1964, after which the trail was widened and sometimes even covered with asphalt to accommodate the thousands of trucks supplied by China and the USSR. The trail was never a single route. There were several branches, along which were dotted repair workshops, stores, depots, hospitals and rest camps. Around 50,000 women were employed at any one time to repair the road. If one part was damaged by American bombing, the traffic would be switched to other branches while repairs were done. Vehicles and parts of the trail were camouflaged with foliage. Giap's trails, troops and trucks melted into the landscape. American bombers perpetually sought to obliterate the trail but failed. Hanoi lost many $6000 trucks, but America lost many several million-dollar bombers, which were far harder and more expensive to replace. The battle of the trail was a vital one, in which people could be said to have triumphed over technology.

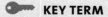

KEY TERM

Booby traps Disguised traps.

What can you infer about the Communist war effort from Source C?

SOURCE C

A scene on the Ho Chi Minh Trail, date unknown.

The role of the US military

Some military experts and historians have argued that the United States fought the Vietnam War in the wrong way. American disunity, the insistence on a 'comfortable' war and problems particular to fighting in Vietnam help explain why the US military role was unsuitable for defeating the Communists.

American disunity

Although many Americans fought with conviction and bravery, the American and allied forces were frequently disunited:

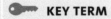 **KEY TERM**

Green Berets US Army special forces.

- Traditionally linked with the navy, Marines were not keen to obey orders from the US Army.
- The unconventional and independent **Green Berets** aroused jealousy and antagonism.
- Americans distrusted the ARVN: at Khe Sanh (see page 165) in 1968, Westmoreland sent for ARVN representation as an afterthought, then deployed them somewhere unimportant.
- Ordinary soldiers served 365 days, Marines thirteen months. This short term of service meant that units never attained the feeling of unity vital to morale and performance. A US Army officer did five months in the front line and would probably be less experienced than some of the soldiers he commanded. Five months was too little to get to know his men properly and he would soon be moved on to a training, organisation or desk job. Unpopular officers were

shot in the back in action or had fragmentation grenades thrown at them. Between 1969 and 1971, there were 730 '**fraggings**', in which 83 officers died. Often they were simply trying to get their men to fight.

- African-Americans constituted 13 per cent of the Americans in Vietnam, but a disproportionate 28 per cent of those in combat units (rather than desk jobs). This led to resentment. Black soldiers often wrote on their helmets, 'NO GOOK [Vietnamese] EVER CALLED ME NIGGER'.

- Many **drafted** soldiers simply did not want to be in Vietnam. Some stencilled their return dates on their helmets, others wrote UUUU, which stood for 'THE UNWILLING, LED BY THE UNQUALIFIED, DOING THE UNNECESSARY, FOR THE UNGRATEFUL'. Some American soldiers disliked their country's manner of waging war; some became confused about why they were fighting; some felt that America had no right to intervene in Vietnam; some disapproved of the mistreatment of civilians on humanitarian or military grounds.

- Disagreement with the war or tactics led to indiscipline. An underground newspaper offered a $10,000 bounty for the death of the officer responsible for Hamburger Hill (see page 159). Things got much worse under President Nixon (see page 193): in 1969 an entire company sat down on the battlefield, while another company refused to go down a dangerous trail in full view of the TV cameras.

There was not only disunity in Vietnam. In the late 1960s anti-war feeling grew back home. Many soldiers returned to America to find themselves ostracised, jeered at ('baby killer' was a favourite insult) and spat on if they wore their uniform. Some found the families they had left at home had been victimised by opponents of the war. Homes belonging to soldiers might have broken glass spread across their lawns, or objects thrown at their windows. The collapse of the home front (see page 162) was a crucial factor in America's failure in Vietnam. It damaged troop morale and hamstrung the government in Washington.

'We soften them up'

Ironically, the American desire to keep their soldiers as comfortable as possible in Vietnam helps to explain their defeat there. President Nixon (see page 175) said, 'If we fail it will be because the American way simply isn't as effective as the Communist way … it may be that we soften them up rather than harden them up for the battle.' Many soldiers spent their whole time in Vietnam organising the American lifestyle for everyone else, for example, running clubs and cinemas. Every week, several thousand combat soldiers were sent for **R&R** to Saigon or Japan. When the last American soldier left Vietnam, there were 159 basketball courts, 90 service clubs, 85 volleyball fields, 71 swimming pools, 40 ice-cream plants and two bowling alleys. All this led to an air of unreality and disorientation. A soldier could be airlifted from the horrors of the jungle to a luxurious base with freezing air-conditioning and comforting, homely fireplaces. He could have steak, French fries, ice-cream and Coca-Cola. Sometimes

KEY TERMS

Fragging When enlisted men tried to kill officers by throwing fragmentation grenades at them.

Draft The enforced call-up of civilians to be soldiers.

R&R Rest and recuperation for American soldiers in Vietnam.

cigarettes and iced beer were dropped by helicopters in mid-siege, and hot meals were landed at remote jungle camps. One colonel got a Silver Star bravery award for delivering turkeys by helicopter for Thanksgiving.

The American soldier fought a different war from his enemy. Every soldier suffers great personal hardship in the field, but while many North Vietnamese and VC spent years away from their families, existed on a basic diet and lacked decent medical treatment, the typical American soldier served a short term in Vietnam, and had good food and medical treatment. One PAVN soldier thought this was the difference between the two sides: 'When we had no water to drink, they had water for showers! We could suffer the hardships much better than they could. That probably was the main reason we won.' Westmoreland said this was the only way you could get Americans to fight.

Frustration with the war led many American soldiers to seek comfort elsewhere. Around a quarter caught sexually transmitted diseases. Drug abuse grew common. In 1970, an estimated 58 per cent of Americans in Vietnam smoked 'pot' (marijuana), and 22 per cent shot up heroin. One colonel was **court-martialled** for leading his squadron in pot parties. In 1971, 5000 needed treatment for combat wounds, 20,529 for serious drug abuse. It was difficult to take action over the drug market as so many prominent government officials in Saigon were involved, including Ky. It was hard to win a war when army discipline deteriorated: the process began under Johnson, then accelerated under his successor as troops were withdrawn and those remaining wondered why they were still there.

Problems for the 'grunts'

Young foot soldiers such as Ron Kovic, whose autobiography *Born on the Fourth of July* was made into a powerful anti-Vietnam War film starring Tom Cruise, were called **'grunts'**. Grunts were often horrified by what they saw in 'Nam' and keen to get out. Many hoped for a small wound and some shot themselves in the foot so as to be sent home. What was particularly awful about this war?

The average age of the grunt in Vietnam was nineteen, compared to a less vulnerable 26 in the Second World War. In the latter, the folks back home cheered their soldiers as they worked their way towards Berlin or Japan, and those soldiers could see clear territorial progress. In contrast, American soldiers in Vietnam fought for ground, won it, then left knowing the VC would move in again, while many folks back home jeered rather than cheered.

The patrolling infantryman was in almost continuous danger, with enemy mines, booby traps or snipers likely to get him at any time. Twenty per cent of American wounded were victims of ubiquitous booby traps such as the 'Bouncing Betty', which shot out of the earth, exploded after being stepped on, and blew away limbs. The VC wired up dead bodies with mines, hoping Americans would trigger them off. They camouflaged holes on trails so Americans would fall in and be impaled on sharpened bamboo stakes,

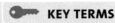

KEY TERMS

Court-martialled Tried by an army court for breaking army regulations.

Grunt Ordinary ground trooper or foot soldier.

positioned so the victim could not get out without tearing off flesh.

Sweat-drenched grunts hated the physical problems of patrolling the ground. They carried 20–30 kg of equipment and were plagued by heat, rain and insects. Metal gun parts burned in the sun as grunts trudged their way through the paddy fields, while in the jungle, thick foliage blotted out the sun and moving air, thorn scratches bled, uniforms rotted because of the dampness and suffocating heat made breathing difficult.

Not knowing which of the local people were the enemy was one of the biggest and most demoralising differences from the Second World War. One admiral said:

> *We should have fought in the north, where everyone was the enemy, where you didn't have to worry whether or not you were shooting friendly civilians. In the south, we had to cope with women concealing grenades in their brassieres, or in their baby's diapers. I remember two of our marines being killed by a youngster who they were teaching to play volleyball.*

It was hard to win the war when so many of the grunts were terrified and demoralised.

US strategy and Viet Cong guerrilla warfare

The American conventional forces struggled to defeat guerrillas. Under Johnson, US troops engaged in 'search and destroy' missions in which they tried to clear areas of VC, but it proved difficult to find the guerrillas. A 1967 CIA report said under 1 per cent of nearly 2 million small unit operations conducted between 1965 and 1967 resulted in contact with the enemy. Furthermore, the ratio of destruction was usually six South Vietnamese civilians for every VC guerrilla.

The large-scale use of helicopters and the blasting of the zones where they were to land was not conducive to searching out guerrillas, who heard all the noise and simply went elsewhere. In Operation Cedar Falls in 1967, twenty American battalions entered an area north of Saigon. Defoliants, bombing and bulldozers cleared the land, and homes and lands were destroyed. Six thousand people were evacuated, 'friendly' civilians were made hostile to Saigon and its American ally, and only a few VC were found. This American reliance upon superior technology simply alienated civilians, both in Vietnam (see page 151) and back home (see page 161).

It is notoriously difficult to try to wipe out a guerrilla movement, particularly when guerrillas are sent in from another country (North Vietnam) and have a sympathetic, supportive or simply apathetic reaction from the local community. Frequently, US troops would 'clear' an area of VC, but the Communists would return as soon as the Americans moved out, as after the American 'victory' in the battle for 'Hamburger Hill' (so-called because of the bloody carnage) in 1969.

The wrong role for the US military?

Americans, particularly ex-soldiers, frequently suggest the United States could have won the Vietnam War with a different role for the US military. Some suggest President Johnson should have gone beyond limited war and declared war on North Vietnam, but the war might have become even more unpopular and the USSR and China might have entered it, which Johnson was determined to avoid. He clearly did not think South Vietnam was worth a third world war, and it is certain that the American public would not have thought so. Congress would probably not have declared war for South Vietnam.

Some, such as General Bruce Palmer (1986), insist the United States should have cut South Vietnam off from Communist infiltration, thereby giving South Vietnam time to build itself up into a viable state, but it was impossible to 'cut off' the jungles and mountains on the Cambodian and Laotian borders. In 1967, the CIA established that most of the supplies used by the Communists originated in the South, so 'cutting off' supplies would have been difficult. The basic problem was that the Saigon regime was so unpopular.

Some, such as the historian Andrew Krepinevich (1986), say the United States Army should have worked harder to win the hearts and minds of the people, but one commander pointed out that if he and his men became 'mayors and sociologists worrying about hearts and minds', they would not be much use if they had to fight the Soviets. A 1990 study of Hau Nghia province, where American troops worked closely with villagers on **pacification**, revealed that pacification still failed to win greater support for the Saigon regime.

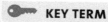

KEY TERM

Pacification Paying greater attention to the security and government of the South Vietnamese people.

Home front problems – aims, methods and McNamara

While many have criticised the US military strategy in Vietnam, others say that the war was lost on the home front, whether by the American public, or the American media, or American politicians.

Many Americans wondered what the United States was doing in Vietnam: nearly half of Americans polled in 1967 did not know for sure what the war was all about. The problem was that the publicly stated aims (see page 146) did not particularly inspire the American public and were probably impossible to achieve – especially with the methods Johnson used and the criticism they aroused. Johnson's methods were to advise, support, and try to strengthen the government in Saigon, both politically and militarily. However, the US military used counter-productive methods in Vietnam ('Bomb, bomb, bomb – that's all they know', Johnson sighed) that failed to bring an American victory and alienated the South Vietnamese and the American home front. Johnson's political methods also alienated many South Vietnamese and some Americans: the US-sponsored Saigon regime had few supporters.

Between 1965 and 1968, the Johnson administration slowly concluded that these aims and methods were inappropriate. It became clear that the escalation of US military involvement in support of the Saigon regime was not going to stop

Hanoi, that the involvement was becoming increasingly unpopular amongst Americans and South Vietnamese, and that Johnson would therefore be forced to retreat.

The loss of McNamara

The Johnson administration was publicly optimistic in late 1967, claiming that the **'cross-over point'** had been reached in South Vietnam: American and ARVN troops were killing the enemy faster than they could be replaced. General Westmoreland said that there were only 285,000 Communists left fighting in the south (the CIA said over 500,000, but the administration kept that quiet to preserve morale).

Privately the administration was pessimistic. 'Rolling Thunder' (see page 145) was deeply divisive and Johnson railed against 'gutless' officials who leaked 'defeatist' stories to the press: 'It's gotten so you can't have intercourse with your wife without it being spread by traitors'. Vietnam was clearly going badly and the administration was losing confidence. Most worrying of all was Secretary of Defence McNamara's change of position.

McNamara had been vital in the formulation of Kennedy and Johnson's Vietnam policies, but the failure to make progress in Vietnam and the passionate anti-war sentiments of his family and friends such as Bobby Kennedy helped destroy his old certainty. McNamara frequently burst into tears during discussions. He told Johnson in early 1967:

> *The picture of the world's greatest superpower killing or seriously injuring 1000 non-combatants a week, while trying to pound a tiny, backward nation into submission on an issue whose merits are hotly disputed, is not a pretty one.*

In August 1967, hawks organised Senate hearings designed to force Johnson into lifting restrictions on the bombing of North Vietnam (opinion polls in spring 1967 revealed that 45 per cent of Americans favoured increased military pressure in Vietnam as opposed to the 41 per cent who favoured withdrawal). During the hearings, the military accused McNamara and Johnson of tying their hands behind their backs by limiting the bombing, but McNamara testified that the bombing was not worth risking a clash with the Soviets, that bombing the Ho Chi Minh Trail did not stop Communist troops and supplies moving south, and that Hanoi would only stop if the bombing totally annihilated North Vietnam and all its people. That infuriated Johnson and the JCS. Johnson thought McNamara had degenerated into 'an emotional basket case', the JCS said he was undermining all the rationale for America's previous and present efforts.

In November 1967, in a last tearful White House conference, McNamara condemned:

> *… the goddamned Air Force and its goddamned bombing campaign that had dropped more bombs on Vietnam than on Europe in the whole of World War II and we hadn't gotten a goddamned thing for it.*

 **KEY TERM**

Cross-over point
The point at which Americans anticipated that Communists would give up because they were being killed faster than Hanoi could replace them.

He did not advocate getting out of Vietnam, only halting the escalation. McNamara resigned and in February 1968 was replaced as Secretary of Defence by Clark Clifford. Clifford questioned the domino theory and the wisdom of US involvement, and the Tet Offensive (see page 164) finally made him conclude America had to get out.

Home front problems – public opinion, the press and the Tet Offensive

Johnson and Congress naturally paid great attention to public opinion. Many believe that opposition to the war from the public and in the press was the main reason why Johnson finally decided on retreat, but polls suggest the objectors were a minority, and supporters of the war also put pressure on Johnson to continue the fighting.

Those who wonder why Johnson continued to escalate for so long often forget how many Cold Warriors criticised Johnson for insufficient escalation. They complained that American boys were being forced to fight the Communists with one hand tied behind their backs, and that America never used more than half of its combat-ready divisions and tactical air power in Vietnam ('Win or get out' was a popular bumper sticker). However, it was the anti-war movement that grabbed the headlines.

Protests

Tens of thousands of Americans participated in anti-war protests. Many hated the thought of themselves or their loved ones having to fight in Vietnam. Some were repelled by the sufferings of Vietnamese non-combatants, or believed America's international image was suffering. There is great debate over whether they were simply a vociferous minority and over the extent to which they affected US and North Vietnamese policy.

1964

The protests began in 1964 when 1000 students from prestigious Yale University staged a protest march in New York and 5000 professors wrote in support. However, the Gulf of Tonkin resolution and the presidential election (see page 142) suggest that at this stage Johnson had near unanimous support for his Vietnam policy from the public and most congressmen.

1965

With the introduction of American ground troops to Vietnam in March, the press and TV networks went to Vietnam in full force in what became America's first fully televised war. People talked of 'the living-room war' as Americans watched it on every evening news. As early as January, one Congressman had reported 'widened unrest' amongst colleagues, but the dispatch of ground troops and rising casualty lists greatly increased criticism of the war. In August, Johnson was informed that increasing numbers of American reporters in Saigon were 'thoroughly sour and poisonous in their reporting'. Many universities held anti-war lectures and debates (20,000 participated in **Berkeley**), although thousands of students signed pro-Johnson petitions, including one-quarter of Yale undergraduates. Thousands of other citizens participated in protests: in April, 25,000 marched on Washington. However, the opposition had little practical impact on American involvement: Johnson continued to escalate and fewer than 25 per cent of Americans believed that the US had erred in sending troops to Vietnam.

1966

Public and congressional support for the war dropped dramatically. Some senators openly criticised the bombing and said Vietnam was not vital to America and withdrawal would do no great harm. Many blamed Vietnam for the dramatic Democrat losses in the congressional elections of November and congressional Democrats urged Johnson to end the war. Congress nevertheless continued to fund the war, unwilling to face accusations of betraying the 400,000 American boys in the field. Westmoreland complained that the media had turned anti-war and made the enemy leaders 'appear to be the good guys'. Johnson felt constrained to limit his public appearances to avoid chants of 'Hey, hey, LBJ, how many boys have you killed today?' On the other hand, there were relatively few marches and only one state governor refused to declare his support for government policy.

1967

As the war escalated, the opposition grew. Tens of thousands protested in the great cities of America. Congressmen put ever more pressure on Johnson, and leading churchmen criticised the war. African-Americans resented the disproportionate number of black casualties in Vietnam and sympathised with the poor, non-white Vietnamese. Civil rights leader Martin Luther King Jr became publicly critical. August tax rises turned more Americans against the expensive war and **draft cards** were openly burned throughout the country in October. Between 4000 and 10,000 Berkeley students tried to close down the draft headquarters in Oakland and clashed with the police. Johnson had 2000 policemen, 17,000 **National Guard** troops and 6000 army regulars to handle 70,000 protesters in Washington. Some extremists were involved in violence outside the **Pentagon**, which McNamara found 'terrifying. Christ, yes, I was scared'. The government's bill for the operations was just over $1 million and 625 were arrested.

On the other hand, in August 1967, hawkish senators conducted hearings aimed at pressurising Johnson into lifting all restrictions on bombing in Vietnam, while the respected and experienced group of elder statesmen nicknamed the '**Wise Men**' all supported Johnson's Vietnam policy. Many middle-class Americans considered the protesters treasonous. Such support for the war and escalation is too often forgotten because it is overshadowed by the drama of the protests.

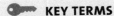

KEY TERMS

Berkeley A leading Californian university.

Draft cards Documents informing an American of compulsory military call-up.

National Guard US armed forces reservists, called up by the President in times of crisis.

Pentagon Headquarters of the US Department of Defence.

Wise Men A group of experienced politicians, generals and others who had previously held high office, frequently consulted by Johnson over the Vietnam War.

Was 1967 a turning point?

Pinpointing turning points in support for the war is difficult, but some consider 1967 crucial because some influential newspapers and TV stations shifted from support to opposition and increased draft calls, deaths in Vietnam and taxes aroused more discontent.

In 1967, 46 per cent of Americans felt that the Vietnam commitment was a mistake, but a massive majority still wanted to stay there and get tougher. After a successful November public relations offensive by the Johnson administration (Westmoreland said, 'We are winning a war of attrition now'), the White House was pleasantly surprised by a poll which showed considerable support for the war in early 1968:

- 49 per cent to 29 per cent favoured invading North Vietnam
- 42 per cent to 33 per cent favoured mining Haiphong (the main port in North Vietnam) even if Soviet ships were sunk as a result
- 25 per cent did not oppose bombing China or using atomic weapons.

There were over 500,000 Americans in Vietnam and nearly 17,000 had died there, but Johnson's policies still had considerable support.

However, the most persuasive argument for 1967 being the great turning point in exiting the Vietnam War is McNamara's resignation (he announced it in November) over his recognition that the war was unwinnable. That recognition was certain to come to others in the Johnson administration. And, after Tet, it did.

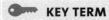

KEY TERM

Tet The most important Vietnamese festival. Americans use the word 'Tet' as shorthand for the 'Tet Offensive'.

The Tet Offensive (1968)

In January 1968, Hanoi broke the traditional **Tet** holiday truce and launched an unprecedented offensive against South Vietnam, hoping to cause the Saigon government to collapse or to demonstrate such Communist strength that America would give up.

When tens of thousands of PAVN and VC attacked cities and military installations in the South, the Americans and South Vietnamese were preoccupied with the Tet festival and taken by surprise. Saigon, Washington and the American public were shocked that the Communists could move so freely and effectively throughout the South. The attackers even hit the US embassy in Saigon (the American ambassador had to flee in his pyjamas) and dramatic scenes there were headline news in America. It took 11,000 American and ARVN troops three weeks to clear Hue of Communist forces, although other cities were regained within days.

The Tet Offensive cost many lives and caused incredible damage: 3895 Americans, 4954 South Vietnamese military, 14,300 South Vietnamese civilians, and 58,373 VC and PAVN died. Out of 17,134 houses in historic Hue, 9776 were totally destroyed and 3169 were seriously damaged.

Military significance

The Tet Offensive was militarily significant. It was the largest set of battles fought in the Vietnam War up to that point, and the first to be fought in the cities of South Vietnam. Although the Communists suffered grievous losses and it took Hanoi several years to get over this great effort, the Communist position in the South Vietnamese countryside was strengthened because of the Communist performance in Tet. Tet seemed to show that although the US could stop the overthrow of the Saigon government, it had failed to make it viable in the face of Communist determination. The South Vietnamese people had not greeted the Communists as liberators, but nor had they rallied to the Saigon regime.

Psychological significance

Tet shook the confidence of US officials and military men in Vietnam. US intelligence officials had failed to notice clear warnings. Westmoreland fell into a Communist trap over the battle of Khe Sanh, which was fought at the same time as the Tet Offensive. Successfully designed to distract the Americans from Tet, Khe Sanh was the biggest and bloodiest battle of the war: 10,000 Communists and 500 Americans died. Westmoreland wrongly perceived Khe Sanh as the great prize and focused upon it. When Westmoreland finally recognised his error, one American official considered him almost broken. Washington 'kicked him upstairs' to a desk job and replaced him.

Tet also had a great psychological impact on American public opinion. Some consider the media coverage of the Tet Offensive in early 1968 the crucial turning point. Walter Cronkite, the most respected TV journalist, had been strongly supportive of the war until a February 1968 visit to Vietnam made him realise it could not be won. 'What the hell is going on?' Cronkite asked. 'I thought we were winning the war.' Johnson knew the significance of Cronkite's change of mind: 'If I've lost Cronkite, I've lost America.' Some saw Cronkite's defection as a great turning point. It was not only Cronkite. A famous photo of a Saigon general shooting a bound captive in the head (see page 166) damaged the faith of Americans that their side was the 'good guys' (it was subsequently discovered that the captive was a VC death-squad member who had just shot a relation of the general). When an anti-war newsman repeated a soldier's saying of the South Vietnamese village of Ben Tre, 'We had to destroy the town to save it', many Americans questioned what was being done in Vietnam. Pictures of destruction and death turned many against the war. The administration had been claiming that America was winning the war but the TV pictures suggested US failure. Tet increased the credibility gap between the Johnson administration's explanations of events in Vietnam and the American public's understanding of those events (one wit said Johnson had lost the most important battle of the war, the Battle of Credibility Gap).

Perhaps most important of all, Tet had a dramatic effect on the Johnson administration. Johnson's approval ratings plummeted from 48 per cent to

36 per cent, and he felt he had to withdraw from the 1968 presidential race. Clifford feared that the President and indeed the whole government of the United States was on the verge of coming apart. Tet forced the administration to re-evaluate US policy. By March, Clifford was totally against the war and even Rusk (see page 100) was wavering. Back in September 1967 the CIA director had said America could get out of Vietnam without suffering any great loss of international standing.

The Treasury said the nation could not afford to send more troops and even hawkish senators said 'no more men'. After Tet, Johnson rejected repeated JCS demands that 200,000 more US troops be sent to Vietnam.

Overall, Tet had destroyed the confidence of the American government and people.

The role of the press and the protesters

Historians disagree over the extent of press responsibility for the US inability to win in Vietnam. Johnson criticised the American press for failing to support the war effort and some have claimed that media coverage of Tet helped to convince Americans that what was actually a victory was instead a US defeat.

? Look at Source D. Why do you suppose this photo shocked Americans and turned so many of them against the war?

SOURCE D

One of the most famous and most misinterpreted photos of the war. South Vietnam's police chief executed a VC in Saigon during the Tet Offensive in 1968.

Others argue that the press reflected rather than shaped opinion and that most reporters were supportive of the war until the public and government members started questioning it.

Historians also disagree as to whether the protests helped bring about the end of the war. It is difficult to trace the interrelationship between the protests and rising dissatisfaction in Congress and in the White House itself, but there is no doubt that politicians were sensitive to the wishes of the voters, and the protesters probably played a part disproportionate to their numbers in bringing the war towards an end. By the spring of 1968, Johnson had lost confidence if not in the rectitude of his policies then at least in his capacity to maintain continued support for them. The protesters and the media had suggested that his war and his way of conducting it were wrong, and this played an important part in the loss of confidence amongst White House officials and the troops in Vietnam. On the other hand, the protests in 1967 did not stop Johnson escalating – it was after Tet and the defection of the 'Wise Men' (see below) that he refused to send any more troops. That suggests that it was the fact that Vietnam was an unwinnable war, rather than protests, that forced Johnson to reverse course.

The defection of the Wise Men

In November 1967, after optimistic briefings from the JCS and CIA, the 'Wise Men' had declared their support for the continuation of US efforts in Vietnam, but after Tet, at their 25 March 1968 meeting, the majority were in the process of changing their minds. Most advocated some kind of retreat in Vietnam. One said that the US could not 'succeed in the time we have left' in Vietnam, because that time was 'limited by reactions in this country'. Johnson could not believe that 'these establishment bastards have bailed out'.

Home front problems – the economy and Johnson's loss of confidence

The war was expensive and it damaged the economy. Fearful that congressional conservatives would cut funding for his Great Society programmes, Johnson was unwilling to admit the cost and slow to ask for the necessary tax rises. As a result, the federal government deficit rose from $1.6 billion in 1965 to $25.3 billion in 1968. That caused inflation and dramatically weakened the dollar on the international money market, which was the final straw for many Americans. Treasury warnings that this should not go on and taxpayer resentment increased the pressure on Johnson to change direction in Vietnam.

The gold crisis, the advice from the Wise Men, congressional pressure to retreat and discouraging polls (78 per cent of Americans believed that America was not making any progress in the war, 74 per cent that Johnson was not handling it well) combined to force Johnson to recognise that there would have to be some sort of a reversal in Vietnam. On 31 March 1968 he said, 'I am taking the first step to de-escalate the conflict'.

The combination of Johnson's loss of confidence, and Hanoi's exhaustion after Tet and hopes that negotiations might divide Americans, improved the prospects for peace talks. Talks began in Paris in May 1968. Johnson demanded a North Vietnamese withdrawal from South Vietnam and rejected Communist participation in the Saigon government. North Vietnam demanded American withdrawal from South Vietnam and insisted on Communist participation in the Saigon government. These mutually exclusive demands explain why the talks continued intermittently for five years. Johnson thought getting out of Vietnam on those terms would damage America, Democrats and his own credibility, and constitute a betrayal of Americans who had fought and died there.

Meanwhile the fighting had reached maximum intensity (in two weeks in May alone, 1800 Americans were killed and 18,000 seriously wounded) and American society seemed near disintegration (protests and riots during the Democratic Party convention in August 1968 were headline news).

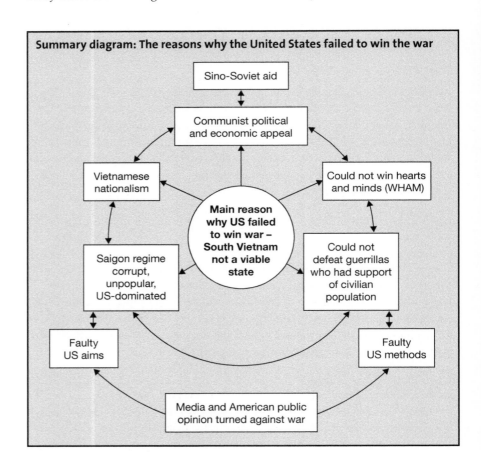

Summary diagram: The reasons why the United States failed to win the war

Sino-Soviet aid

Communist political and economic appeal

Vietnamese nationalism

Could not win hearts and minds (WHAM)

Main reason why US failed to win war – South Vietnam not a viable state

Saigon regime corrupt, unpopular, US-dominated

Could not defeat guerrillas who had support of civilian population

Faulty US aims

Faulty US methods

Media and American public opinion turned against war

Interpretations

▶ *Why did the United States fail to win the Vietnam War?*

Most historians believe the main reason America failed to win the war was that the establishment of a viable South Vietnamese state was beyond American capabilities. Johnson rejected real escalation because it might bring in the Soviets and Chinese and attacking a small state such as North Vietnam would damage America's international image. Americans therefore continued to fight a limited and ineffective war to support a series of unpopular Saigon regimes. The nature of the warfare and criticism back home led to the apparent collapse of the home front and the American forces in Vietnam.

However, those who fought in Vietnam and subsequently wrote about it often disagree. In his memoirs, Westmoreland (1976) claimed that he was too restricted by orders from Washington and that more ground troops and air power would have defeated Hanoi. Historians who accept that US intervention was morally justifiable in the struggle against Communism argue that greater use of force would have been acceptable and more likely to lead to victory. Others contend that Westmoreland should have concentrated more on pacification and counter-insurgency, rather than on the war of attrition. However, a study of Hau Nghia province, where American troops worked closely with villagers on pacification, revealed that they still failed to win greater support for the Saigon regime. Most historians argue that it is an error to imagine that military solutions could have solved the political problems of the unpopular Saigon regime. Indeed, many historians actually blame overuse of American military power for the US failure. They point out that the bombing in particular served to alienate the South Vietnamese people. Others criticise US confidence in high-tech warfare and managerial techniques.

Some historians contend that the outcome of the Vietnam War was not so much an American failure, but rather a Vietnamese success. They emphasise the Communist advantages: their undoubted patriotism, superb organisation, ruthlessness when necessary and effective military strategy. Interestingly, a few historians suggest the Saigon regime was not as bad as is often thought, and many point out the frequently unpleasant nature of the Communist government after Vietnam was reunified in 1975 (see page 201).

Some historians have adjudged Chinese and Soviet aid to Hanoi to be a major reason for the US failure. China gave North Vietnam weapons, ammunition, trucks, gasoline, trains, clothing, grain and soldiers (170,000 of which the US was aware in 1967), and warned the United States against invading North Vietnam. The Soviets provided MiG jets from 1965 and around 800 anti-aircraft guns.

The significance of the Tet Offensive is much debated. Although most historians agree that it marked the start of an American de-escalation process that eventually got the United States out of Vietnam, they disagree over whether or not it was a US defeat. Some claim it was a military victory for the US, upon which feeble politicians failed to capitalise. They consider Tet a costly Communist miscalculation because no popular rising occurred in South Vietnam and many men and much materiel were lost. However, the US Army Chief of Staff felt the offensive showed the limits of US military power. Furthermore, many historians believe Tet was exactly what Hanoi wanted – a psychological victory over the Americans.

Historians debate the influence of the press. Several journalists claim that for the first time ever, the media rather than battlefield events determined the outcome of a war, especially when the media convinced the American public that Tet was a defeat when it was actually a victory. On the other hand, some scholars have found no evidence that TV reporting had a negative impact on public opinion (only one-third of Americans watched the TV news) and therefore consider that it did not affect the outcome of the war. However, there is no doubt that coverage of Tet exposed the credibility gap and exacerbated doubts about American policy that had begun to develop within the Johnson administration since the autumn and the resignation of McNamara. Some historians reject claims of media bias in American reporting, and argue that it was not the impact of Tet on the public that was significant, but rather the impact of Tet on senior officials in the Johnson administration. Some studies found most reporters supportive of the war until the public and government members started questioning it, and concluded that the press reflected rather than shaped public opinion.

Studies of the anti-war movement suggest that the protests did not end the war but did restrain Johnson and his successor. It has been argued that presidents were more influenced by protests than they cared to admit, but it has also been claimed that the radicalism of some protesters alienated the majority of Americans, discredited the anti-war movement, and may even have helped to prolong the war.

Chapter summary

President Johnson continued the US involvement in Vietnam because he believed in containment and the domino theory and felt that US prestige (and his own aspirations) depended upon seeing through the commitment that his predecessors had bequeathed him. Although clearly a victim of the 'commitment trap', he has been much blamed for 'Johnson's war', because he was the President who sent in American ground troops and initiated Rolling Thunder.

President Eisenhower had created a South Vietnamese state that was not viable, and that was the main reason why the United States could not defeat the Communist forces in South Vietnam. While ruthless when necessary, the Communists had far greater popularity and nationalist appeal than the corrupt, incompetent and unrepresentative Saigon regime. The Communists fought a highly effective guerrilla war, with which the Americans and the flawed ARVN simply could not cope.

Once the US ground troops were sent to Vietnam, the American press followed. Anti-war protests began in 1964, and large numbers were involved by 1967. Despite the protests, Johnson continued to escalate, so that over 500,000 ground troops were in Vietnam by January 1968. Then the Tet Offensive confirmed what McNamara had recognised in autumn 1967: the war was simply not winnable and not worth the toll it was taking upon the American economy and upon the relationship between the Johnson administration, the press, some members of the public and the rest of the world. Johnson therefore rejected the military's request to send more ground troops.

Refresher questions

Use these questions to remind yourself of the key material covered in this chapter.

1 Why did President Johnson continue the US involvement in Vietnam?

2 Who was Diem's successor as leader of South Vietnam?

3 What did the Gulf of Tonkin resolution say?

4 What was the Working Group?

5 Why did President Johnson introduce ground troops to Vietnam?

6 What was Rolling Thunder?

7 How many US troops were in Vietnam by Christmas 1967?

8 What was Giap's strategy?

9 Why was Agent Orange used?

10 Why did the ARVN often perform badly?

11 Why was the Ho Chi Minh Trail important?

12 What was fragging?

13 What problems faced the grunts?

14 What did Operation Cedar Falls illustrate?

15 Why was the United States unable to defeat the Vietnamese Communists?

Question practice

ESSAY QUESTIONS

1 Who bore greater responsibility for Johnson's continuation of the war in Vietnam? i) Eisenhower. ii) Kennedy. Explain your answer with reference to both i) and ii).

2 'The United States failed to defeat the Communists because it never won the hearts and minds of the South Vietnamese people.' How far do you agree?

3 To what extent was the Vietnam War lost because of the anti-war protests?

INTERPRETATION QUESTION

1 Read the interpretation and then answer the question that follows. 'All the logic and rationale of the Cold War and containment called for escalation [in Vietnam in summer 1965].' (From D. Schmitz, *The Tet Offensive*, 2005.) Evaluate the strengths and weaknesses of this interpretation, making references to other interpretations that you have studied.

CHAPTER 5

Nixon's policies in Vietnam, Cambodia and Laos

Richard Nixon came to the presidency in January 1969 determined to end the Vietnam War and to improve relations with the Soviets and China. The prospects for such improved relations had greatly improved thanks to the Sino-Soviet split. Detente with the Soviets and Chinese helped end the Vietnam War, but Nixon also needed large-scale bombing of North Vietnam, Laos and Cambodia to help force Hanoi to accept what he called 'peace with honour'. Even as Nixon withdrew American troops, many Americans perceived him as having dramatically extended the war through his interventions in Laos and Cambodia, and this led to the biggest anti-war protests yet. The United States finally signed a peace treaty ending its involvement in Vietnam in January 1973, but the Communists continued to fight the Saigon regime and in spring 1975, they reunified Vietnam and triumphed in Laos and Cambodia.

These developments are covered in the following sections:

★ Nixon's changing views on Vietnam

★ Nixon and the changing Cold War world

★ Nixon and the Vietnam War

★ Assessment of Nixon's Vietnam policy

★ Interpretations

Key dates

1969	Feb.	Communist offensive in Vietnam
	March	Nixon secretly bombed Cambodia
	April	Nixon suggested secret Washington–Hanoi negotiations
	May	Nixon offered Hanoi concessions
	Summer	First US troop withdrawals
	Sept.	'Great silent majority' speech
	Oct.–Nov.	Anti-war protests; My Lai massacre
1970	Jan.	North Vietnam and Ho Chi Minh Trail heavily bombed
	Feb.	Communist offensive in Laos; US/ARVN invasion of Cambodia
1970	April	'Pitiful, helpless giant' speech
	May	Large-scale protests; Kent State shootings
1971	Feb.	Vietnamisation tested at Lam Son
	May	More Nixon concessions
1972	March	Communist offensive in Vietnam
	April	Nixon bombed Hanoi and Haiphong
	Aug.	More Nixon concessions
	Oct.	'Peace is at hand'
	Nov.	Nixon re-elected but running out of money
	Dec.	Christmas bombing
1973	Jan.	Paris Peace Accords
	Aug.	US bombing ended
1975		Vietnam, Laos and Cambodia became Communist

1 Nixon's changing views on Vietnam

▶ *When and why did Nixon's views on the Vietnam War change?*

Between 1953 and 1968 Nixon's views on the US involvement in Vietnam changed dramatically.

Cold Warrior (1953–67)

As Eisenhower's Vice President, Nixon advocated helping the French at Dien Bien Phu with an American air strike. He was even willing to use (small) atomic bombs (see page 103). He said that if sending American boys to fight in Vietnam was the only way to stop Communist expansion in Indochina, then the government should take the 'politically unpopular position' and do it. After his defeat in the 1960 presidential race, Nixon held no political office for eight years but kept himself in the political news by foreign policy pronouncements. He criticised the anti-war protesters as a traitorous minority and advocated escalating the war in Vietnam, saying, 'Victory is essential to the survival of freedom.' As the recognised leader of the Republican opposition on foreign policy, Nixon spurred the Democrat Johnson to greater involvement in Vietnam. Whatever President Johnson did, Nixon urged him to do more. 'The United States cannot afford another defeat in Asia', Nixon said. 'When [President] Nixon said, in 1969, that he had inherited a war not of his making, he was being too modest', said his biographer Stephen Ambrose.

Presidential candidate and Vietnamisation (1968)

In 1967, Republican presidential hopeful Nixon seemed the last man likely to advocate withdrawal from Vietnam, but the Tet Offensive (see page 164) of early 1968 was a great turning point for Nixon. He realised that there would have to be changes in American policy and started to call (like Kennedy and Johnson before him) for the increased use of South Vietnamese soldiers. This policy became known as **Vietnamisation**:

> *The nation's objective should be to help the South Vietnamese fight the war and not fight it for them. If they do not assume the majority of the burden in their own defence, they cannot be saved.*

Nixon said that American forces should be withdrawn while the ARVN was built up. He ceased talk of escalation and spoke instead of **'peace with honour'**.

Did Nixon really believe that Thieu could maintain a strong South Vietnam without the ever-increasing American aid Nixon himself had so strongly advocated until Tet? Perhaps not, but his main concern was to get America out, through more American bombing and a radical change of diplomatic direction.

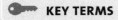 **KEY TERMS**

Vietnamisation A phrase/ policy introduced by the Nixon administration; the idea was that the South Vietnamese government and forces should take the main responsibility for the war against Communism.

'Peace with honour' Nixon always claimed he would get 'peace with honour' in Vietnam, by which he meant that Thieu's government must stay in power in a viable South Vietnamese state.

Richard Nixon

1913	Born in California
1947–50	Congressman
1950–3	Senator
1953–61	Vice President
1954	Advocated tactical nuclear weapons to help French at Dien Bien Phu (see page 103)
1967	Advocated improved relations with China
1968	Tet convinced him US involvement must end (Jan.–Feb.)
	Presidential election victory (November)
1969	First US troop withdrawal from Vietnam
1970	Extended Vietnam War to Cambodia; anti-war protests
1972	Visited the People's Republic of China (February)
	Re-elected in landslide victory (November)
1973	Ended Vietnam War (January)
	Arms limitation treaty with the USSR (May)
1974	Resigned over Watergate affair (August)
1994	Died

Background

Richard Nixon was born to a struggling family in California. Academically able, he practised law in California before naval service in the Second World War. As Congressman (1947–50) and Senator (1950–3), he gained national fame for hounding Communists. His defeat of Helen Douglas in the 1950 Californian Senate race owed much to his accusations that she had 'pink' (Communist) sympathies – he said she was 'pink right down to her underwear'. A loyal and impressive Vice President to President Eisenhower (1953–61), Nixon was narrowly defeated by the Democrat John F. Kennedy in the 1960 presidential election. Defeated in the Californian gubernatorial election in 1962, he told the press he was retiring from politics, so they would not 'have Richard Nixon to kick around any more'. Although 'retired', he continued to do sterling work for the Republican Party, and in 1968 was the successful Republican candidate for the presidency.

Achievements

President Nixon (1969–74) had many positive foreign policy achievements. He ended two decades of dangerous estrangement from China, signed an arms limitation treaty with the USSR and finally ended the American involvement in Vietnam. He has been much criticised for his painfully slow exit from Vietnam (and also for his disgrace and enforced resignation from the presidency after the **Watergate affair**). Faced with the problem of getting out of Vietnam yet retaining US international credibility, his tactics included the promotion of **detente** and the massive bombing of Vietnam, Cambodia and Laos. Bombing damaged his reputation, but his farsighted China policy is generally admired.

Nixon hoped that America could replace the era of confrontation with the era of negotiation, and get Soviet and Chinese help in forcing Hanoi to accept American peace terms.

Paris peace talks, 1968

The final months of Johnson's presidency were dominated by the Paris peace talks, and some have accused Nixon of sabotaging the negotiations in order to stop the Democrats getting the credit for peace. Hanoi offered Thieu an opportunity to remain in power with a coalition government and Nixon privately encouraged Thieu not to participate in the talks. 'We don't want to play politics with peace', said Nixon, but subsequently admitted, 'that was inevitably what was happening'. So, had Nixon sabotaged the talks? Although Nixon might have tried to do so, Thieu needed no persuasion to reject the idea of a coalition government.

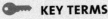

KEY TERMS

Watergate affair During Nixon's re-election campaign, Republicans authorised burglary and wiretapping of Democratic national headquarters at the Watergate building in Washington, DC; the Nixon administration tried a 'cover-up'.

Detente Relaxation of tension between the USA and the USSR in the Cold War in the 1970s.

Why Nixon decided to exit Vietnam

As a Congressman and Senator, Richard Nixon made his name as an extreme anti-Communist, but he got America out of Vietnam and drew closer to the Soviets and Chinese than any previous Cold War President. The Tet Offensive, idealism, political ambition and the changing Cold War world all combined to make the old Cold Warrior ready to end the Vietnam War.

The Tet Offensive (see page 164) convinced Nixon that the Vietnam War was unwinnable and that America needed to withdraw as soon as possible. He wanted to bring peace at home and abroad, saying in his inaugural address, 'The greatest honour history can bestow is the title of peacemaker'. Improved relations with China and the USSR and peace in Vietnam would reinvigorate America and ensure Nixon's place in the history books and his re-election in 1972. He knew the Vietnam War had ruined Johnson's presidency and upon learning of Johnson's bugging and wiretapping in the White House, said privately, 'I don't blame him. He's been under such pressure because of that damn war, he'd do anything. I'm not going to end up like LBJ … I'm going to stop that war. Fast!'

The US withdrawal from Vietnam and detente with both the Soviets and the Chinese were facilitated by the **Sino-Soviet split**. The Cold War world had changed. Sino-Soviet disagreements shattered the threat of a **monolithic Communist bloc** that had first caused Truman then Eisenhower to initiate and sustain the US involvement in Vietnam. Nixon decided that America could play off the two rival Communist giants against each other and he hoped that if he improved American relations with both China and the USSR, he could enlist their support in pressing Hanoi to a 'peace with honour' settlement in Vietnam. The Soviets in particular had considerable leverage over Hanoi because of the vast amounts of aid they contributed.

The USSR's influence in Southeast Asia

Initially, Soviet attention in Southeast Asia had focused upon Burma and Indonesia, but little was achieved. The Soviets had more success in Vietnam, where Moscow rather than Beijing was Hanoi's main ally in the war against the Americans. Soviet aid to North Vietnam was motivated by ideology, anti-Americanism and rivalry with China. Moscow supplied diplomatic support and several billion dollars worth of economic and military aid, including high-quality jet fighters, bombers, anti-aircraft systems, tanks and artillery.

The relationship between Hanoi and Moscow was sometimes uneasy. Khrushchev infuriated Hanoi when he called for the admission of both Vietnams to the United Nations in 1957, and he was reluctant to provide Hanoi with sufficient diplomatic and military support for the reunification of Vietnam. A second great period of tension arose from the developing Sino-Soviet split, which prompted deep divisions amongst the Communist leadership in Hanoi. In 1963, Ho Chi Minh praised Khrushchev's policy of peaceful coexistence with

---

🔑 **KEY TERMS**

Sino-Soviet split In the early 1960s, Chinese–Soviet mutual hostility became increasingly obvious to the rest of the world.

Monolithic Communist bloc During the 1950s, many Americans believed that Moscow and Beijing were united in their foreign policies; by the 1960s, it was increasingly clear that with the Sino-Soviet split (in which other Communist nations took sides) there was no longer a united/monolithic Communist bloc.

the West, but soon after retired from day-to-day politics, suggesting he was pushed upstairs by the pro-Chinese faction. Soviet aid increased again after Khrushchev's fall, and by late 1968, the Soviets were clearly the major suppliers of aid to North Vietnam. Nevertheless, the Chinese continued to be a vital source of food, consumer goods, military equipment, anti-aircraft weaponry, troops and foreign currency.

Moscow had always advised Hanoi to negotiate a peace settlement with South Vietnam and the Americans, but Hanoi always disregarded such advice until Nixon's detente policy prompted heavy Sino-Soviet pressure on North Vietnam to allow the Americans to exit Vietnam with some honour. During the Nixon era, as at the Geneva conference in 1954 (see page 107), both the Soviet Union and China put their own concerns before those of any Communist ally.

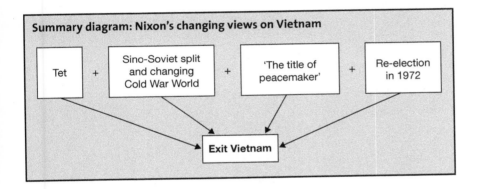

Summary diagram: Nixon's changing views on Vietnam

Tet + Sino-Soviet split and changing Cold War World + 'The title of peacemaker' + Re-election in 1972 → **Exit Vietnam**

2 Nixon and the changing Cold War world

▶ *How, why and with what results had the Cold War world changed between 1945 and 1968?*

Although many Americans perceived the USSR and the People's Republic of China as working together in Asia, the Soviet attitude toward the Chinese Communists had frequently been ambivalent.

The USSR's attitude toward China, 1945–68

The long history of antagonism between Russia and China, neighbouring and expansionist powers, dated from the nineteenth century. After Russia became Communist, the Soviets were not particularly helpful to the Chinese Communists. Stalin's advice nearly ruined the fledgling Chinese Communist Party in the 1920s and Stalin's ambassador was the last to recognise that Jiang Jieshi was no longer ruler of mainland China in 1949 (see page 30).

Figure 5.1 Cold War China.

Uneasy allies

After China became Communist in October 1949, a Sino-Soviet Treaty of Friendship, Alliance and Mutual Assistance was signed in Moscow on 14 February 1950. Nevertheless, Stalin maintained a cautious attitude:

- Soviet economic aid to China was minimal, because Stalin considered Mao Zedong (see page 6) a potential rival for the leadership of world Communism
- the Soviets were the main supplier of the Communist forces in the Korean War, but they let China do the blood-shedding and take all the risks
- after the Korean War, the USSR made China repay the massive loans borrowed to finance Chinese fighting in the war.

Sino-Soviet relations did not improve under Stalin's successor Khrushchev, who recorded a clear personality clash between himself and Mao: 'His chauvinism and arrogance sent a shiver up my spine … The Chinese have little in common with our people.' At the 1955 Bandung conference (see page 90), Chinese Foreign Minister Zhou Enlai persuasively aligned China with other nations who (unlike the Russians) had suffered at the hands of imperialists. While the Soviets gave diplomatic support for the non-aligned movement, Khrushchev was desperately competitive with the United States over the Third World, and irritated that the Chinese seemed to be muscling in.

Ideological differences

There were ever-increasing ideological differences between the Chinese and the Soviets:

- Mao's insistence on the importance of the peasantry in a Communist revolution annoyed the Soviets, who followed the **Marxist–Leninist** emphasis on the industrial proletariat.
- When Khrushchev criticised Stalin without any consultation with Mao in 1956, Mao was greatly offended. He considered himself the world's leading Communist after the death of Stalin, resented not having been consulted about this dramatic ideological statement, and had emulated many of Stalin's policies.
- Mao and Khrushchev disagreed about relations with the West. Khrushchev spoke frequently about peaceful coexistence and considered Mao's aggressive anti-Western rhetoric dangerous and provocative.

Along with the ideological differences, Mao resented the lack of Soviet support during the Quemoy and Matsu crises in 1955 and 1958 and during Sino-Indian crises in 1959 and 1962.

The Quemoy and Matsu crises

Although nearer to mainland China than Taiwan, the Quemoy and Matsu Islands in the Taiwan Strait were occupied by Jiang Jieshi's Nationalist forces (see Figure 2.1, page 54). Mao Zedong repeatedly threatened to invade Taiwan and incorporate it into Communist China and it seemed that he was about to do this in 1954 and again in 1958, when he ordered the shelling of Quemoy and Matsu. In both cases, the Eisenhower administration clarified its defence commitment to Taiwan and the Chinese backed down and stopped the shelling.

During both the Quemoy and Matsu crises, the Soviets declared their support for China and made it clear that they would fulfil their defence obligations under the 1950 treaty. Indeed, on 7 September 1958, Khrushchev warned Eisenhower that any US attack on China would be considered an attack on the Soviet Union. However, there were tensions behind the scenes. Moscow disliked China's way of proceeding: it was not so much that Mao had been provocative as that he had failed to consult Moscow about his actions. Furthermore, Zhou Enlai told Soviet Foreign Minister Andrei Gromyko in September 1958 that the Soviets should not respond to American use of tactical nuclear weapons against China. The Soviets disliked China taking this lead in foreign and defence policy and dictating when they should or should not use nuclear weapons.

 **KEY TERM**

Marxist–Leninist
Communist theories as established in the nineteenth century by the philosopher Karl Marx and the early twentieth century by the Russian revolutionary and then Soviet leader Vladimir Lenin.

Sino-Indian disputes

Sino-Indian border tensions came to a head in 1959 after an unsuccessful Tibetan rising against Chinese rule. The Tibetan leader, the Dalai Lama, took sanctuary in neighbouring India, which helped prompt Sino-Indian border clashes that culminated in a war in September–November 1962, in which the Chinese humiliated the Indian Army.

China rightly perceived the USSR as unsupportive in its struggles with India. Moscow had no wish to alienate India, one of the leaders of the non-aligned movement with which Moscow sought good relations. The Chinese, furious when in September 1959 the Soviet news agency Tass called for a peaceful resolution of the Sino-Indian dispute, wrote a stiff letter to the Soviets.

SOURCE A

From a letter from the Central Committee of the Chinese Communist Party to the Soviet Communist Party's Central Committee, September 1959.

The Tass statement showed to the whole world the different positions of China and the Soviet Union in regard to the incident on the Indian–Chinese border, which causes a virtual glee and jubilation among the Indian bourgeoisie and the American and the English imperialists who are in every way driving a wedge between China and the Soviet Union.

> Who or what does Source A blame for increasing Sino-Soviet tension?

Sharing the bomb

During the mid-1950s, the Soviets signed several agreements with the Chinese in which they promised to aid China's development of nuclear weapons, but by 1959 Khrushchev had become uneasy about that prospect. When Mao described imperialist America as a 'paper tiger', Khrushchev pointed out that the tiger had nuclear teeth. In October 1959, Khrushchev visited Beijing to celebrate the tenth anniversary of the People's Republic of China, but discussions over Taiwan and the Sino-Indian border issues went badly. Moscow opposed any Chinese attack upon Taiwan and was concerned about Sino-Indian tensions. The Soviets wanted to control Chinese foreign policy and nuclear warheads and when this appeared an unlikely eventuality, withdrew 1390 scientific and technological advisers from China in late 1960. The Soviets explained this by pointing out that Chinese officials had tried to indoctrinate the Soviet advisers on disputed ideological issues. The departure of the advisers damaged Chinese economic development and increased Chinese determination to go ahead without Soviet aid.

The propaganda war

Khrushchev's withdrawal of the Soviet advisers had its roots in the growing Sino-Soviet war of words:

- In spring 1960, the Chinese published an article in the newspaper *Red Flag* entitled 'Long Live Leninism'. The article contained a coded attack on Khrushchev's policy of peaceful coexistence.
- During the conference of Communist parties at Bucharest in June 1960, the Chinese delegates attacked Khrushchev and his policies. Khrushchev responded by threatening that he would withdraw his scientific and technological advisers from China.
- In October 1960, the official Soviet newspaper *Pravda* made its first major criticisms of China.
- In November 1960, when Deng Xiaoping (see page 31) visited Moscow, Khrushchev described Mao as a 'megalomaniac warmonger' who wanted 'someone you can piss on … If you want Stalin that badly, you can have him – cadaver, coffin and all!'
- Each side made veiled criticisms of the other, usually through attacks on each other's allies. When Chinese publications attacked 'revisionist' East European ideological errors, it was a veiled attack on the Soviets, and Soviet criticisms of 'ultra-leftism' and 'adventurism' were aimed at Chinese policies.

Moscow tried to end the propaganda war in 1962–3, but then infuriated the Chinese by signing a Nuclear Test Ban Treaty with the United States, which Beijing saw as a Soviet attempt to stop China becoming a nuclear power (China became one in 1964).

Border clashes

Given the history of antagonism, it is not surprising that there were Sino-Soviet border clashes in 1962. By 1969, when 658,000 Soviet troops faced 814,000 Chinese troops in Xinjiang and there were border clashes on the Ussuri River, China and the USSR each regarded the other as the world's greatest threat to peace. This dramatic deterioration in Sino-Soviet relations gave Nixon the opportunity to improve Sino-American relations.

Sino-American relations to 1968

Prior to 1968, Sino-American relations were extremely hostile. There were many reasons for this. Mao found it difficult to forgive and forget US involvement in the Chinese civil war during 1945–8, when the United States had aided Jiang Jieshi and the Chinese Nationalists in their struggle against Mao and the Chinese Communists (see page 30). While Mao hated capitalism, the United States hated Communism, particularly resented their erstwhile protégé China becoming Communist, believed that Beijing was Moscow's puppet, and feared other Asian countries might follow China's lead. However, it was Taiwan and the Korean War that really embittered Sino-American relations.

US policies towards Taiwan to 1968

When the State Department publicly declared Taiwan strategically unimportant to America in December 1949, it seemed America had lost interest in a Chinese civil war in which the US had backed the losing side. The United States still recognised Jiang Jieshi as representing 'China' in the United Nations, but so did most of the rest of the world.

It was Korea that caused a dramatic deterioration in Sino-American relations. While the United States interpreted the Korean War as a sign that Chinese-sponsored Communism was expansionist and threatened US security, China interpreted the Korean War as a sign that America was aggressive, anxious to get a foothold on the Asian mainland, and likely to attack China itself. Not only had the Americans sent troops to Korea, which bordered on China, but Truman had sent the US 7th Fleet to the Taiwan Strait (see page 53). As far as Mao was concerned, the United States had thereby reinjected itself into the Chinese civil war. Mao's fears of American aggression were confirmed when American forces neared the Yalu River. That led to two years of bitter fighting between American and Chinese troops on the battlefields of Korea. Their bloody clashes dramatically intensified Sino-American antagonism.

When the Korean War ended in 1953, the United States put a trade embargo on China, ensured its continued exclusion from the United Nations, and established bases on Taiwan. The US–Taiwan Defence Treaty of 1954 infuriated Mao. He never gave up hope of regaining Taiwan, as demonstrated during the Quemoy and Matsu crises.

The Quemoy and Matsu crises

The US–Taiwan Treaty prompted Mao to shell the Chinese Nationalist islands of Quemoy and Matsu (see Figure 2.1, page 54) in 1954–5, but when President Eisenhower publicly hinted that he was considering the use of tactical atomic weapons to protect Taiwan, the furious and humiliated Chinese backed down. In 1958, there was a similar Quemoy and Matsu crisis. Mao shelled the islands, America made threatening noises, Mao backed down.

Taiwan was clearly a major factor in the Sino-American enmity, but it was not the only one. Eisenhower's Secretary of State John Foster Dulles considered Chinese Communism more threatening than Soviet Communism: China had more people, greater cultural influence and prestige in Asia, and major Chinese minorities in all Asian nations, and other Asian nations were relatively weak. The United States was convinced by the Chinese involvement in Vietnam and Malaya (see page 34) that China was determined to aid revolutions worldwide, and by the Chinese occupation of Tibet (1950) and invasion of India (1962) that China was aggressively expansionist. For their part, the Chinese viewed the US intervention in Vietnam as conclusive proof of imperialist aggression.

Clearly, in the context of past Sino-American hostility, Nixon's policy of Sino-American detente was revolutionary.

Nixon's visit to China in 1972

During 1969–70, President Nixon relaxed trade and passport restrictions on China. In April 1971, China invited the American table tennis team to China and amidst much talk of 'ping-pong diplomacy', Nixon lifted the 21-year-old trade embargo on China and in February 1972, visited Beijing.

Nixon's China visit made worldwide headlines. As a crowd of thousands gathered to watch his plane take off for China, the President compared his trip to the moon flights. His plane was full of newsmen, and his visit, after twenty years with no pictures coming out of China, left American audiences spellbound. When Nixon got off the plane in Beijing, he shook hands with Zhou Enlai, which John Foster Dulles had famously refused to do at Geneva in 1954. When Nixon and Henry Kissinger (see page 185) visited Mao in his study, Kissinger was shocked to find a sick old man, barely able to stand.

Little specific was agreed upon, but the final communiqué at the end of the visit was significant. First, the joint communiqué said that both opposed any country attempting to seek hegemony in Asia (the Chinese repeatedly accused the Soviets of doing just that, so this was a coded reference to the Soviets). Second, each inserted a separate paragraph on Taiwan. The Chinese paragraph said the Communists were the sole legitimate government of China, that Taiwan was a part of China, and that US military forces should be withdrawn from Taiwan. The American paragraph was carefully phrased, and did not give much away.

SOURCE B

President (right) and Mrs Nixon (left) on the Great Wall of China, February 1972.

Why was President Nixon so keen for photographs such as Source B to be headline news in the United States?

How could the words in Source C be interpreted as recognising Jiang Jieshi as the ruler of all of China?

SOURCE C

From the American paragraph in the final Sino-American communiqué of February 1972, quoted in Stephen Ambrose, *Nixon: The Triumph of a Politician, 1962–1972*, Simon & Schuster, 1989, p. 516.

The United States acknowledges that all Chinese on either side of the Taiwan Strait maintain there is but one China and that Taiwan is a part of China. The United States Government does not challenge that position. It reaffirms its interest in a peaceful settlement of the Taiwan question by the Chinese themselves. With this prospect in mind, it affirms the ultimate objective of the withdrawal of all US forces and military installations from Taiwan. In the meantime, it will progressively reduce its forces and military installations on Taiwan as the tension in the area diminishes.

The State Department considered the joint communiqué a disaster because it contained no American reaffirmation of the defence treaty with Taiwan, but Kissinger got over this by an oral commitment before the American party left China in what Nixon called 'the week that changed the world'.

Nixon's relations with China

How had Nixon been able to bring about this amazing *rapprochement*? First, conservatives considered Nixon's Cold Warrior pedigree impeccable. Many Americans thought that if Nixon said detente was right, it must be. Nixon's conversion to detente deprived the conservatives of their leader. Second, Mao believed Chinese trade and industry would benefit from the stimulus afforded by contact with the West. Mao could see that Nixon was determined to get American troops off the Asian mainland, which made the United States less of a threat to China than the USSR was. In a speech in September 1973, Zhou Enlai said it was acceptable to negotiate with the United States, because it was a decreased threat to world peace, having declined in power since the Korean War.

Why had this leading Cold Warrior brought about such an amazing *rapprochement*? Nixon

- believed that allowing ideology to dominate foreign policy was a great and unrealistic error
- knew American power was in relative decline, due to budgetary problems, Soviet nuclear and naval parity, and the economic rise of the European Community and Japan. Making a friend out of an enemy made sense. By 1968, Nixon had concluded that the Cold War had changed. It was no longer a bipolar world, so America had to adjust its foreign policy. New friends were needed because relationships with old friends were deteriorating (the West Europeans were critical of the Vietnam War)

- recognised that the Sino-Soviet split meant America was no longer faced with a monolithic Communist bloc and it made sense to change America's relationship with the two leading Communist nations
- wanted to use China to counter Soviet power, to force Moscow into detente, and to help America win peace with honour in Vietnam
- felt it was foolish and even dangerous to leave a potential superpower such as China outside the community of nations
- rightly anticipated that detente with China would make him look like a peace-loving world statesman, help him win re-election in November 1972 and end the Vietnam War.

The results and significance of Sino-American detente

China considered Sino-American detente a success in that it greatly increased China's international standing and prestige. In October 1971, soon after the detente process began, the People's Republic of China took its seat in the United Nations, and Taiwan was expelled.

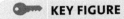

KEY FIGURE

Henry Kissinger (1923–)

Head of the National Security Council (1969–75) and Secretary of State (1973–7) under Presidents Nixon (1969–74) and Ford (1974–7). He contributed greatly to detente and Vietnamisation, and received the Nobel peace prize for his contribution to the Paris Peace Accords which ended the Vietnam War.

Soviet–American detente

By 1968, it suited the two most powerful nations in the world to improve their relationship. Why?

The American viewpoint

- Some commentators detected a growing American desire to retreat from international affairs.
- **Kissinger** said detente was a new tactic for 'managing' the emergence of the USSR as a truly global power (by the late 1960s the Soviets had attained nuclear and naval parity). Nixon knew that the American public and economy made it impossible to counter increased Soviet power by a massive arms race or by increased US global commitments. Containment had to be pursued in a different manner – by making a deal with the enemy. Kissinger wanted America to forget the old idealistic and legalistic foreign policy style that had sometimes gone against American national interest. He felt America's prime concern should be maintaining the world balance of power, while recognising that American power was limited.
- Nixon had privately concluded 'there is no way to win the [Vietnam] war'. He knew that decreased involvement in Vietnam would make it easier to improve relations with the Soviets, who could then be used to put pressure on North Vietnam to agree to a settlement, which would enable the US to get out of Vietnam without losing face.
- As America seemed to be losing old friends within the Western alliance (for example, there was increasing anti-American feeling within France), it made sense to gain new friends. Nixon believed that the increasing economic and military power of Western Europe and Japan had created a multipolar world wherein America would have to readjust its position and policies.

The Soviet viewpoint

The Soviets:

- wanted detente in order to cut their military expenditure, which had left them with great economic problems
- wanted more economic contacts with the West because of Soviet technological backwardness
- believed they had attained nuclear parity and therefore felt more secure about negotiations
- feared China and therefore wanted to decrease tension with the West
- wanted to gain recognition of the European *status quo* – especially their domination of Eastern Europe.

**Gerald Ford
(1913–2007)**

Long-serving Republican Congressman Gerald Ford became Richard Nixon's Vice President in 1973, after Vice President Spiro Agnew had to resign because of corruption. When President Nixon resigned over the Watergate affair, Ford became President (August 1974 to January 1977).

It pleased the United States (and its allies) that a dialogue had at last been opened with a potentially dangerous power, and Chinese pressure was helpful in pushing Hanoi towards a peace settlement (see page 195).

However, America and China remained wary of each other, particularly over the Taiwan issue. China was resentful when Nixon insisted that he would maintain the close US–Taiwanese relationship. The tenuous nature of the detente was demonstrated in December 1975, when President **Gerald Ford** got a luke-warm welcome on a visit to Beijing. The reason for this cooling of Sino-American relations was that the Chinese felt that the Soviet–American detente was too successful.

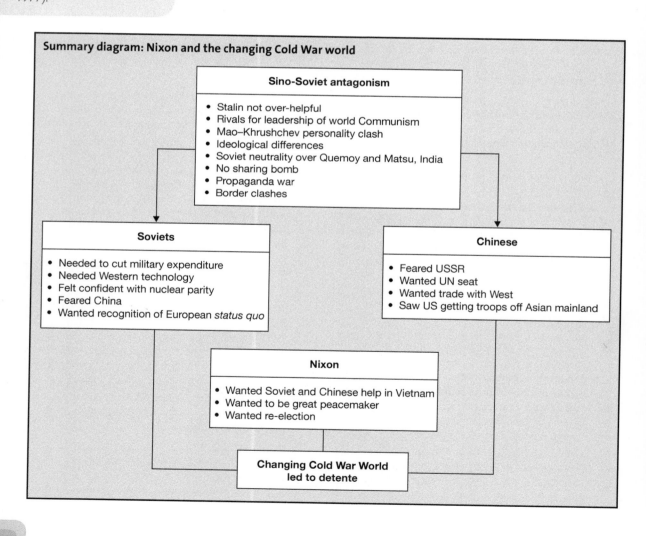

Summary diagram: Nixon and the changing Cold War world

Sino-Soviet antagonism

- Stalin not over-helpful
- Rivals for leadership of world Communism
- Mao–Khrushchev personality clash
- Ideological differences
- Soviet neutrality over Quemoy and Matsu, India
- No sharing bomb
- Propaganda war
- Border clashes

Soviets

- Needed to cut military expenditure
- Needed Western technology
- Felt confident with nuclear parity
- Feared China
- Wanted recognition of European *status quo*

Chinese

- Feared USSR
- Wanted UN seat
- Wanted trade with West
- Saw US getting troops off Asian mainland

Nixon

- Wanted Soviet and Chinese help in Vietnam
- Wanted to be great peacemaker
- Wanted re-election

**Changing Cold War World
led to detente**

Nixon and the Vietnam War

▶ *How and with what results did Nixon extricate America from
Vietnam?*

Nixon considered foreign policy the most important and interesting task of any
President and in Henry Kissinger he chose a National Security Adviser who
agreed with him. In order to ensure he and Kissinger kept control of foreign
policy, Nixon chose his old friend and supporter William Rogers to be Secretary
of State. Rogers knew little about foreign policy and was amazed when he got
his first pile of foreign policy papers to read: 'You don't expect me to read all this
stuff, do you?'

Kissinger was a great believer in personal and secret diplomacy. He distrusted
bureaucrats and it was commonly said in Washington that he treated his staff
as mushrooms: kept in the dark, stepped on, and frequently covered with
manure. Like Nixon, Kissinger considered foreign policy 'too complex' for 'the
ordinary guy' to understand. This conviction proved a weakness in that they
did not always explain their policies and thereby ensure popular support for
them (see page 191). Led by two such hard-headed realists, American foreign
policy became what some considered immoral in its emphasis upon the ultimate
survival and strength of American power. Unlike Johnson, neither seemed to
worry about the deaths of Vietnamese civilians or even of American soldiers.

Vietnam – the problems and solutions

Vietnam was Nixon's greatest single problem. He sought a peace settlement that
would allow America to save face. That required Communist agreement that
Thieu remain in power in an independent South Vietnam. He hoped to achieve
this through 'Vietnamisation' and improved relations with the USSR and China.
He guessed that the desire of both Communist powers for detente with the
United States would encourage them to press Hanoi to make peace with honour.
Nixon also had another ploy, according to one of his advisers, who recalled
Nixon saying:

> I call it the '**Madman Theory**' ... I want the North Vietnamese to believe ...
> I might do anything ... We'll just slip the word to them that, 'for God's sake, you
> know Nixon is obsessed about Communism. We can't restrain him when he's angry
> – and he has his hand on the nuclear button' – and Ho Chi Minh himself will be in
> Paris in two days begging for peace.

America also needed peace at home, as demonstrated during Nixon's
presidential inaugural parade, when thousands of anti-war demonstrators
chanted 'Ho, Ho, Ho Chi Minh, the NLF [see page 114] is going to win', and
some demonstrators burned small American flags and spat at police. Nixon
hoped that peace in Vietnam would restore calm in the United States.

 KEY TERM

Madman Theory President
Nixon's depiction of himself
as an unpredictable leader
in order to intimidate the
Vietnamese.

Vietnam – the exit strategy

Although determined to end the war, Nixon wanted 'peace with honour'. It took time and tremendous effort to persuade Hanoi to agree to allow Thieu to remain in power. Nixon had to use great military and diplomatic pressure to gain a settlement in which Thieu was given a reasonable chance for survival and about which it could not be said that America had wasted its time and effort in Vietnam. While applying the military and diplomatic pressure, Nixon had also to take into account American left-wing opposition to the war, and right-wing opposition to losing it.

1969 – military solutions

In February 1969, the Communists launched another offensive on South Vietnam. 'Rolling Thunder' (see page 145) and the American ground offensive of 1966–8 (see page 148) had clearly not worked, so Nixon tried a secret bombing offensive against the Ho Chi Minh Trail (see Figure 4.1, page 137) in Cambodia in March. Nixon hoped the bombing offensive would

- sever enemy supply lines
- encourage Hanoi to agree to an acceptable peace
- destroy the supposed Vietnamese Communist headquarters in Cambodia – **COSVN** (the Central Office for South Vietnam).

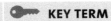

KEY TERM

COSVN Central Office for South Vietnam – small, mobile Vietnamese Communist headquarters in Cambodia.

When the bombing failed to destroy COSVN or slow traffic on the trail, Nixon escalated it in late April. 'I can't believe', said the exasperated Kissinger, 'that a fourth-rate power like North Vietnam does not have a breaking point'. He advocated blockading Haiphong and invading North Vietnam. Nixon feared domestic opposition to this but deliberately leaked to the press that he was considering it – his 'madman' tactic.

1969 – the Paris peace talks and diplomacy

Nixon's first diplomatic initiative was the April 1969 suggestion that, as the Paris peace talks had stalled amidst the public posturing by the representatives from Saigon and Hanoi, there should be secret Washington–Hanoi negotiations. Hanoi had always favoured that option, because it excluded Saigon.

In secret talks in Paris in May, Nixon offered Hanoi new peace terms. Although still insistent that Thieu remain in power, he dropped Johnson's insistence that American troops would only withdraw months after the PAVN and he offered simultaneous withdrawal. The North Vietnamese delegation was unimpressed. Nixon told Kissinger to warn them that as America was withdrawing troops and was willing to accept the results of South Vietnamese elections, they must do likewise or Nixon would have to do something dramatic. Kissinger set Hanoi a 1 November deadline, but Hanoi insisted that they had no troops in South Vietnam and that Thieu must give way to a coalition government.

Making little progress with Hanoi, Nixon turned to Moscow and in October, promised detente in exchange for Soviet assistance in ending the Vietnam War (he called this exchange '**linkage**'). He warned them, 'The humiliation of a defeat is absolutely unacceptable to my country.'

1969 – the home front

Nixon used several tactics to keep the home front quiet:

- He made a series of troop withdrawals from Vietnam, timing the announcements to defuse public opposition: for example, as anti-war activists and Congressmen prepared to protest in September, Nixon announced the withdrawal of 60,000 troops. Kissinger opposed the troop withdrawals, saying it would decrease American bargaining power with Hanoi and be like giving salted peanuts to the American public – they would just want more. Nixon said public opinion gave him little choice.
- He judged that the heart of the anti-war movement was male college students threatened with the draft. He therefore adjusted it so that older students (whom he presumably considered more confident and articulate) were less hard-hit. This temporarily decreased protests and Nixon got a 71 per cent approval rating.
- Nixon tried to keep his actions secret in order to forestall the anti-war protesters, as with the bombing of Cambodia. When a British correspondent in Cambodia publicised it, Nixon, convinced it was an internal leak, ordered large-scale wiretapping.

These tactics failed to halt the protests. Nixon rightly claimed that the protesters were a minority, but their numbers were growing. Furthermore, Congress was increasingly obstructive.

1969 – protests and congressional opposition

In October 1969, the campuses were in uproar and the largest anti-war protest in American history took place. In this '**Moratorium**' protesters took to the streets in every major city. Millions participated, many middle class and middle aged. The more radical waved VC flags, chanted defeatist slogans and burned American flags. Although such behaviour proved unpopular, it made Nixon drop the 1 November ultimatum to Hanoi. He backed down to keep the public happy, despite saying that:

> *… to allow government policy to be made in the streets … would give the decision, not to the majority, and not to those with the strongest arguments, but to those with the loudest voices … It would invite anarchy.*

KEY TERMS

Linkage Linking US concessions to the USSR and China to their assistance in ending the Vietnam War.

Moratorium In this context, suspension of normal activities, in order to protest.

Nixon used speeches to try to keep the home front quiet and on 3 November delivered one of his best. He asked for time to end the war:

And so tonight, to you, the great silent majority of my fellow Americans – I ask for your support. Let us be united for peace. Let us be united against defeat. Because let us understand: North Vietnam cannot defeat or humiliate the United States. Only Americans can do that.

Nixon's approval rating shot up to 68 per cent, but although he exulted, 'We've got those liberal bastards on the run now, and we're going to keep them on the run', protests soon began again.

Between 14 and 16 November, 250,000 peaceful protesters took over Washington. As 40,000 marchers carrying candles filed past the White House, each saying the name of an American soldier, Nixon wondered whether he could have thousands of helicopters fly low over them to blow out their candles and drown their voices. Simultaneously, news of the My Lai massacre (see page 151) surfaced. Although Nixon reminded everyone that the VC often behaved similarly, many thought that the price of war was too high if it was making murderers out of American youths.

Meanwhile, torn between the demands of the protesters and the need to be seen as loyal to American boys in the field, Congress responded to unconfirmed press reports of US activity in Laos. In October, closed congressional hearings on the US involvement in Southeast Asia resulted in the first detailed official information on Laos and demonstrated congressional unease about the 'secret war'.

> ## The secret war in Laos
>
> In spring 1970, heavily edited transcripts of the October 1969 congressional hearings were published. A White House statement admitted to 1040 Americans working in Laos, but emphasised the presence of 67,000 North Vietnamese troops there. The statement said no Americans had been killed, but press reports to the contrary forced the Nixon administration to admit 27 American deaths in Laos since 1964.

1970 – Vietnam and the Cambodian offensive

Nixon was no nearer to peace in 1969, and 1970 proved no better. His goals were clear. He wanted to be out of Vietnam before the presidential election of November 1972, leaving pro-American governments in South Vietnam, Cambodia and Laos. He also wanted Hanoi to release American prisoners of war (POWs). His only means of persuasion were 'Mad Bomber' performances and linkage, and neither worked in 1970.

Having announced the withdrawal of 150,000 American troops from Southeast Asia, Nixon nevertheless appeared to be extending the war in January 1970, when he escalated the air offensive. He ordered heavy bombing of the trail in

Laos and Cambodia and of North Vietnamese anti-aircraft bases, believing that demonstrations of American power would

- counter Saigon's pessimism about American troop withdrawals
- help protect the remaining Americans in Vietnam
- intimidate Hanoi
- gain better peace terms.

Nevertheless, the North Vietnamese launched another great offensive in Laos on 12 February. Desperate for some success, especially as Congress was considering cutting off his money, Nixon sent 30,000 American and ARVN forces into southwestern Cambodia (less than 50 miles from Saigon), but they encountered neither enemy resistance nor COSVN.

Nixon argued that his Cambodian offensive had been successful. The capture and destruction of vast quantities of Communist war materiel rendered Hanoi incapable of launching another major offensive in South Vietnam for two years, which theoretically gave the ARVN time to also grow stronger. Nixon claimed that intervention in Cambodia had occupied PAVN troops who would otherwise have been killing Americans.

On the downside, COSVN had not been found. Perhaps it had never existed. The Americans had expected to find a miniature Pentagon, but there were just a few huts. Furthermore, 344 Americans and 818 ARVN died, and 1592 Americans and 3553 ARVN were wounded. Nixon's critics said that it had widened the war. The *New York Times* queried whether the offensive had won time for America or just boosted Hanoi by revealing American divisions and the restraints on the President. One totally unexpected result of the Cambodian invasion was that it forced the Communists further inland, where they destabilised the Cambodian government. Furthermore, American bombing increased the popularity of the Cambodian Communists (see Chapter 6).

From Nixon's viewpoint, the most undesirable result of the Cambodian offensive was the opposition on the home front.

1970 – home front problems

The invasion of Cambodia caused unrest within the United States. Nixon tried to defuse it with a speech in April. He said America had respected Cambodian neutrality for five years (he lied) but that as Vietnamese Communists had vital bases there, the US had to do a clean-up operation. He denied that this constituted an invasion of Cambodia and said America's first defeat in its 190-year existence would be a national disgrace:

> *If, when the chips are down, the world's most powerful nation, the United States of America, acts like a pitiful, helpless giant, the forces of totalitarianism and anarchy will threaten free nations and free institutions throughout the world.*

This emotive language was effective. The speech proved quite popular but the success was short-lived: the Cambodian offensive caused student protests across America.

Kent State and campus riots

When Secretary of State Bill Rogers was finally told about the planned invasion of Cambodia, he said, 'This will make the students puke.' The Cambodian offensive did indeed cause trouble on campuses across America. On 5 May 1970, four students at Kent State University, Ohio, were shot dead by the National Guard. Some had been participating in an anti-war rally, some just changing classes. Student protests increased, leading California's conservative Governor Ronald Reagan to close down Californian colleges. As students rioted, Nixon backed down and declared that he would get American troops out of Cambodia by June. Government policy was made in the streets again. That infuriated the military, while in New York City, 100,000 pro-Nixon people demonstrated. Amongst the demonstrators were traditionally Democrat construction workers who, in support of the Republican President's policies, clashed with and beat up students from the East's leading colleges.

President, public opinion and Congress

Polls showed how Nixon's Cambodian offensive had divided Americans: 50 per cent approved, 39 per cent disapproved. As the Cambodian offensive appeared to be a dramatic escalation of the war authorised solely by the President, it aggravated relations between the President and Congress. Under pressure of the Cold War, the President had been acquiring ever greater power and America had been developing what contemporaries christened the **'imperial presidency'**. It was inevitable that Congress would attempt to reassert its power, especially when presidential policies were unpopular. Congress rightly said that the constitution gave them alone the power to declare war and to raise and to finance the armed forces, although Nixon also had a good point when he said that he had inherited a war and the constitution gave him powers as Commander-in-Chief. Whatever the constitutional rectitude, the Senate enthusiastically supported bills to stop Nixon waging war in Cambodia, Laos and Vietnam throughout 1970–1. 'Virtually everybody wants out', said one hawk.

Nixon felt he was in an awful dilemma: he could not get re-elected unless he extricated America from Vietnam, but he would not be able to save Thieu and American honour if he just withdrew.

1971 – the Lam Son Offensive

Determined not to be the first President to lose a war and desperate to gain peace with honour, Nixon decided to go on the military offensive again. The May 1970 US/ARVN invasion of Cambodia and Cambodia's closure of its ports

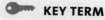

KEY TERM

'Imperial presidency'
Some Americans felt that under the pressure of the lengthy Cold War, the President gained greater power and became like some old European King or Emperor.

to Communist shipping had left the North Vietnamese Communists heavily reliant upon the Ho Chi Minh Trail. The JCS had long been tempted to attack the trail in southern Laos, but when on 1 January 1971 Congress forbade the use of American ground troops in Laos and Cambodia, the Lam Son Offensive became a test of Vietnamisation. Although Westmoreland had said that it would require four American divisions, the JCS argued that the ARVN could do it if protected by American air power. Cutting the Trail would

- help ARVN morale
- show Vietnamisation was working
- damage Hanoi's ability to stage an offensive in 1971.

Rogers warned that Hanoi expected it (there had been leaks in Saigon), and that Nixon was sending only one ARVN division to do a job which Westmoreland had refused to do without four American divisions, but Nixon and Kissinger ignored him, and the Lam Son Offensive began on 8 February 1971.

Backed by 600 US helicopters, 17,000 ARVN troops faced 30,000 PAVN troops, who were supported by 20,000 logistics troops. The ARVN did well at first, but then the PAVN got the upper hand, mostly because of new armoured units using Soviet equipment. Within two weeks, the ARVN was heavily defeated. American TV viewers saw ARVN troops fighting each other for places on American helicopters lifting them out of Laos. American crews coated the skids with grease so the South Vietnamese would stop hanging on in numbers sufficient to bring down the choppers. Kissinger was particularly furious with Thieu, who had refused to send the number of troops the US recommended. 'Those sons of bitches. It's their country and we can't save it for them if they don't want to.'

> ## Morale amongst the anti-Communist forces
>
> The casualty rate in the Lam Son Offensive was exceptionally high: 1402 Americans and 7683 ARVN; 100 US helicopters were destroyed, 618 damaged. Lam Son hit ARVN morale hard. Laotian Prime Minister Souvanna Phouma refused to participate in the offensive, because he was keen to be seen as neutral. His Royal Lao Army was unenthusiastic and unimpressive in fighting the Communists. The Hmong tribe bore the brunt of the anti-Communist operations in Laos, but as early as 1970 they suffered manpower problems and were reduced to calling up 13–14-year-olds.
>
> By 1971, the morale of the American forces in Vietnam had plummeted, with 18-year-olds being asked to fight a war that everyone in America agreed was just about finished, in order to allow time for the army of a corrupt dictatorship in Saigon to improve. Nixon warned the West Point graduating class that it was no secret that they would be leading troops guilty of drug abuse and insubordination.

1971 – the Paris peace talks and diplomacy

Although Nixon appeared not to have made any progress on the military front, it seemed as if linkage might be working by spring 1971 – detente with both the USSR and China was becoming a reality and Moscow and Beijing were urging Hanoi to stop insisting upon Thieu's removal as a prerequisite for peace.

At the Paris peace talks in May, Nixon offered Hanoi another concession: the United States would get out by a set date without demanding mutual withdrawal. In return, Hanoi should stop sending additional troops or materials to South Vietnam, observe a ceasefire, and guarantee the territorial integrity of Laos and Cambodia (just when the Communists were about to win in both). Thieu would stay in power and the American POWs would be returned. Hanoi was unimpressed, especially as there was no mention of stopping the bombing.

1971 – the home front

With his approval rating down to 31 per cent, Nixon was depressed by the home front in 1971. Influenced by the spring protests (300,000 marched in Washington, DC), some senators tried to halt all aid to South Vietnam unless there was a presidential election. Thieu held one in October, with one candidate – himself. Nixon could only say that democracy took time to develop.

After three years, Nixon seemed no closer to bringing peace to America or Vietnam. Public opposition was hampering the military offensives he hoped would get Hanoi to make concessions at the peace talks and his diplomatic offensives were not paying off. The USSR and China could not or would not persuade Hanoi to give in. Aware of American national honour and credibility, and fearful of alienating the right wing, Nixon insisted that Thieu remain in power, but Hanoi said 'No'.

1972 – the presidential election year

Nixon needed some great breakthrough to ensure re-election, but a breakthrough looked unlikely in early 1972. The USSR and China were pressing Hanoi to let Nixon exit with honour and to let Thieu remain for a while, but Hanoi did not want to face a superbly equipped ARVN perpetually supplied by America. The PAVN therefore began a great March offensive against South Vietnam, using tanks and artillery in unprecedented quantities. The ARVN crumbled. His policy of Vietnamisation discredited in the presidential election year, Nixon decided that these 'bastards have never been bombed like they are going to be bombed this time'.

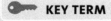

KEY TERM

B-52s Large American bomber planes.

B-52s were used on North Vietnam for the first time since 1968 and inflicted heavy casualties. When the PAVN still advanced, Nixon escalated the bombing. He bombed oil depots around Hanoi and Haiphong. On 16 April, American bombers hit four Soviet merchant ships at anchor in Haiphong, but as Nixon anticipated, the Soviets were so keen to have the planned Moscow **summit** that their protests were low key. Linkage was working.

Nixon then mined North Vietnam's ports. One Democrat spoke of flirting with a third world war to keep General Thieu in power and save Nixon's face for a little longer, but it was Nixon who understood the Soviets best. Moscow was tired of financing Hanoi's war, desperate for detente, and impressed by a great Nixon concession (he hinted that he was willing to accept a coalition containing Communists).

Meanwhile, Nixon tried to rally the American public, saying:

> If the United States betrays the millions of people who have relied on us in Vietnam … it would amount to renunciation of our morality, an abdication of our leadership among nations, and an invitation for the mighty to prey upon the meek all around the world.

He said that if America was strong, the world would remain half rather than wholly Communist. His approval rating shot up to 60 per cent.

Bombing, concessions, time and money

One of the ways in which Nixon hoped to obtain 'peace with honour' was by disguising concessions with simultaneous shows of force. So, while continuing the bombing throughout the Moscow summit (May 1972), he secretly offered Hanoi yet another vital concession: the PAVN would be allowed to stay in South Vietnam.

Hanoi was finally being driven towards a settlement by a combination of

- American concessions
- Soviet and Chinese pressure
- the failure of their offensive to take big cities
- Operation Phoenix (see page 196)
- the destructiveness of the B-52s
- the probable re-election of the unpredictable 'Mad Bomber'.

After three years, Nixon's combination of military and diplomatic pressure and concessions appeared to be working. It was just as well. By the second half of 1972, he was running out of time and money. Troop withdrawals meant Congress could no longer be shamed into granting funds to help 'our boys in the field'. Nixon begged them not to damage his negotiating capabilities, and claimed it would be immoral to walk away from Vietnam as there would be a bloodbath for former Thieu supporters. Polls showed that most Americans agreed with Nixon: 55 per cent supported continued heavy bombing of North Vietnam, 64 per cent the mining of Haiphong and 74 per cent thought it important that South Vietnam should not fall to the Communists.

KEY TERM

Summit During the Cold War, meetings or conferences between the US and Soviet leaders were known as summit meetings.

Operation Phoenix

In 1968 the CIA introduced a system codenamed 'Operation Phoenix', whereby tens of thousands of VC were sought out and interrogated. Few taken for interrogation came out alive. Torture was the norm. An American officer testified before Congress about the methods used:

> the insertion of the 6-inch dowel into the canal of one of my detainee's ears and the tapping through the brain until he died. The starving to death [in a cage] of a Vietnamese woman who was suspected of being a ... cadre ... the use of electronic gear ... attached to ... both the women's vaginas and the men's testicles [to] shock them into submission.

Nixon had been delighted by the success of Operation Phoenix, saying, 'We've got to have more of this. Assassinations. Killings. That's what they [the Communists] are doing.' However, when the press exposed the programme, there was considerable American outrage, so Nixon had to cancel Phoenix operations in 1972.

The Paris peace talks

Both sides now compromised. Hanoi would let Thieu remain in power while America would let the PAVN stay in South Vietnam and not insist upon a ceasefire in Cambodia and Laos. However, Hanoi insisted on a voice in the Saigon government and Thieu refused to accept that, despite Nixon's promise that America would never desert him. Kissinger rejected the idea of a coalition government but offered a Committee of National Reconciliation (to be one-third South Vietnamese, one-third Communist and one-third neutral) to oversee the constitution and elections. Kissinger thereby agreed that the Communists were a legitimate political force in South Vietnam, which Thieu had always denied. Nixon shared Thieu's doubts but felt that his ally had to make some concessions and threatened him with the withdrawal of American support. 'We're going to have to put him through the wringer ... We simply have to cut the umbilical cord and have this baby walk by itself.' Nixon threatened the tearful Thieu with a reminder of what had happened to Diem (see page 130).

In October, Kissinger thought he had an agreement:

- America would withdraw all its armed forces but continue to supply the ARVN.
- There would be a National Committee of Reconciliation with Communist representation.
- Hanoi would release American POWs.
- Thieu would remain in power.
- The PAVN would remain in South Vietnam.
- America would help with the economic reconstruction of North Vietnam as a humanitarian gesture.

Nixon claimed this was 'a complete capitulation by the enemy', then got cold feet and rejected the terms. He feared accusations that he had given in to protesters, or that peace at this time was an electoral ploy. Some advisers feared that if peace came before the election, people might vote Democrat as the Democrats were often considered better at peacetime governing. American Cold Warriors opposed the National Committee, as did Thieu, who loathed it, and was also desperate to have the PAVN out of South Vietnam. Nixon himself was unsure that this constituted peace with honour.

Kissinger was as keen as Nixon that Nixon be re-elected. It meant four more years for both of them. However, when on the eve of the American presidential election, Kissinger assured the press that 'Peace is at hand', Nixon was furious, believing that it would make Hanoi and Thieu more intransigent. He also resented Kissinger's gaining the glory from the announcement. Some Democrats were cynical. Why was peace suddenly at hand on the eve of the election? Nixon had had four years to do this. Kissinger pointed out that Hanoi's recent concessions allowing Thieu to remain in power were the difference. He omitted to mention that America had also made concessions.

In the November 1972 presidential election, Nixon defeated Democrat liberal George McGovern, but the Democrats controlled Congress and they were not going to carry on funding the war. The only way forward was to force Thieu to accept the unacceptable. Nixon gave Thieu his 'absolute assurance' that if Hanoi broke the peace, he would take 'swift and severe retaliatory action'. Thieu knew that any agreement was inevitably going to be a temporary ceasefire so long as the PAVN remained in South Vietnam, and that the American political system could invalidate Nixon's promise of future aid against North Vietnamese aggression. Some of Kissinger's staff were so exasperated by Thieu's stubbornness that they suggested assassinating him.

Hanoi remained willing to accept the October agreement that Nixon and Kissinger had initially considered satisfactory, but having once rejected that agreement, America could hardly accept it now without looking foolish.

Christmas bombing

On 18 December, Nixon bombed and mined Haiphong again. Although American planes tried to avoid civilian casualties, 1000 died in Hanoi. The North Vietnamese shot down fifteen B-52s with 93 American airmen, a rate of losses the US Air Force could not sustain for long. There was no public explanation for this Christmas 1972 bombing, which caused worldwide uproar. Kissinger was cracking: he leaked to the press that he opposed the Christmas bombing (that was untrue). One adviser thought that 'we look incompetent – bombing for no good reason and because we do not know what else to do'.

Why did Nixon do it? He was probably trying to:

- reassure Thieu of American strength and support
- weaken Hanoi so that it could not speedily threaten South Vietnam after peace was concluded
- disguise American retreats and compromises in the negotiations.

Several Congressmen and influential newspapers disapproved. Some questioned Nixon's sanity and accused him of waging 'war by tantrum'.

The Paris Peace Accords, January 1973

The peace settlement of January 1973 was basically the same as that of October 1972 with a few cosmetic changes for both sides (one Kissinger aide said, 'We bombed the North Vietnamese into accepting our concessions'). Knowing his funding would soon be cut off, Nixon had to tell Thieu that he was going to sign with or without him. On 22 January, Thieu agreed, although he regarded it as virtual surrender.

The 27 January 1973 Paris Peace Accords declared a ceasefire throughout Vietnam (but not Cambodia or Laos). POWs would be exchanged, after which America would remove the last of its troops. The PAVN was not required to leave the South, but had to promise not to 'take advantage' of the ceasefire or increase its numbers. Thieu remained in power, but the Committee of National Reconciliation contained Communist representation and would sponsor free elections. Nixon secretly promised billions of dollars worth of reconstruction aid to Hanoi.

Kissinger was awarded the highly prestigious Nobel peace prize for ending the Vietnam War. Some denied that he deserved it more than Nixon, others denied that he deserved it at all.

Summary diagram: Nixon and the Vietnam War

Aim
Peace settlement that leaves Thieu in power

Methods
Military + diplomatic + keep home front onside

Progress		
Military	**Diplomatic**	**Home front**
1969 • Vietnamisation • Bombed trail in Cambodia	• Excluded Saigon from Paris peace talks • Concession – simultaneous US/PAVN withdrawal	• Withdrew troops to pre-empt protests • Moratorium • Appealed to public
1970 • Bombed trail in Laos and Cambodia • Bombed North Vietnam heavily • US/ARVN force in Cambodia	• Planning detente	• Campus riots against Cambodian offensive
1971 • Lam Son Offensive in Laos • US Army morale plummeting	• Linkage operating – but Hanoi ignored Moscow/Beijing • Concession – US would get out without PAVN withdrawal	• Spring protests • Congressional opposition
1972 • Communist spring offensive → Nixon bombed as never before	• Great Chinese/Soviet pressure on Hanoi • Both sides compromised – Hanoi said Thieu could remain, Washington recognised Communists as legitimate political force in South Vietnam • 'Peace is at hand' – October	• Congressional opposition = running out of time and money
1973	Paris Peace Accords	

4 Assessment of Nixon's Vietnam policy

▶ *Does Nixon's Vietnam policy deserve condemnation?*

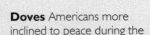
At the very least, critics of Nixon have to admit that he got the American troops out of Vietnam. Nixon did not always get much thanks for it (**doves** criticised his slowness) and he perhaps did not have much choice, but it was highly significant. It was difficult for any President to preside over the retreat of American power and from America's uncompromising and impossibly expensive Cold War militancy. Managing this retreat was perhaps one of Nixon's greatest achievements.

Some felt that Nixon and Kissinger were barely rational in their Vietnam policies, but they were motivated by the desire to do what they thought was best for America (which for the most part was what they thought was best for themselves too). Although one might not agree with their interpretation and be sickened by what it meant for the victims of their slow withdrawal and saturation bombing, one cannot help but conclude that all was accomplished with rational calculation of what was politically acceptable and best for America and the Western world.

Why did Nixon take so long to get out of Vietnam?

During 1968, Nixon had decided that America had to get out, but it took him four years to do it, during which time 300,000 Vietnamese and 20,000 Americans died. Having decided on retreat, would it not have been less painful if Nixon had done it speedily? The slow retreat damaged the morale of American forces in Vietnam and antagonised American anti-war activists, and some argue that it created the division, discontent and the presidential paranoia that helped to bring about the Watergate scandal (see page 175) that cost Nixon the presidency. However, Nixon believed American honour required North Vietnam's agreement that Thieu be left in power and that South Vietnam be left with a good chance of survival. Why else had America fought at such great cost in men and money? Nixon wrote to Rogers: 'We simply cannot tell the mothers of our casualties and the soldiers who have spent part of their lives in Vietnam that it was all to no purpose.' He was convinced that a first American defeat would lead to a collapse of confidence in American leadership and to Communist expansion throughout the world. He wanted peace, but not at any price.

It took until late 1972 before North Vietnam agreed that Thieu could remain in power and although the slow withdrawal was painful, there were clearly many who understood what Nixon was trying to do and sympathised with him. Like so many Americans, Nixon genuinely believed that the USSR and China presented a threat to America and its allies. Given the lack of political freedom within those two countries and Eastern Europe, those American fears were comprehensible and vital to understanding why America got into Vietnam and insisted on getting out 'with honour'. Although Kissinger and Nixon believed in detente, they thought that it was dangerous if the Soviets and Chinese thought that America was weak. They were probably right.

Had Nixon gained peace with honour?

Nixon had got the American ground forces out without abandoning Saigon. He had forced Hanoi to agree that Thieu could remain in power with the world's fourth largest air force and an improved ARVN. On the other hand, Nixon had failed to get the PAVN to withdraw and he had failed to nullify the VC in South Vietnam. By late 1972, his freedom was limited: he knew that Congress would cut off his money early in 1973, so he had to make peace on whatever terms he could get, and thanks to his 'mad bomber' and linkage tactics the terms were quite probably better than he could have got in 1969. However, they surely did not constitute peace with honour. '"Exit with face saved" would have been a more accurate phrase than peace with honour', opined the *Toronto Star*. Furthermore, Nixon had not really won peace for Indochina in January 1973.

1975 – the victory of North Vietnam and the fall of Saigon

Hanoi remained determined to reunify Vietnam and Thieu remained determined to maintain a South Vietnamese state. As a result, the fighting continued in South Vietnam. By spring 1973, the American troops were withdrawn and only 159 Marines remained to guard the embassy, although of the 10,000 US civilians remaining, many were military men who had been hastily discharged in order to enable them to stay. Nixon had promised continued aid to South Vietnam and he bombed Communist sanctuaries in Cambodia until 15 August 1973 when Congress cut off his money.

Hanoi had problems – the Soviets and Chinese were less forthcoming with aid because the Americans had left and both powers wanted to maintain improved relations with the United States. However, Hanoi's problems paled into insignificance alongside those of Thieu:

- Although the ARVN's million soldiers outnumbered the 100,000 PAVN and PLAF forces in South Vietnam, the Communists soon sent tens of thousands of reinforcements down the Ho Chi Minh Trail.
- The ARVN, trained in US-style warfare, ran short of petrol, ammunition and spare parts when the Americans lost interest in Vietnam.
- The South Vietnamese economy was badly hit by the loss of American money, the poor rice harvest of 1972, and the global rise in oil prices in 1974.
- The economic hardship contributed to large-scale protests against government corruption.

In December 1974, the Communists began probing. They attacked the lightly defended Phuoc Long province and then moved south when the Americans did nothing. South Vietnam's speedy collapse in the face of this Communist advance shocked Americans but no help was forthcoming. Nixon had resigned because of Watergate in 1974 (see page 175). Had he still been President, would Nixon have saved Saigon? Or had he (like Kissinger) just wanted a decent interval to elapse before the inevitable Saigon collapse? In 1977 Nixon said that he did not think he could have saved South Vietnam because Congress was opposed to any more American actions there. Congress rejected President Ford's requests for aid for South Vietnam. When Ford sent Army Chief of Staff Frederick Weyand to visit South Vietnam in April 1975, Weyand reported that even with increased American aid, the Saigon regime's chances of survival were 'minimal at best'. He might have added that it had always been so.

On 21 April 1975, President Thieu resigned and fled the country, blaming the Americans for the collapse of South Vietnam. With the Communists just outside Saigon, US helicopters airlifted 5000 people (900 Americans, 4100 South Vietnamese) out of Saigon, via the US embassy roof. On 25 April 1975, the Communists took Saigon. Vietnam was now a united nation, with a Communist government.

> ### Estimated deaths and casualties in the Vietnam War
> - Communist military deaths – at least 1 million.
> - Communist civilian casualties – at least 2 million.
> - South Vietnamese military deaths – at least 100,000.
> - South Vietnamese military casualties – 500,000.
> - South Vietnamese civilian deaths – 415,000.
> - American deaths – 58,000.
> - American casualties – 153,000.
> - South Korean and allied deaths – 5200.

Laos and Cambodia

When the Americans departed Vietnam, the Communists triumphed in Laos and Cambodia. Although Laos was supposedly neutral from 1962 (see page 120), the North Vietnamese and the Americans continued to support the factions they favoured in the Laotian civil war. The Americans dropped over 2 million tons of bombs on Laos, which caused large-scale devastation, and they supported anti-Communist forces (see page 147). North Vietnam aided the Pathet Lao and transported men and materials on the parts of the Ho Chi Minh Trail that wound through Laos.

Johnson's and Nixon's involvement in Laos was dominated and motivated by events in Vietnam. As a result, the 17,000 US-financed Thai troops left Laos after the Americans exited Vietnam in January 1973. After signing the Paris

Peace Accords, Kissinger visited Souvanna Phouma and told him there would be no more American aid and that he should make the best deal possible with the Pathet Lao. The Royal Laotian government speedily negotiated a coalition with the Pathet Lao in February 1973. However, when South Vietnam fell to the Communists in spring 1975, the Pathet Lao, assisted by the Vietnamese Communists, moved to take control of Laos. By August 1975, they had succeeded. Caught in the crossfire of the struggle between the Vietnamese Communists and the United States, Laos had suffered destabilisation, devastation and deaths. Had it not been for Vietnam and the Cold War, Laos might not have gone Communist in 1975.

The new Communist regime in the 'Lao People's Democratic Republic' killed as many as 100,000 of the Hmong who, with CIA aid and encouragement, had fought against them (see page 147). Over 20,000 civilian supporters of the old Royal Laotian government were sent to 're-education camps'. However, their sufferings were nothing compared to those of the Cambodians (see Chapter 6).

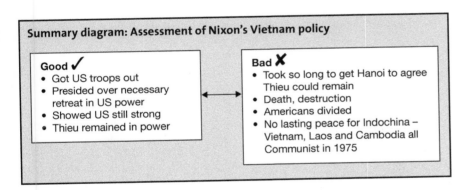

Summary diagram: Assessment of Nixon's Vietnam policy

Good ✔
- Got US troops out
- Presided over necessary retreat in US power
- Showed US still strong
- Thieu remained in power

Bad ✘
- Took so long to get Hanoi to agree Thieu could remain
- Death, destruction
- Americans divided
- No lasting peace for Indochina – Vietnam, Laos and Cambodia all Communist in 1975

⑤ Interpretations

▶ *How have historians interpreted Nixon's Vietnam policies?*

Nixon felt that, 'History will treat me fairly. Historians probably won't, because many historians are on the left.' He was right in guessing that historians would usually be hostile towards him.

Historians such as Iwan Morgan (2002) have criticised the 'madman theory', arguing that it constituted dangerous brinkmanship. However, it is not difficult to imagine that Vice President Nixon had watched President Eisenhower successfully manage crises by threatening to use American force, and that he decided to do likewise when President, while describing the policy in more extravagant terms than Eisenhower ever did.

Most historians, for example Larry Berman (2001), contend that Nixon failed to achieve peace with honour, given that South Vietnam collapsed within two years of the departure of US troops. On the other hand, it was a considerable achievement to preside over the retreat of American power and to get Hanoi to agree to allow the continued existence of Thieu and South Vietnam. Nixon accomplished this while managing to retain the support of a majority of Americans for his Vietnam policy, as seen in his landslide victory of 1972.

Nixon has been much criticised for extending the war to Cambodia, and many historians believe that Laos and Cambodia (see Chapter 6) went Communist because of Nixon's bombing. Some critics, such as Christopher Hitchens (2001), find Kissinger equally if not more culpable for the destructive bombing. The sacrifice of lives, whether American or otherwise, in the cause of American 'face', is seen by some as indefensible, although there have been occasional defences of the Nixon administration's determination that the Soviets and the Chinese should not consider the United States to be weak.

Overall, the vast majority of historians are highly critical of Nixon's policies in Southeast Asia.

Chapter summary

Although he had urged President Johnson to escalate the war in Vietnam, Nixon had decided by 1968 that America had to exit Vietnam. His change of mind was due to the Tet Offensive, his desire to go down in history as a peacemaker, and the changing Cold War world.

Nixon believed that the Communists were no longer such a threat, due to the Sino-Soviet split that became evident during the 1960s. Relations between the Chinese Communists and the Soviets had always been uneasy, due to ideological and territorial disagreements, and rivalry over leadership of the Communist world. The 1969 Sino-Soviet border clashes demonstrated how each viewed the other as a great security threat. That led both to seek detente with the United States. Sino-American relations had been embittered by the Korean War, but Nixon revolutionised American foreign policy with his 1972 China visit. Nixon sought and obtained Chinese and Soviet help to press Hanoi to make peace.

Four years of American bombing, concessions by both sides, and Soviet and Chinese pressure on Hanoi combined to lead North Vietnam and the United States to agree to end the Vietnam War in January 1973. In that Hanoi allowed President Thieu to remain in power in South Vietnam, it could be claimed Nixon had achieved peace with honour, but Nixon had been forced to agree that Communist forces could stay in South Vietnam. As a result, Communist–ARVN clashes continued throughout 1973 and 1974, and in spring 1975, the Communists launched a great and successful offensive on South Vietnam and reunited the country. After the US exit from Vietnam, Communist forces also triumphed in Laos and Cambodia in 1975.

Refresher questions

Use these questions to remind yourself of the key material covered in this chapter.

1 Why did Nixon change his ideas on Vietnam between 1954 and 1969?

2 How did Nixon plan to win peace with honour?

3 Why did Nixon secretly bomb Cambodia in spring 1969?

4 What was 'Vietnamisation'?

5 What was the Moratorium of autumn 1969?

6 What happened at Kent State University in May 1970?

7 Why did President Nixon visit China in February 1972?

8 How did Nixon think detente could help bring peace with honour?

9 What motivated Nixon's Christmas bombing?

10 What were the main terms of the Paris Peace Accords of January 1973?

11 Why did the PAVN attack Phuoc Long province in January 1975?

12 Why did the United States do nothing when South Vietnam fell to the Communists?

13 When did Laos become Communist?

14 Who were the Hmong?

 Question practice

ESSAY QUESTIONS

1 Which was more important in Nixon's desire to exit Vietnam? i) The changing Cold War world. ii) The Tet Offensive. Explain your answer with reference to both i) and ii).

2 How important was detente in achieving the Paris Peace Accords?

3 To what extent was the failure of Vietnamisation in the years 1969–75 due to President Thieu?

INTERPRETATION QUESTION

1 Read the interpretation and then answer the question that follows. 'Because of his faith in mad strategies and triangular diplomacy, Nixon had unnecessarily prolonged the war [in Vietnam].' (From Jeffrey Kimball, *Nixon's Vietnam War*, 1998.) Evaluate the strengths and limitations of this interpretation, making references to other interpretations that you have studied.

CHAPTER 6

Cambodia

After gaining independence from France in 1954, Cambodia was governed by King Sihanouk until 1970. He tried to maintain Cambodian Cold War neutrality, but his country suffered Vietnamese and American incursions as the war in neighbouring Vietnam spilled over into Cambodia. After General Lon Nol led a coup against Sihanouk, President Nixon greatly escalated US involvement and carpet-bombed Cambodia. American intervention and aid ceased after the Vietnam War ended in 1973, which left the incompetent Lon Nol regime vulnerable and led to the establishment of Pol Pot's Communist government in 1975. The murderous regime of Pol Pot and the Khmer Rouge was overthrown by the Vietnamese in 1978, which elicited international condemnation and prompted a punitive invasion of Vietnam by Pol Pot's Chinese allies. After a decade of Vietnamese occupation, the United Nations organised a new coalition government in 1993. The tearing apart of Cambodia by internal factions and external intervention is covered in the following sections:

★ Sihanouk (1955–70)

★ US bombing and the fall of the Khmer Republic (1970–5)

★ Pol Pot and Democratic Kampuchea (1975–8)

★ The Vietnamese invasion (1978) and its consequences

★ Interpretations

Key dates

1920s–30s		Anti-colonialist movement emerged
1941		Sihanouk crowned
1954	**July**	Cambodian independence from France
	Sept.	SEATO established
1955		Sihanouk advocated neutrality at Bandung
1967		Cambodian Communist Party's armed insurgency began
1969	**March**	US secretly bombed Cambodia
1970	**Mar. 18**	Lon Nol overthrew Sihanouk
	Mar.–Apr.	ARVN and US attacked Communist bases in Cambodia
	June	US ground forces withdrew from Cambodia
1971	**Jan.**	US Congress prohibited use of American troops in Laos or Cambodia
1973	**Aug.**	US stopped bombing Cambodia
1975	**April**	Pol Pot's Democratic Kampuchea established
1978		Vietnamese invaded Cambodia
1979–85		Vietnamese-installed Heng Samrin headed People's Republic of Kampuchea
1985		Vietnamese-backed Hun Sen headed PRK
1991–3		UN involvement in Cambodia
1993		Elections resulted in co-premiership of Hun Sen and Prince Ranarriddh

1 Sihanouk (1955–70)

▶ *How important was Sihanouk in Cambodian and Cold War politics?*

Early twentieth-century Cambodia was a quiet backwater in the French colonial empire, a small, landlocked, predominantly Buddhist nation, in which 80 per cent of the population were peasants and ethnic **Khmers**. The capital, Phnom Penh, was only 20 per cent Khmer. Its other inhabitants were mostly the Chinese traders and Vietnamese workers who dominated all Cambodian cities. Other minority populations included Lao, Thais, and a large Islamic Cham community. France allowed the Cambodian monarch to retain his traditional status as a demi-god, which retarded the development of a strong anti-colonialist movement for independence.

From 1940 to 1945, Cambodia was administered by France, under Japanese supervision. In 1941, the French chose eighteen-year-old Norodom Sihanouk as the next King. Although a withdrawn, sheltered child, Sihanouk grew increasingly interested in political participation and his royal status gave him great political influence. Keen to be seen as a moderniser, Sihanouk encouraged the formation of Cambodian political parties. In 1946, the Democratic Party won Cambodia's first national election, but Sihanouk suppressed the National Assembly in 1948 because he found the Democratic Party too challenging.

Anti-colonial movements

As yet, Sihanouk considered French colonialism the best way to protect Cambodia from other foreigners. However, there were anti-colonialist movements throughout French Indochina, and they co-operated with each other in order to weaken the French. The Viet Minh were the most effective opponents of French colonialism and they encouraged the Cambodian independence movement or **Issarak** (established in 1940) and worked to win the support of the Vietnamese population of Cambodia. The Viet Minh were motivated by the desire to:

- increase the number of French opponents
- secure sanctuaries from the French within Cambodian territory
- ensure that the weaponry they obtained in Bangkok could be transported through Cambodia
- spread Communism.

In 1947, French Colonel Yves Gras said the Cambodian Issarak movement was 'creating a serious problem in Cambodia', mostly due to Viet Minh support. He estimated there were around 1200 armed Cambodian Issaraks (mostly Communists), supported by a similar number of Viet Minh. Chea Soth, the future Minister of Planning in the Communist People's Republic of Kampuchea (see page 229), recalled how closely 'we worked with' the Viet Minh, who

KEY TERMS

Khmer Ethnic Cambodian.

Issarak Cambodian independence movement/supporter.

'explained things to us. I did not even know what Communism meant. If anybody had asked me whether I was afraid of Communism then, I would have said "yes".' In 1949, the first significant Vietnamese intervention in Cambodia occurred: big units of 'Viet Minh Troops to Help Cambodia' brought the total Viet Minh force in Cambodia to 3000. The anti-Communist Sihanouk admitted, 'these disruptive foreign elements … have managed to win to their cause a great number of our compatriots.' For their part, the Communists despised Sihanouk, calling him 'the fascist novice', because he had been put on the throne as an eighteen-year-old by the French in 1941. The Viet Minh radio station, the Voice of Nambo, declared that 'King Sihanouk, already gone to fat, who shamelessly makes use of sensuous perfumes … must not rule.'

In September 1951, the Cambodian Communists established the Khmer People's Revolutionary Party (**KPRP**). By December, it had 1000 Khmer and 3000 Vietnamese members. The KPRP Constitution reflected the priorities of the Cambodian Communists: there was no mention of Marxism–Leninism or land reform, only of anti-colonialism. The anti-colonial rebellion was brutal. Issaraks cut open the stomachs of Cambodians suspected of spying for the French, tore out their livers, then fried and ate them (they believed that if you ate an enemy's internal organs you acquired his strength). By 1952, the rebels in arms numbered nearly 10,000 (around 2500 non-Communist Issarak groups, over 3000 Cambodian Communists and roughly 3000 Viet Minh units) and the French admitted that well over half of Cambodia was 'insecure'. By early 1954, around 5000 Cambodian Communists were fighting against the colonial government. The policies of a Western colonial power had made the Communists a serious political force.

Sihanouk and Cambodian independence

The rebel strength was such that in 1952, Sihanouk dismissed the Democratic Party government (characterised by factional struggles, corruption and incompetence), instituted personal rule and promised independence within three years. By now he had concluded that the best way forward was to put himself at the head of the nationalist movement – his 'Royal Crusade for Independence'. Independence was granted at the Geneva conference as a result of the Viet Minh defeat of the French at Dien Bien Phu (see page 103).

While the participants at the Geneva conference (1954) agreed to the independence of Vietnam, Laos and Cambodia, the agreements were made without the participation of the Cambodian Communists, who relied upon the Viet Minh to represent them. Hoping to keep the Americans out of Southeast Asia, China pressed the Viet Minh to stay out of Cambodian (and Laotian) affairs, and for the next decade the Vietnamese Communists duly distanced themselves from Cambodian Communism. The Cambodian Communists were further weakened after Geneva because many of their former supporters felt that further struggle was unnecessary as the French had been defeated.

Norodom Sihanouk

1922	Born in Phnom Penh
1941	Became King
1954	Cambodian independence recognised at Geneva
1954–70	Ruled Cambodia
1970–5	Allied with Khmer Rouge against Lon Nol's government
1975–8	Khmer Rouge puppet then prisoner
1979–91	Allied with Khmer Rouge against Vietnamese-backed Cambodian government
1993–2004	King again
2012	Died

Background

When King Monivong died in 1941, the French colonial regime chose his grandson Sihanouk as King. The 'Playboy Prince' slowly grew interested in politics and from 1952 pressed the French to grant Cambodian independence. That was conceded during the 1954 Geneva conference. Sihanouk ruled Cambodia from 1954 to 1970. His greatest preoccupations were the maintenance of Cambodian Cold War neutrality and the repression of threats to his authority. That repression contributed to the civil war (1967–70) between Sihanouk's regime and the Cambodian Communists, whom he christened the **Khmer Rouge**. While out of Cambodia in 1970, Sihanouk was deposed by Prime Minister Lon Nol and the National Assembly. Sihanouk then collaborated with the Khmer Rouge in order to overthrow Lon Nol's regime (1970–5). In the early months of Pol Pot's Khmer Rouge government, Sihanouk was titular head of state, but Pol Pot soon placed him under house arrest. When the Vietnamese invasion ousted Pol Pot in 1978, Sihanouk made another uneasy alliance with the Khmer Rouge in opposition to the Vietnamese-established governments of Heng Samrin and Hun Sen. When the United Nations and the great powers promoted a Cambodian settlement, Sihanouk returned to Cambodia (1991), but his health was failing. He abdicated again in 2004. He had several wives and concubines in his younger days and produced an estimated fourteen children, four of whom were killed by the Khmer Rouge.

Achievements

Sihanouk claimed to have won independence from France, but in reality the Vietnamese drove the French out of Indochina. His Cold War neutrality policy failed to stop Cambodia suffering from the Vietnam War. His authoritarian rule helped destroy the middle ground in Cambodian politics and left the country at the mercy of extreme right-wingers such as Lon Nol and extreme left-wingers such as the Khmer Rouge. Sihanouk was always motivated by what he thought best for Cambodia and for himself (he saw the two as inseparable) and his support for the Khmer Rouge in 1975 probably convinced many Cambodians to accept their rule. His continued support in the 1980s helped prolong Khmer Rouge activism. Nevertheless, he was much loved by many Cambodians because of his nationalism, his concern for Cambodians (so long as they did not oppose him), and because he represented continuity. When 'Papa King' died, tens of thousands mourned in the streets of Phnom Penh.

Significance

Sihanouk was an influential figure in the Non-Aligned Movement (see page 91), but proved unable to shield Cambodia from Cold War fallout. While undeniably a patriot, his authoritarian rule distorted independent Cambodia's political development and contributed to Pol Pot's brutal regime.

Sihanouk's problems

Sihanouk faced many great problems in the governance of independent Cambodia:

- some Cambodians felt he had too much power
- the fighting in Vietnam impacted upon Cambodia
- from 1967, Cambodian Communist opposition plunged Cambodia into civil war.

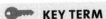

KEY TERM

Khmer Rouge 'Khmer Reds', Sihanouk's name for the Cambodian Communists.

Domestic politics

After Geneva, Sihanouk began silencing opposition groups through censorship, arrests, executions and his referendum on his 'Royal Crusade', which he claimed had won independence from the French: 99.8 per cent of voters approved him, but turnout was low and voters were intimidated. Then, in March 1955, he dropped what he called his 'atomic bomb'. He announced his abdication and consequent freedom to participate in politics as 'citizen Sihanouk'. A brilliant move, it gave him the best of both worlds: the traditional respect afforded a Cambodian monarch minus the ceremonial duties and limitations on his freedom his crown had necessitated. He then declared the formation of a new political movement, his People's Socialist Community. Membership was open to people from across the political spectrum, so long as they pledged loyalty to Sihanouk and his policies.

Sihanouk tried to make his government inclusive. For example, in 1958 he brought some young leftists into the government. However, his government was undemocratic (as demonstrated when he shamelessly rigged the elections in 1955) and intermittently repressive. One Democrat commented, 'The Khmers have been slaves for centuries. In the face of authority, they bow down. Those who use violence know that – they know how the people react.' In 1960, the French ambassador wrote that Sihanouk 'is so thirsty for power that he can admit no opposition', and that 'the police impose a sort of reign of terror.' A fifteen-minute government film of the execution of a twenty-year-old 'traitor' was shown before the main event at every cinema in Cambodia for a month.

Sihanouk deserved praise for improving educational opportunities. The French had paid little attention to Cambodian education, but under Sihanouk the number of high schools rose from eight in 1953 to 200 by 1967. Mass education was new to Cambodia and it contributed to the growing political ferment. Some literate young Cambodians, especially those who found it difficult to obtain employment commensurate with their qualifications in the underdeveloped Cambodian economy, turned to Communism. So did some of the poorest peasants. The peasantry failed to prosper under Sihanouk: over half were chronically in debt and between 1950 and 1970, the proportion of landless farmers rose from 4 to 20 per cent. Pol Pot (see page 219) subsequently claimed this was a crucial factor in his rise to power.

Overall though, the years 1956–66 were years of relative calm in Cambodia. An American resident said that for once there was 'complete peace and internal security'. The calm owed much to what the Viet Minh considered best for Vietnam. It seems likely that Sihanouk made a deal with the Viet Minh: they would be allowed to operate secretly on the Cambodian–Vietnamese border but would not interfere in Cambodia. The pro-Vietnamese faction dominated the KPRP (renamed the Communist Workers' Party of Kampuchea or **WPK** in 1960) and they acquiesced in Sihanouk's rule. Meanwhile, Sihanouk carried out

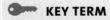

KEY TERM

WPK Workers' Party of Kampuchea or Cambodian Communist Party, 1960–6.

The Royal Court

Sihanouk's court was characterised by venality. His mother and his wife Monique's relatives so enriched themselves at the expense of the nation that Sihanouk wrote in 1962 that 'corruption will finish by bringing me down'. Nevertheless, he did nothing about it. More straitlaced Cambodians still considered him a playboy prince and his behaviour and policies were sometimes strange. In 1966, he wrote, directed and starred in a series of romantic movies, with his favourite wife Monique as his leading lady and members of the government in supporting roles. The French ambassador considered some of his policies laughable (see Source A below).

SOURCE A

Observations on Sihanouk's court by the French ambassador, Jean De Beausse, quoted in Philip Short, *Pol Pot: The History of a Nightmare*, Hodder, 2004, p. 153.

The Prime Minister, members of the Cabinet, MPs, civil servants, no one is spared! All have to stop their official business and submit to the Prince's fantasies. Last year it was manual labour [everyone had to spend one day a month working on dams and irrigation canals]. *This year it's sport. A small thing, you may say … but infuriating for middle-aged men who have to display themselves in volley-ball and basket-ball matches, which naturally the Head of State's team* [Sihanouk's] *… always wins.* [They] *make a sorry spectacle in athletics shorts … and roundly jeered by the good people of Phnom Penh, whom the Prince invites to watch … The country, or rather the Prince, is in a frenzy. Everything is sacrificed to sport. A fifth of the annual budget is being spent on preparing the South-East Asian Games which are to be held in Phnom Penh in December* [1963*] *… At a time of financial crisis … where hospitals are cruelly lacking, such expenditure is scandalous.*

* The Games were eventually cancelled due to regional rivalries and Cambodian domestic instability.

> Judging from Source A, how would you characterise Sihanouk's government?

harsh and effective repression of the urban Cambodian Communist movement, so that by 1960 the Cambodian Communists were in retreat in the rural areas dominated by the Vietnamese and the NLF.

Foreign policy

Several factors encouraged Sihanouk to try to maintain Cold War neutrality:

- Cambodia's Communists had been helpful in the war for Cambodian independence and they had the potential to disrupt a pro-Western regime
- neutrality appealed to moderate nationalists and to the older generation of Communists
- neutrality might prevent the conflict in Vietnam from impacting upon Cambodia.

Sihanouk refused to join SEATO (see page 109), but accepted US military aid from May 1954. He took a leading role in the development of the new Non-Aligned Movement at the Bandung conference in April 1955 (see page 89), then visited China in February 1956 and signed a Sino-Cambodian Friendship Declaration. Cambodia was the first non-Communist leader to receive Chinese aid, to which Thailand, South Vietnam and the United States responded with a brief economic embargo.

US–Cambodian relations deteriorated further as the US involvement in Vietnam increased. In 1958, troops from Washington's puppet Saigon regime entered a Cambodian province in pursuit of Communists. Then the CIA co-operated with Saigon in assassination attempts on Sihanouk. Diem's assassination confirmed Sihanouk's belief that the Americans could not be trusted: 'Look what happens when you put your trust in the Free World,' he said. 'The Americans have so many ways to eliminate those they no longer need.' When President Kennedy and the pro-American Prime Minister of Thailand were assassinated soon after, Sihanouk said, 'Our enemies have departed one after the other … Now they are all going to meet in hell, where they will build military bases for SEATO … The gods punish all the enemies of peaceful and neutral Cambodia.' Sihanouk suggested the neutralisation of all of Indochina, which frightened Ambassador

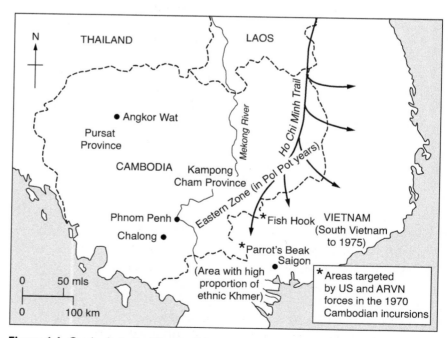

Figure 6.1 Cambodia in the Vietnam War years.

Lodge (see page 129) and Washington. Lodge said it would 'undermine the confidence of the new Vietnamese leadership [under General 'Big' Minh] in the firmness of purpose' and 'foment and encourage the neutralism which is always present in varying degrees here in Vietnam.'

In 1964, Sihanouk dispensed with American aid, expelled American citizens, and leaned towards Hanoi and Beijing. The United States retaliated by seeking support amongst Cambodian Army officers and the social elite. In May 1965, Sihanouk broke off diplomatic relations with the United States primarily because of the recent introduction of American ground troops into the Vietnam War (see page 146) (some wondered whether it was also pique over a *Newsweek* article that claimed that his family ran brothels in Phnom Penh). At the same time, he allowed the NLF (see page 114) to establish permanent sanctuaries inside Cambodia.

Reasons for North Vietnamese intervention

The greater US involvement in Vietnam under Johnson increased North Vietnamese activity in Cambodia and destabilised Sihanouk's regime:

- Events in Vietnam damaged the government's finances. The Vietnamese rice harvest suffered during the Vietnam War, so huge quantities of Cambodian rice were smuggled into Vietnam, avoiding the export duties on rice that were Sihanouk's main source of revenue.
- Thousands of ethnic Khmer living in the Mekong Delta fled the Saigon regime's hostility and entered Cambodia.
- From 1965, General Westmoreland's 'search and destroy' tactics (see page 159) drove North Vietnamese Communist forces into Cambodia in search of sanctuary. The Americans then pursued them into Cambodia.
- Although Sihanouk had little choice but to tolerate Vietnamese Communist incursions and their increased use of the Ho Chi Minh Trail in Cambodia, US aircraft responded by strafing the Cambodian–Vietnamese border area. In 1966, Sihanouk claimed that 'hundreds of our people' had been killed by American bombs.

The North Vietnamese intervention in Cambodia that resulted from the escalation of the Vietnam War coincided with the growing insurgency by Cambodian Communists led by Pol Pot (see page 219). Sihanouk called the Cambodian Communists the Khmer Rouge or the 'Cambodian Reds', but after 1966 they called themselves the Communist Party of Kampuchea or **CPK**. Initially, Cambodian Communists had been pro-Vietnam and they and Hanoi had accepted Sihanouk's Cold War neutrality, but Pol Pot and the younger generation of Cambodian Communists were anti-Vietnamese and pro-Chinese.

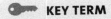 **KEY TERM**

CPK Kampuchean (Cambodian) Communist Party from 1966.

Reasons for the first civil war, 1967–70

From 1967, the CPK waged war on Sihanouk's government. The reasons for this Cambodian civil war were:

- the increased government repression of the left in the years 1962–6 was sufficient to inspire the Communists, but insufficient to destroy them. When Sihanouk allowed relatively free elections in 1966, those elected were very conservative. Conservative Prime Minister Lon Nol's troops angered the peasants when they expropriated peasant land and when many, having been promised money for each rebel head that they presented at military headquarters, simply brought in non-rebel peasant heads for payment.
- the increasing influence of the anti-Vietnamese Pol Pot (see page 219) and his followers within the Cambodian Communist movement.
- Pol Pot's more militant stance was encouraged by China.
- the increasingly obtrusive US involvement in Cambodia.

The rebellion failed for several reasons:

- The pro-Vietnamese amongst the Cambodian Communists were unenthusiastic participants.
- Although the rebels criticised Sihanouk, telling villagers that he 'thinks only of going to live the good life in France' at their expense, and that he and Lon Nol had 'sold out their country to the United States', it proved impossible to overcome Sihanouk's prestige and nationalist credentials.
- Sihanouk's response was ruthless: for example, some rebels were beheaded and/or disembowelled, and 40 teachers suspected of subversion were reportedly thrown off a cliff. Sihanouk personally and proudly ordered the roasting of a captured Vietnamese Communist (he was wrongly convinced that it was the Vietnamese rather than the Chinese who encouraged the Khmer Rouge).
- The rebel forces were not numerous: they only numbered between 2000 and 4000 in 1969, and around 10,000 by 1970.

However, while the rebels were not a great military threat to Sihanouk's regime, they helped alter its character: their rebellion pushed the government to the right, so that Lon Nol and the Americans gained greater influence.

Increased US involvement in Cambodia

By 1968, Sihanouk was convinced the Communists were his greatest threat. After Sino-Cambodian relations deteriorated with the Chinese **Cultural Revolution** and consequent unrest amongst ethnic Chinese-Cambodians, Sihanouk moved to repair relations with the United States. His first step was to invite President John F. Kennedy's widow, Jacqueline Kennedy, to visit Cambodia's spectacular Angkor temples. Sihanouk indicated to President

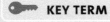
KEY TERM

Cultural Revolution
Mid-1960s' effort by Mao to revitalise and purify Chinese Communism, characterised by extremism.

SOURCE B

Jacqueline Kennedy, widow of President Kennedy, with King Norodom Sihanouk in 1967.

Johnson that significant American anti-Communist activity in Cambodia would be acceptable and the JCS urged an invasion of Cambodia in order to stop the Vietnamese Communist operations there. However, Johnson feared a Sino-Soviet reaction and confined himself to bombing the Cambodian–Vietnamese border. Johnson also agreed to mine-laying and reconnaissance missions conducted by Americans dressed as VC.

President Nixon proved far more enthusiastic about involvement in Cambodia and the result was Operation Menu in 1969 (see page 188): over 3600 secret B-52 raids dropped around 160,000 tons of bombs on Cambodia between March 1969 and March 1970. Nixon doubled the number of reconnaissance and mine-laying missions in 1969, which caused the Communists to move deeper into Cambodia and further destabilised Sihanouk's regime. The North Vietnamese responded by increased support for the Khmer Rouge. 'We are a country caught between the hammer and the anvil,' Sihanouk said.

> Why do you suppose Sihanouk was keen for scenes such as that in Source B to be photographed and published?

The overthrow of Sihanouk

By 1970, Sihanouk's regime had been destabilised from within by the Khmer Rouge, and from without by the activities of:

- the Vietnamese Communists, who moved at will throughout the borderlands between Vietnam and Cambodia. In 1969, Lon Nol estimated that nearly 40,000 of them were on Cambodian territory (in March 1970, Sihanouk and Lon Nol encouraged student protests against the presence of VC on Cambodian territory).
- the Saigon regime, which repressed South Vietnam's Khmer Krom minority from the early 1960s and caused 17,000 Khmers to flee Vietnam for Cambodia between 1965 and 1968.
- the Americans, who responded to North Vietnamese activity in Cambodia with covert sabotage operations there (by 1970, the number of operations approached 2000).

Although the Khmer Rouge began armed resistance against Sihanouk in 1967, his overthrow in March 1970 was the work of right-wingers. Sihanouk had gone to France for his annual obesity treatment, then visited Moscow in search of aid for his beleaguered nation. In his absence, the National Assembly replaced him with the pro-American faction led by General **Lon Nol**. Why was Sihanouk overthrown?

- Although the Cambodian economy was in dire straits, Sihanouk was personally extravagant and his court was expensive.
- While the peasantry still revered Sihanouk as a god-king, the middle class in Phnom Penh and senior military men disagreed with his policies and sought to fully align Cambodia with the United States.
- Lon Nol and many other Cambodian military leaders had profited from selling supplies to the North Vietnamese but they anticipated greater gains from the Americans.
- Lon Nol knew that the mercurial Sihanouk was likely to turn on him at any time and he was encouraged in his coup by the US military and the right-wing National Assembly, which supported the overthrow by 91 votes to 1.
- Sihanouk remained out of the country for too long.

Although thousands of urbanites welcomed the overthrow of the playboy prince with what one called 'his damn film shows and endless radio speeches in that singing voice', Lon Nol's Khmer Republic was ominously short of popular support.

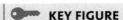

KEY FIGURE

Lon Nol (1913–85)

A general in the Cambodian Army, he was Prime Minister of Cambodia (1970–2) then President of the Khmer Republic (1972–5).

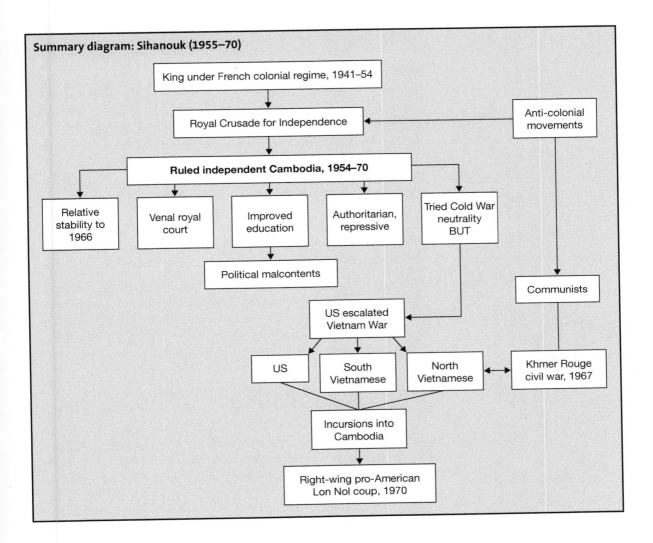

Summary diagram: Sihanouk (1955–70)

King under French colonial regime, 1941–54

Royal Crusade for Independence ← Anti-colonial movements

Ruled independent Cambodia, 1954–70

Relative stability to 1966

Venal royal court

Improved education

Authoritarian, repressive

Tried Cold War neutrality BUT

Political malcontents

Communists

US escalated Vietnam War

US

South Vietnamese

North Vietnamese ↔ Khmer Rouge civil war, 1967

Incursions into Cambodia

Right-wing pro-American Lon Nol coup, 1970

2

US bombing and the fall of the Khmer Republic (1970–5)

▶ *To what extent was Pol Pot's rise to power due to US bombing?*

During spring 1970, Cambodia appeared to be on the verge of anarchy. Tens of thousands across the nation participated in pro-Sihanouk demonstrations, while rival gangs attacked each other and ate the hearts and livers of their opponents. The North Vietnamese and the South Vietnamese made incursions into Cambodia at will, which encouraged anti-Vietnamese sentiment. Vietnamese residents of Cambodia were attacked both by ordinary citizens and by Lon Nol's government (the Mekong River became clogged with thousands of dead bodies, prompting 300,000 ethnic Vietnamese to flee to Vietnam or Thailand). Then, with the assent of the Lon Nol regime, 30,000 US and 50,000 ARVN (see page 115) forces invaded Cambodia. Why?

- General Abrams warned President Nixon that US troop withdrawals left the remaining American forces in Vietnam more vulnerable. They would be safer if Vietnamese Communist sanctuaries in Cambodia were eliminated.
- Nixon thought a Cambodian incursion would demonstrate that 'we were still serious about our commitment in Vietnam'.
- There was great Communist activity near Phnom Penh and Nixon feared that Cambodia would 'go down the drain' unless he acted.
- Although CIA analysts warned Nixon that aiding Lon Nol would 'probably' not stop the Communists fighting, Nixon said 'we must do something symbolic' because at last, after 25 years, a Cambodian regime had 'the guts to take a pro-Western, pro-American stand.'

Lon Nol's government in Phnom Penh received nearly $2 billion in American aid, but large-scale US bombing strikes aimed at the Communists destroyed large areas of Cambodian territory and killed and alienated many Cambodians. The North Vietnamese Communists responded to the US/South Vietnamese invasion of Cambodia by stepping up their activities there and by close co-operation with the Khmer Rouge and the exiled Sihanouk.

By January 1971, the Communists controlled half the country: 15,000 Khmer regulars and 60,000 Khmer guerrillas fought Lon Nol's regime. There were also 40,000 Vietnamese Communist troops in Cambodia, along with a similar number of South Vietnamese forces. During 1972, the total number of Khmer rebels opposing Lon Nol rose from around 125,000 to 200,000. By 1975, they had overthrown Lon Nol's regime in a civil war in which both sides had perpetrated atrocities.

SOURCE C

From a US Defence Intelligence Agency Appraisal, 8 July 1971, quoted in Ben Kiernan, *How Pol Pot Came To Power*, Yale University Press, 2004, p. 322.

The Communists have found some backing among the Khmer peasantry, and the Chinese and Vietnamese minorities … It is estimated that the Communists control some two to three million people in Cambodia out of a total of about seven million … For the most part, however, the Vietnamese Communists have apparently acceded to Khmer demands for autonomy …

Khmer Communist cadres have resorted where necessary to coercion, intimidation and assassination. Some have used their new positions to settle old scores with government officials who formerly opposed them when they were 'bandits' under the Sihanouk regime. On the whole, however, they have attempted to avoid acts which might alienate the population, and the behaviour of Vietnamese Communist soldiers has generally been exemplary when compared with the South Vietnamese.

How far would you trust Source C's assessment of the Communist position?

Pol Pot

1925	Born Saloth Sar to a prosperous Cambodian peasant family
1949–53	Studied in Paris
1963	Fled to countryside to avoid Sihanouk's repression of leftists
1967	Clearly emerging as Khmer Rouge leader
1968	Unsuccessful rebellion against Sihanouk's regime
1970	Rebelled against Lon Nol regime
1975–9	Ruled Democratic Kampuchea
1977	Declared Democratic Kampuchea a Communist state
1978	Vietnam attacked Cambodia
1979	In hiding and exile, but still recognised by UN, China and West as Cambodia's ruler
1993	Refused to recognise new Cambodian government
1998	Died (possibly murdered)

Background

Pol Pot was born Saloth Sar to a rich Khmer peasant family of Sino-Khmer descent. As two of his relations were concubines of King Monivong, he was frequently in the royal palace. Educated at an elite Catholic school, he proved academically limited, but won a French government scholarship to study in Paris, where he joined the French Communist Party. He subsequently admitted that when he read 'the big thick works of Marx … I didn't really understand them at all'. According to his brother Suong, Pol Pot 'would not have killed a chicken then'. Contemporaries considered him gentle, shy and charming. Sar christened himself the 'Original Khmer' at this time, suggesting a nationalist preoccupation. Having failed his exams for three years in a row, he lost his scholarship and returned to Cambodia in 1953. He worked as a History teacher (he proved popular

and gifted) and simultaneously engaged in secret leftist political activity. Democrat politicians said Sar became sexually and politically frustrated and embittered after his beautiful girlfriend dumped him for a prominent, right-wing politician in 1955 (Sar married a fellow revolutionary instead). When Sihanouk's persecution of leftists escalated, Sar fled to the countryside.

Sar visited Vietnam in 1965, and chafed at the Vietnamese Communists' attitudes towards Cambodians. He spent the winter of 1965–6 in a Chinese training camp for Third World revolutionaries near Beijing and was impressed by the Chinese government's programme to transform the thinking of the peasantry. By 1967, he was clearly the leader of the Communist Party of Kampuchea, which attempted an unsuccessful uprising against Sihanouk. Sihanouk's alliance with the Khmer Rouge after his deposition helped bring about the downfall of Lon Nol's right-wing government. In April 1975, Sar's forces took the capital, Phnom Penh. By now he was calling himself Pol Pot (perhaps because the Pols were royal slaves and old Khmers) and purging the pro-Vietnamese Cambodian Communists.

Achievements

As leader of Democratic Kampuchea, Pol Pot's policies were responsible for the deaths of roughly 2 million of the nation's 8 million population. Ethnic minorities and the educated were particularly targeted by the regime, which sought control, uniformity and the excision of foreign influences from Cambodia. In later life, Pol Pot admitted that between 1975 and 1979, the Khmer Rouge were 'drunk with victory and incompetent'.

Significance

Pol Pot's policies were a disaster for much of the Cambodian population. The international community's support for him from 1979 demonstrated how the Cold War produced strange bedfellows and could perpetuate instability within small nations.

Reasons for the fall of the Khmer Republic

In 1975, Pol Pot's Khmer Rouge forces overthrew the Khmer Republic and Pol Pot came to power. Why?

- The Lon Nol regime was an unpopular, corrupt and incompetent military dictatorship, the titular leader of which was irreparably damaged by his stroke in 1971.
- The regime's Communist opponents were well organised, more determined than the government's conscripts, and popular with the poorest Cambodian peasants who benefited from their land redistribution and helpfulness.
- The Communists were supported by Sihanouk, whom the superstitious peasants still revered (when Lon Nol declared the abolition of the monarchy in April 1970, peasants asked a French missionary, 'How shall we tend our rice-paddies, now that the king is not here to make it rain?'). From his exile in Beijing, Sihanouk urged his subjects to join the Khmer Rouge. The Khmer Rouge kept him out of Cambodia for as long as possible because, as one cadre said, 'If Sihanouk comes back, all the people will unite behind him, and we will be left bare-ass.'
- The Khmer Rouge were assisted by the Vietnamese Communists, even as Pol Pot began to purge both pro-Vietnamese and pro-Sihanouk cadres.
- The South Vietnamese helped the Communist cause in Cambodia: after the invasion of Cambodia in spring 1970, the American ground troops soon withdrew, but the South Vietnamese forces remained for two years and did great damage to the population (their behaviour was notably worse than that of the North Vietnamese and Cambodian Communist forces).
- The historian Ben Kiernan argued that because of its involvement in Vietnam and then its intervention in Cambodia, the United States destabilised the Sihanouk and Lon Nol regimes.

American bombing and the rise of Pol Pot

American bombing alienated many Cambodians. In 1970, US aerial and tank attacks in the province of Kampong Cham killed 200 people and a peasant remembered that 'some people ran away … others joined the revolution'. Another peasant recalled that when twenty people died in Chalong village in 1972, 'Many monasteries were destroyed by bombs. People in our village were furious with the Americans, they did not know why the Americans had bombed them.' Seventy people from Chalong joined the fight against Lon Nol. In April 1973, one villager pointed out, 'The bombers may kill some Communists but they kill everyone else too.' It has been estimated that half the population became refugees in this period and that somewhere between 50,000 and 150,000 civilians were killed by the 3 million tons of American bombs dropped between 1969 and 1973.

SOURCE D

From a CIA report of 2 May 1973, quoted in Ben Kiernan, *The Pol Pot Regime*, Yale University Press, 2008, p. 22.

[The Communists] *are using damage caused by B-52 strikes as the main theme of their propaganda. The cadre tell the people that the Government of Lon Nol has requested the air strikes and is responsible for the damage and the 'suffering of innocent villagers' … The only way to stop 'the massive destruction of the country' is to … defeat Lon Nol and stop the bombing.*

This approach has resulted in the successful recruitment of a number of young men … Residents … say that the propaganda campaign has been effective with refugees and in areas … which have been subject to B-52 strikes.

To what extent could it be argued that Source D offers conclusive proof that the American bombing played a vital part in Pol Pot's rise to power?

After the Americans exited Indochina through the Paris Peace Accords of January 1973 (see page 198), the Khmer Rouge launched a great and successful offensive against Lon Nol's pro-American government. Lon Nol fled, leaving a caretaker government, the head of which sent a note to the Americans rejecting their offer of evacuation and saying, 'I have only committed this mistake of believing in you.'

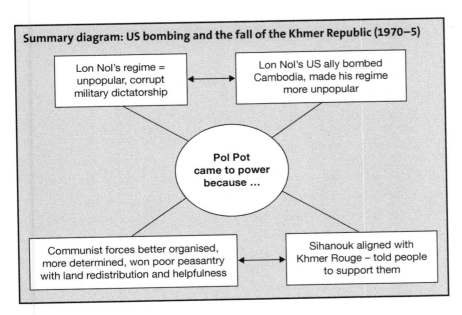

Summary diagram: US bombing and the fall of the Khmer Republic (1970–5)

Lon Nol's regime = unpopular, corrupt military dictatorship

Lon Nol's US ally bombed Cambodia, made his regime more unpopular

Pol Pot came to power because …

Communist forces better organised, more determined, won poor peasantry with land redistribution and helpfulness

Sihanouk aligned with Khmer Rouge – told people to support them

Pol Pot and Democratic Kampuchea (1975–8)

▶ *What were aims and methods of the Pol Pot regime?*

In April 1975, the Communists, led by Pol Pot, established **Democratic Kampuchea (DK)**. The Pol Pot regime aimed to make Cambodia

- free of the corrupting influence of foreigners and their 'depraved cultures'
- self-sufficient in food production
- a 'new community', socialist and cleansed of 'social blemishes'
- great again.

The process had already begun in Khmer Rouge-held areas before 1975, but 1975 was 'Year Zero', the year in which the regime would begin to remake the whole country. The regime's methods included

- the exclusion of foreign visitors and foreign influence
- the demolition of urban life
- the elevation of the social status of the poorest peasantry
- the creation of huge agricultural co-operatives
- the enforcement of uniformity amongst the Khmers and especially amongst the ethnic minorities
- mass executions.

Chinese models

In many ways, it seemed that the Khmer Rouge and the Chinese shared belief in

- the triumph of the human will
- the downgrading of intellectuals
- the sanctity of manual labour and the peasantry
- collectivisation
- the countryside 'surrounding' the city.

However, nationalism was more important than Communist ideology and fraternity to the Pol Pot regime, which was always anxious to emphasise its unique nature. In spring 1975, **Ieng Sary** told an interviewer the Khmer Rouge would build socialism 'without reference to any existing model' and that Cambodia would go where 'no country in history has ever gone before.' In 1975, Mao himself urged Pol Pot to 'create your own experiences yourself', although he also warned him to be less extreme and suggested he learn from the Chinese Communist Party's increased moderation after 1934. For their part, the Khmer Rouge felt that Mao had compromised when he had allowed money ('an instrument which creates privilege and power', according to Pol), wages, learning and family life. Furthermore, Pol Pot did not believe in a Mao-style personality cult.

KEY TERM

Democratic Kampuchea (DK) The name by which Cambodia was known under the Pol Pot regime.

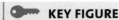

KEY FIGURE

Ieng Sary (1925–2013)

Studied with Pol Pot in Paris and became a leading member of the WPK, the CPK and Pol Pot's regime. In 1996, he left the Khmer Rouge and was pardoned by Sihanouk, but was under arrest and investigation by an international tribunal in his last six years.

Sometimes, Khmer Rouge policies that seemed to be influenced by Chinese models were also due to pragmatic reasons. For example, the Khmer Rouge introduced collectivisation in areas under their control from 1973, and while ending private ownership seemed to be pure Communism, collectivisation was also practical in that it would (supposedly) ensure food supplies for the armed forces and help promote control of the population.

Evacuation to the rural areas

From 1973, the Khmer Rouge started evacuating urban centres in areas under their control. When the Khmer Rouge troops entered Phnom Penh in April 1975, the urban residents were shocked by the behaviour of the peasant troops: some drank from toilet bowls, believing that they were urban wells, others tried eating toothpaste. For their part, these troops loathed the corrupted urbanites, were jealous of their wealth, and resented their superior attitude and their supposed complicity in US bombing. The Khmer Rouge quickly deported 2 million residents of overcrowded Phnom Penh (refugees from American bombing had quadrupled the capital's population to 2.5 million by 1975), telling them that the Americans were about to bomb the city. Pol Pot described the urban evacuation as 'an extraordinary measure … That one does not find in the revolution of any other country.'

The motivation behind the evacuation was

- ideological (cities were centres of capitalism and Pol Pot said even cadres might be tempted by the 'sugar coated bullets of the bourgeoisie')
- economic (Pol Pot claimed that 'a food shortage was imminent' and more field labourers were needed)
- military (the capital was vulnerable to an invasion from nearby Vietnam).

Observers found the mass exodus pitiful to behold. The evacuees included over 15,000 people who had been in the city's hospitals. Some lay on beds pushed by their families, with plasma and intravenous drips bumping alongside them. The population were told they would soon be able to return, but they were forcibly resettled in the countryside and worked like slaves in agricultural labour camps.

Khmer Rouge supervisors forced the poorly fed relocated urbanites to work, frequently with bare hands, at planting crops and digging irrigation channels in the countryside. By early 1979, roughly 650,000 of these evacuees had died, whether from execution, overwork, disease, lack of medical care or starvation (a similar number of Khmer peasants died for the same reasons). Food was short because the dispirited population produced less, crops were exported to gain the regime foreign currency and foraging for food was considered 'anti-revolutionary' and a manifestation of 'individualism'. The hunger was so bad that cannibalism grew rife in the province of Pursat and one mother was seen eating her own child. Some contemporaries estimated that more died from disease or malnutrition than from executions.

Study Source E. What can you infer about Democratic Kampuchea from this anthem?

SOURCE E

The national anthem of Democratic Kampuchea.

Bright red Blood covers the towns and plains
of Kampuchea, our Motherland,
Sublime Blood of the workers and peasants,
Sublime Blood of the revolutionary men and women fighters!
The Blood changes into unrelenting hatred
And resolute struggle,
[Which] … frees us from slavery.

Anti-intellectualism

Dissent was unacceptable and punishable by death. It is been estimated that 2 million of Cambodia's roughly 8 million population died under Pol Pot, and somewhere between 500,000 and 1 million of them were executed. Most Khmer Rouge supporters were illiterate peasants, so the executed were mostly the educated elite and the urban population. Urbanites were more likely to voice or organise dissent (and they had looked down upon Pol Pot for his academic failures). Those who spoke a foreign language or wore spectacles were accused of being 'parasitical intellectuals'. Eighty per cent of teachers and 95 per cent of doctors were murdered under the Pol Pot regime, along with anyone else perceived as educated. For example, Dr Haing Ngor survived the Pol Pot years by discarding his spectacles and demonstrating no evidence of his medical qualifications (he let his wife die in childbirth rather than reveal his profession). Public buildings were converted into torture chambers such as S-21

SOURCE F

Do you consider it appropriate for tourists to visit sites such as the one photographed in Source F?

A Cambodian visits Cambodia's 'Killing Fields', where the remains of victims of the Pol Pot regime can be seen. There are many sites such as this one.

(a former high school) where men, women and children were liquidated. After Cambodian journalist Dith Pran escaped the Pol Pot regime, he called its mass grave sites the 'killing fields'.

The Killing Fields and ethnicity

Some historians have concluded that many Khmer Rouge executions were motivated by racism, but most of Pol Pot's victims were ethnic Khmers. During 1976, the Pol Pot regime killed thousands of Khmer Republic officials, army officers, ordinary soldiers and schoolteachers. The purges were renewed in 1977, when most of the victims were peasants related to local officials who had been purged. The government's secret security apparatus, the Santebal, was in charge of the purges. There had been many arrests and massacres in the Eastern Zone, and in 1978, Heng Samrin led an ethnic Khmer rebellion, but the rebels were soon forced into retreat.

While hundreds of thousands of ethnic Khmers were executed in the Pol Pot years, proportionately more died from ethnic minorities. The Khmer Rouge said ethnic minorities constituted only 1 per cent of the population, it but was actually 15–20 per cent. Khmer racism had a long tradition. When the young Pol Pot spent a year studying at a Buddhist monastery, he was taught that the Vietnamese and Chinese always duped the Khmer. All Khmer children were taught that the Vietnamese were the enemy who had taken over the formerly Khmer Mekong Delta. The French colonial administration's employment of Vietnamese bureaucrats increased Khmer resentment and hostility. An essential element of the Khmer Rouge regime was, as cadres said, that 'There are no Vietnamese, Chinese … only the Khmer race. Everyone is the same.' One Muslim Cham said the extermination of those from an ethnic minority was not ethnic cleansing, 'but just that the Khmer Rouge wanted total control of our activities'. Ethnic minorities constituted a threat to uniformity.

The Muslim Cham

The Muslim Cham constituted the largest ethnic minority in Cambodia. From as early as 1950, many joined the Communists. When the Khmer Rouge gained control of Muslim Cham areas in the early 1970s, one Muslim recalled their propaganda as persuasive: 'The Khmer Rouge said that if we don't struggle, our religion and nation will all disappear … The US imperialists would take our country and abolish our religion and race.' However, from 1973, Khmer Rouge policies changed.

In November 1973, some Cham revolted against Khmer Rouge attempts to make them abandon their customs and religion. They revolted again in summer 1975, and Pol Pot ordered 150,000 of them to be dispersed. This ethnic repression was justified by the claim that all Cham were middle class (many had resisted the establishment of co-operatives). With their different customs, they were a threat to uniformity: the Khmer Rouge told other Khmers that 'the Muslims devoted too much time to religious matters and not enough time to revolution'. The Cham particularly opposed communal eating, fearing that they might be forced to eat the pork their religion prohibited. Some Muslims were forced to eat pork on pain of death, mosques were closed, Islam was banned. 'Some Cham villages completely disappeared, leaving only two or three people. We were persecuted much more than the Khmers', one Cham peasant recalled. By January 1969, roughly 100,000 of Cambodia's 250,000 Chams had been killed or worked to death. However, any religion threatened Khmer Rouge uniformity: along with Islam, the Buddhist religion of ethnic Khmers was abolished.

Chinese Cambodians

The Khmer Rouge considered both the Cham and the Chinese diehard capitalists. Most of the 500,000 ethnic Chinese in Cambodia were involved in trade or moneylending. Over half of them died because of Khmer Rouge policies in 1975–9, even though the People's Republic of China gave generous financial aid to Pol Pot's regime. There were pragmatic rather than ethnic reasons for many Chinese deaths: the Chinese found it hardest to adjust to peasant life, so the Khmer Rouge branded them 'lazy' and treated them with exceptional harshness. Many Chinese survivors of the Pol Pot regime did not attribute Chinese-Cambodian deaths to ethnic cleansing.

Vietnamese Cambodians

During 1974, roughly three-quarters of the estimated 450,000 ethnic Vietnamese in Cambodia fled to Vietnam in order to escape the racist attacks perpetrated under the Lon Nol regime. In 1975, the Khmer Rouge expelled most of the remaining Vietnamese from Cambodia. Most of the 10,000 Vietnamese left in Cambodia were hunted down and murdered in 1977–8. As Vietnam was historically Cambodia's national enemy, it seems likely that the Vietnamese were more victims of ethnic cleansing than of the drive for uniformity.

The Khmer Krom and the tribal minorities

Perhaps the most persuasive evidence that for the most part uniformity rather than racism motivated the Khmer Rouge lies in the treatment of the Khmer Krom and the tribal minorities. The Khmer Krom were ethnic Khmers who had lived in Vietnam. Ieng Sary, born in Vietnam's Mekong Delta, was a Khmer Krom. Although ethnic Khmers, they spoke Cambodian with a Vietnamese accent. Many were massacred between 1975 and 1977. While the small Thai and Lao minorities were persecuted, hill tribes such as the Jarai were even allowed to continue using their own languages, perhaps because Pol Pot had lived amongst them between 1967 and 1970, or because, as one Cambodian recalled, the Khmer Rouge 'said the hill-tribes were faithful to the revolution, were not traders, and they had class hatred'.

Pol Pot's foreign policy

Pol Pot broke off diplomatic relations with the USSR and with all capitalist states in 1975, and subsequently with four Communist nations – Albania, Vietnam, Cuba and Laos. China was the most supportive foreign power, but some CPK cadres considered China an enemy. From the first though, Pol Pot was most wary of the Vietnamese – the ancient foe. Beginning in spring 1977, Cambodian–Vietnamese border clashes prompted Pol Pot to:

- execute those with 'Vietnamese minds in Khmer bodies'
- conduct purges in the zones bordering Vietnam, because these were 'people who follow the Vietnamese'
- show the people Sihanouk, who had been kept in luxurious confinement in Phnom Penh
- make the regime more open and tolerant in order to win more foreign and domestic support
- appeal to the Chinese.

These actions had unhelpful results. First, Deng Xiaoping promised support but scolded Pol Pot humiliatingly for excessive radicalism, for the 'anarchic behaviour' of Cambodian troops on the Vietnamese border, and for the failure to unite the country behind the Khmer Rouge. Second, the purges of 'people who follow the Vietnamese' constituted in effect another Cambodian civil war that greatly weakened the Khmer Rouge. Third and most importantly, they contributed to the Vietnamese invasion of 1978.

President Ford and the *Mayaguez* incident

In May 1975, Cambodian naval units seized an American cargo ship, the *Mayaguez*, and its 38-man crew. President Ford sent an American force to raid Cambodian territory. Some 40 Americans died in the raid. Even before they had landed, the Cambodian government released the crew. Polls showed popular support in the United States for Ford's actions.

Summary diagram: Pol Pot and Democratic Kampuchea (1975–8)

Pol Pot and Democratic Kampuchea, 1975–8	
Aims	**Methods**
No foreign influence	• Empty cities • Executions of urbanites, intellectuals • Elevate peasantry • Ethnic cleansing? • Closed society
Self-sufficiency	• Collectivisation • Sanctify manual labour
Uniformity – no individualism, socialist community	• Collectivisation • Executions • Dispersal • Torture • Abolished money
Avoid Vietnamese influence/domination	• Friendship with China • Border raids • Executions of 'Vietnamese minds in Khmer bodies' • Kill/drive out ethnic Vietnamese

The Vietnamese invasion (1978) and its consequences

▶ *How did the international community react to the Pol Pot regime?*

The Pol Pot regime collapsed as a result of the Vietnamese invasion of Cambodia that began on Christmas Day, 1978. There have been various suggestions for the Vietnamese motivation, including:

- the Khmer Rouge's anti-Vietnamese purge
- the influx of 375,000 Cambodian refugees fleeing from Pol Pot's brutal regime into Vietnam
- Khmer Rouge-initiated border clashes throughout 1977, which suggested Cambodian designs upon Vietnamese territory (the Khmer Rouge claimed the Vietnamese initiated the clashes)
- the Vietnamese recorded that during the Khmer Rouge incursions, their forces committed 'most barbarous crimes … women were raped, then disembowelled, children cut in two, pagodas and schools were burned down' (believable accusations, given the behaviour of Khmer Rouge troops within Cambodia itself)

- the Khmer Rouge rejection of Vietnamese suggestions for talks on disputed border regions
- fear of the Sino-Cambodian alliance and the encirclement of Vietnam ('When we look at Cambodia, we see China, China, China,' a Vietnamese Communist official told American journalist Stanley Karnow)
- the desire to dominate Indochina.

Whatever their motivation, the Vietnamese possessed one of Asia's best armies and the first result of their invasion was that the poorly organised Khmer Rouge forces were quickly forced to retreat to the jungle. Madame In, mother of two Khmer Rouge supporters, said the Khmer Rouge 'would not treat people properly, so now they have lost everything. Band of cretins!' Many Cambodians welcomed the Vietnamese intervention, but the vast majority of foreign nations reacted with unease when the Vietnamese established a new Cambodian government under **Heng Samrin**. Pol Pot's Democratic Kampuchea now became the People's Republic of Kampuchea.

The People's Republic of Kampuchea (PRK)

A 140,000-strong Vietnamese occupation force remained in Cambodia and supported Heng Samrin's pro-Vietnamese People's Republic of Kampuchea (**PRK**). The PRK was opposed by China, the United States and **ASEAN** (see page 230), all of which declared support for Pol Pot's deposed government and condemned Vietnam.

Throughout the 1980s, nearly 30,000 Khmer Rouge guerrillas, many based in Thailand, opposed the PRK. Other Cambodian opponents of the PRK included the Khmer People's National Liberation Front (KPNLF), established in Paris in March 1979 and led by Son Sann. The KPNLF deployed an 8000-strong army, led by officers of Lon Nol's army, but failed to win the support of the peasantry. A third opposition group was led by Sihanouk, who, despite having had some of his family killed by the Khmer Rouge, nevertheless joined with the KPNLF and the Khmer Rouge (which by now had renounced Communism in order to win the support of Khmer nationalists and the anti-Communist world) in a Coalition Government of Democratic Kampuchea (CDGK) in June 1982. These anti-Vietnamese forces received American aid. Indeed, the international reaction to events in Cambodia was the most important consequence of the Vietnamese invasion.

The international consequences

The Vietnamese invasion of Cambodia generated international interest and tension. The most significant response came from China, which invaded Vietnam to demonstrate support for Pol Pot.

KEY FIGURE

Heng Samrin (1934–)

A Khmer Rouge defector in 1978, he was the Vietnamese-backed leader of Cambodia from 1979 to 1985, and has remained politically active and influential ever since.

KEY TERMS

PRK People's Republic of Kampuchea (1979–89).

ASEAN Association of Southeast Asian Nations, established in 1967 to promote political and economic co-operation.

China's response

The Chinese supported the overthrown Pol Pot because of:

- traditional Chinese support for the Khmer Rouge. The Chinese gave the Khmer Rouge forces an estimated $100 million worth of weapons each year during the 1980s.
- Soviet support for Vietnam (in exchange, the Soviets were given control over the Vietnamese naval base at Cam Ranh Bay). The Chinese claimed that 'it is to serve the Soviet Union in its expansionist strategic plan that the Vietnamese have invaded Kampuchea so recklessly.'
- the Chinese belief that the Vietnamese should defer to Chinese supremacy.
- the several warnings China had issued since 1975 against Vietnamese expansionist ambitions.
- Sino-Vietnamese territorial disputes over their borders and the Paracel and Spratly Islands in the South China Sea. These mostly barren islands gave strategic command of the South China Sea and contained great offshore oil reserves. In 1974, China occupied the Paracels, and Vietnam and the Philippines each occupied several of the Spratly Islands.
- the over 1 million Vietnamese of Chinese ethnicity (the 'boat people'), who fled the persecution of the Hanoi government.

In February 1979, the Chinese invaded Vietnam. Their aim was to teach Vietnam a lesson for having invaded Cambodia, which was why the Chinese called the war the 'Punitive War'. China sent 33,000 ground troops into Vietnam. Although hampered by antiquated equipment, their brief incursion destroyed six Vietnamese missile sites and countless bridges, roads, railways and buildings. However, the Vietnamese fought well, and the Chinese suffered heavy casualties (the numbers are disputed). Both sides claimed victory. The United Nations criticised the Chinese, while the Soviets supported Vietnam.

ASEAN's response

ASEAN was established in 1967 in order to promote economic co-operation. Its pro-Western members were Indonesia, Malaysia, the Philippines, Singapore and Thailand. The Communist takeover of all of Indochina in 1975 inspired ASEAN to hold its first summit (1976). The Vietnamese invasion of Cambodia in 1978 and the Chinese invasion of Vietnam in 1979 worried ASEAN and further strengthened its determination to co-ordinate political and economic policies. Although members disagreed about the Chinese threat (Indonesia, Malaysia and the Philippines considered China their greatest threat; Singapore and Thailand feared the USSR), ASEAN issued a joint statement deploring Vietnamese intervention in Cambodia and subsequently supported opponents of Heng Samrin's regime.

US response

In his inaugural address, President **Jimmy Carter** (1977–81) had said that his policy on human rights would be 'absolute' and indicated that any nation that abused human rights would arouse American wrath. However, although in 1979 Carter referred to Pol Pot as the 'worst violator of human rights in the world', his representative at the United Nations

- condemned the Vietnamese invasion that had overthrown the mass murderer Pol Pot
- supported a Chinese attack on Vietnam, even though that attack was designed to restore Pol Pot to power
- declared the Khmer Rouge to be Cambodia's true government.

The United States also

- obtained international aid for Khmer Rouge camps
- supported Khmer Rouge possession of Cambodia's UN seat.

Why? The answer lay in Carter's pro-China policy.

Carter, China and Taiwan

The USSR had entered a great expansionist phase in the wake of America's failure in Vietnam, so Carter considered it the greatest threat to US security and sought to improve Sino-American relations. As China was Pol Pot's ally, Carter found himself in the bizarre position of appearing to be pro-Pol Pot. Improved relations with the People's Republic of China also necessitated what some Americans considered to be the betrayal of Taiwan (see page 232).

President Reagan and Pol Pot

The **Reagan** administration (1981–9) supported Khmer Rouge possession of Cambodia's UN seat, and persuaded many US friends and allies to do likewise, prompting Sihanouk to say America was bringing Pol Pot 'back to life'. The United States sought to weaken Hanoi and Moscow – and Pol Pot helped in that. However, US policy changed with the end of the Cold War, a result of dramatic developments in the USSR.

The Soviet response

Under the Soviet leader, **Leonid Brezhnev** (1964–82), the role of the USSR in Asia had increasingly become that of rival to China. Both China and the USSR wooed Vietnam, but the Soviets triumphed. In 1978, Vietnam became a full member of **Comecon** and signed a Treaty of Friendship and Co-operation with the USSR. As Vietnam was the only pro-Soviet state in Southeast Asia, the Soviets staunchly supported the Vietnamese and their invasion of Cambodia, sending a naval force to the Vietnamese coast and providing the Vietnamese with armaments. Although the Vietnamese had ended Pol Pot's murderous regime, Western nations criticised Vietnam and withheld economic aid, leaving Vietnam isolated and even more dependent upon the USSR.

 **KEY FIGURES**

James ('Jimmy') Carter (1924–)

Democrat President of the United States from 1977 to 1981, he spent his retirement working for world peace and humanitarian causes.

Ronald Reagan (1911–2004)

Republican President of the United States from 1981 to 1989, he was militantly anti-Soviet until the mid-1980s, when his close relationship with Soviet leader Mikhail Gorbachev was vital in bringing about the end of the Cold War.

Leonid Brezhnev (1906–82)

One of the leaders of the 1964 coup against Nikita Khrushchev, Brezhnev led the USSR from 1964 until his death. He built up the Soviet nuclear arsenal, gained parity with the United States, then pursued a policy of detente, motivated by fear of China and the desire to improve the Soviet economy.

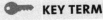 **KEY TERM**

Comecon Soviet-dominated economic organisation for Communist nations.

The United States and Taiwan, 1949–79

Recap: Taiwan timeline

- 1949 – After defeat in the Chinese civil war, Jiang Jieshi and the Chinese Nationalists fled to Taiwan, where they set up an alternative Chinese government (see page 30).
- 1950 – Truman initially opposed any close association with Taiwan, but when North Korea attacked South Korea, he sent the 7th Fleet to the Taiwan Strait in order to defend Taiwan and to restrain Jiang Jieshi from any attempt upon the mainland. The Korean War made the US–Taiwanese relationship far closer (see pages 53–4).
- 1954 – Chinese artillery bombarded the Nationalist island of Quemoy (September) (see page 179).
- US–Taiwanese mutual defence treaty (December).
- 1955 – At Bandung (see page 89), the Chinese offered to discuss the Quemoy–Matsu crisis with the United States, then stopped talking about 'liberating' Taiwan and finally stopped the bombardment (April) (see page 182).
- 1958 – The second Quemoy–Matsu crisis began with another Chinese bombardment and attempt to blockade the islands. Eisenhower

stood firm and the Chinese eventually backed down again (August) (see page 182).
- 1971 – Nixon sought Sino-American detente and did not resist the UN vote to give Taiwan's UN seat to Communist China (October) (see page 185).
- 1972 – Nixon visited China, and the Sino-American Shanghai Communiqué cagily acknowledged continuing differences over Taiwan (February) (see pages 183–4).
- 1975 – Jiang Jieshi died.
- 1978 – The end of recognition for Taiwan: Carter normalised Sino-American relations and ended the defensive pact and 'official relations' with Taiwan, while China undertook not to invade Taiwan (December). However, the Carter administration said it would continue military sales to Taiwan, and in March 1979, Congress forced Carter into strong US guarantees of Taiwan's independence. Republicans accused Carter of selling out Taiwan: Senator Barry Goldwater called Carter's decision on China 'one of the most cowardly acts ever performed by a President of the United States'.
- 1980 – Sino-Taiwanese economic co-operation began.

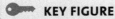
Soviet policies greatly changed under **Mikhail Gorbachev** (1985–91), who advocated 'New Thinking' in Soviet foreign policy. Gorbachev emphasised global interdependence and believed he could make the USSR and the world safer by decreasing Soviet–American and Sino-Soviet tensions. That in turn would help the struggling Soviet economy, which had been greatly distorted by Cold War expenditure. Interdependence, national security, economic recovery and his determination to improve Sino-Soviet relations combined to encourage Gorbachev to cut aid commitments to countries such as Vietnam and to press the Vietnamese to withdraw their forces from Cambodia. For their part, the Vietnamese were glad to exit in 1989, because the withdrawal of Soviet aid left their economy in dire straits.

A Vietnamese joke

From 1979, the Vietnamese were highly dependent upon Soviet aid. A favourite Vietnamese joke told of Hanoi begging Moscow for economic aid. When Moscow replied, 'Tighten your belts', the Vietnamese responded, 'Send belts.'

The role of the United Nations and the Paris Peace Settlement

The United Nations played a far from admirable role over Pol Pot. In 1979, the General Assembly condemned the Vietnamese overthrow of Pol Pot's murderous regime by 71 to 35 votes. From 1979 to 1992, the United States and the People's Republic of China persuaded the United Nations to support Pol Pot's exiled Khmer Rouge as Cambodia's legitimate government, rather than the Vietnamese-sponsored regimes of Heng Samrin (1979–85) and **Hun Sen** (from 1985).

In Jakarta in 1988, ASEAN initiated international negotiations on the future governance of Cambodia. Their final communiqué recorded opposition to a return to 'the genocidal policies and practices of the Pol Pot regime'. With the Cold War over, it was easier for the great powers to agree on the future of Cambodia, and in 1989 they joined in the talks, located by now in Paris. In March 1990, the UN Security Council proposed the formation of a new Cambodian coalition government containing representatives from all the warring Cambodian factions, which would hold elections supervised by a UN peacekeeping force. A UN-sponsored agreement was signed in Paris in October 1991.

The Paris Peace Settlement (1991–3)

The Paris Peace Settlement said

- all competing Cambodian factions would demobilise
- national elections would be held in 1993
- the United Nations would administer Cambodia until the elections took place, with Sihanouk as head of state.

Under the UN 'occupation' of Cambodia between 1992 and 1993, Cambodia was supposedly a UN protectorate – the first and, as yet, only time that the UN ever adopted such a solution. Although it deployed 16,000 troops and 5000 civil servants, the UN Transitional Authority in Cambodia (UNTAC) was insufficiently funded because countries such as the United States and Britain did not want an open-ended financial commitment to Cambodia. The Khmer Rouge and Hun Sen refused to demobilise their forces, so Hun Sen continued in power alongside the UN, while Khmer Rouge guerrillas kidnapped and killed UN workers. Sihanouk declared that he had been made a puppet and retired sulkily to Beijing.

Despite Khmer Rouge attacks on voters and polling stations, the UN managed to stage elections in 1993 in which 90 per cent of the electorate voted. The party of Prince Ranariddh (Sihanouk's son) won 58 seats, while Hun Sen (aided by violence, intimidation and bribery) won 51 seats. The UN declared the election a success, and Sihanouk, Hun Sen and Ranariddh agreed to govern together. Theirs proved to be a corrupt and undemocratic government, plagued by Khmer Rouge resistance until the late 1990s. As Ranariddh said in 1995, 'The Western

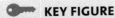

KEY FIGURE

Hun Sen (1952–)

A Khmer Rouge defector in 1977, he was the Vietnamese-backed leader of Cambodia from 1985. Sihanouk christened him the 'one-eyed lackey of the Vietnamese' (he lost an eye during his military career). He has remained in power since the Vietnamese departure.

brand of democracy and freedom of the press is not applicable in Cambodia.' Cambodia degenerated into anarchy again.

The significance of Cambodian history from 1955 to 1993

After more than half a century of domination by the French colonialists, the history of 'independent' Cambodia was dominated and distorted by the Cold War. Tellingly, Cambodia finally regained control over its own destiny soon after the Cold War ended. The bitter Sino-Soviet rivalry also impacted upon hapless Cambodia in the late 1970s and early 1980s, as China supported the overthrown Pol Pot, and the Soviets backed the Vietnamese and their puppet regime in Cambodia. When Gorbachev decided to improve Soviet relations with the United States and China and to cut overseas commitments, the Soviets ceased support for the Vietnamese-sponsored regime in Cambodia and the Chinese decided to abandon the Khmer Rouge. At that point, the three superpowers were finally willing to work upon a Cambodian settlement.

Cambodia constitutes a particularly tragic example of the impact of the Western powers upon Asia. French colonialism assisted the development of Khmer Communism and then the French departure brought little respite from foreign domination for Cambodia. Other countries, such as Vietnam, Laos, Korea and the Philippines, also experienced varying degrees of suffering due to the intervention and activities of the West, the USSR and China. However, out of all the foreign interventionists, the United States was probably the most intrusive, dangerous and destructive, and Cambodia was perhaps its greatest victim, because US policies were a major reason for the rise to power of Pol Pot.

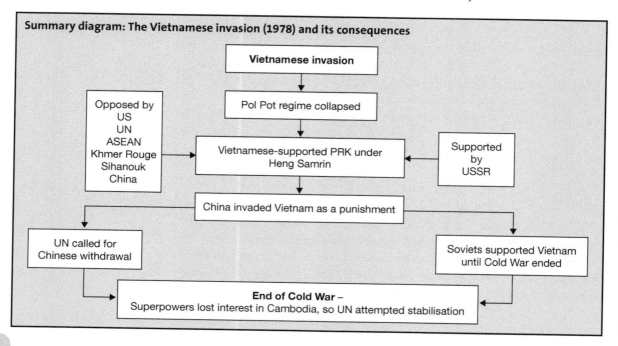

Summary diagram: The Vietnamese invasion (1978) and its consequences

5 Interpretations

▶ *How do historians explain Pol Pot's rise to power and policies?*

The main debate about Pol Pot is how he came to power. The first explanations were written in a period when intellectuals were full of disgust over Nixon and Kissinger's Vietnam policies. As a result, accounts such as that of the British journalist William Shawcross (1979) blamed the American bombing for driving the Cambodian peasantry towards the Khmer Rouge. The historian Ben Kiernan (2008) agreed, but while the journalist Joel Brinkley (2011) also blamed the United States, he emphasised that it was US support for Lon Nol's coup that paved the way for Pol Pot. Either way, it was all America's fault.

In contrast, the journalist Philip Short (2004) argued that Cambodian agency should not be denied and that the Cambodians were not simply helpless victims of a foreign power. Some employed traditional methods toward enemies (see page 208) that reflected a society both violent (a Cambodian government soldier recalled how in the 1950s he and his fellow soldiers had tested their strength by pulling off the legs of babies) and superstitious (Lon Nol ordered military aircraft to sprinkle 'magic sand' around Phnom Penh in order to ward off enemies). Short pointed out that Vietnam suffered far heavier bombing than Cambodia, but did not produce a Pol Pot. However, Short's attempts to explain Pol Pot were not always persuasive, especially when he saw Buddhist beliefs as helping to explain Pol Pot's policies. For example, Short felt Pol Pot's

- drive for uniformity was rooted in Buddhism's goal of the demolition of the individual and egotism
- forced labour policies were necessary to overcome the Cambodian indolence that owed much to Buddhism's rejection of wealth
- Communism was rooted in the Buddhist creation myth, when life was idyllic and there was no greed for private possessions.

The other great debate on Pol Pot concerns the nature of his regime. The historian David Chandler (1992) described it as 'the purest and most thorough-going Marxist–Leninist movement', but Michael Vickery (1984) thought it an anti-Marxist 'peasant revolution' (Marx anticipated the industrial proletariat in the forefront of Communist revolutions). Hanoi criticised the Pol Pot regime as a Maoist deviation from Orthodox Marxism, as did the Soviet historian Vladimir Simonov (1979). Ben Kiernan (2008) emphasised that racism was more important than Communism to the Khmer Rouge, as proved by the murder of non-Khmer Cambodians with extensive revolutionary experience and Cambodian Communist Party seniority, and by the persecution of non-Khmer peasants. Philip Short quoted Pol Pot saying socialism was a means of making Cambodia great again. Pol Pot told an interviewer in the 1980s,

> We chose Communism because we wanted to restore our nation. We helped the Vietnamese, who were Communist. But now the Communists are fighting us, so we have to turn to the West and follow their way.

Chapter summary

After Cambodia gained independence from France, King Sihanouk dominated Cambodian politics from 1955 to 1970. He tried to pursue a policy of Cold War neutrality, but the Vietnam War spilled over into Cambodia when the Americans escalated their involvement in neighbouring Vietnam during the 1960s. Cambodia then suffered incursions by Vietnamese Communist, American and South Vietnamese forces.

Although the peasantry in particular revered Sihanouk, his authoritarian rule aroused opposition. The Khmer Rouge insurgency began in 1967, and Lon Nol and other right-wingers overthrew Sihanouk during his absence in 1970. Lon Nol's brutal right-wing regime of 1970–5 colluded in US bombing of Cambodian–Vietnamese border regions, designed to destroy Vietnamese Communist trails and sanctuaries in Cambodia.

The combination of the American bombing, the nature of the Lon Nol regime, and the positive appeal of the nationalistic Khmer Rouge and their promised land redistribution enabled Pol Pot to come to power. His regime introduced collectivisation and was anti-intellectual and anti-urban. While ethnic minorities suffered disproportionately, ethnic Khmers were also likely to be executed or imprisoned. Many simply starved to death because of food shortages or died because of lack of medical treatment. An estimated 2 million of Cambodia's 8 million population died under Pol Pot.

In 1978, the Vietnamese overthrew the Pol Pot regime, which had persecuted Vietnamese Cambodians and staged border incursions into Vietnam. The Soviets helped fund the Vietnamese-backed governments of Heng Samrin (1979–85) and Hun Sen (from 1985). China, along with America and its Western allies, supported the exiled Pol Pot as the legitimate ruler of Cambodia, until Gorbachev eased Sino-Soviet and Soviet–American tensions. With the Cold War over, the great powers were willing to try to settle Cambodia, and between 1991 and 1993, the government of Hun Sen uneasily coexisted with a UN regime that organised nationwide elections in 1993. They failed to bring stability to Cambodia.

Refresher questions

Use these questions to remind yourself of the key material covered in this chapter.

1 When did Cambodia gain independence from France?

2 Which nation were Cambodian school children taught to perceive as their national enemy and why?

3 What was Sihanouk's position on the Cold War?

4 What did Sihanouk call Cambodian Communists?

5 At which 1955 conference did Sihanouk play a leading role?

6 What did Sihanouk advocate at that conference?

7 When did the Khmer Rouge's armed insurgency begin?

8 Why was Sihanouk more popular amongst the peasants than in cities such as Phnom Penh?

9 Why did America bomb Cambodia from 1969 to 1973?

10 How and why was Sihanouk overthrown?

11 How did Pol Pot come to power?

12 What policies were adopted by the Khmer Rouge, 1975–8?

13 Which ethnic groups suffered most under Pol Pot?

14 Why did the Vietnamese invade Cambodia in 1978?

15 What role was played by the United Nations in Cambodian history from 1979 to 1993?

Question practice

ESSAY QUESTIONS

1 Which was more important in Sihanouk's overthrow? i) The Khmer Rouge. ii) Cambodian right-wingers. Explain your answer with reference to both i) and ii).

2 How important was the United Nations in ending the conflict in Cambodia in the years 1979–93?

3 To what extent were Khmer Rouge policies determined by nationalism rather than by Communism?

INTERPRETATION QUESTION

1 Read the interpretation and then answer the question that follows. 'Pol Pot's revolution would not have won power without US economic and military destabilization of Cambodia ... 1966 ... [to] 1973.' (From Ben Kiernan, *The Pol Pot Regime*, 2008.) Evaluate the strengths and limitations of this interpretation, making references to other interpretations that you have studied.

OCR A level History

Essay guidance

The assessment of OCR Units Y252 and Y222: The Cold War in Asia 1945–1993 depends on whether you are studying it for AS or A level:

- for the AS exam, you will answer one essay question from a choice of two, and one interpretation question, for which there is no choice
- for the A level exam, you will answer one essay question from a choice of two and one shorter essay question, also from a choice of two.

The guidance below is for answering both AS and A level essay questions. Guidance for the shorter essay question is at the end of this section. Guidance on answering interpretation questions is on page 243.

For both OCR AS and A level History, the types of essay questions set and the skills required to achieve a high grade for Unit Group 2 are the same. The skills are made very clear by both mark schemes, which emphasise that the answer must:

- focus on the demands of the question
- be supported by accurate and relevant factual knowledge
- be analytical and logical
- reach a supported judgement about the issue in the question.

There are a number of skills that you will need to develop to reach the higher levels in the marking bands:

- understand the wording of the question
- plan an answer to the question set
- write a focused opening paragraph
- avoid irrelevance and description
- write analytically
- write a conclusion which reaches a supported judgement based on the argument in the main body of the essay.

These skills will be developed in the section below, but are further developed in the 'Period Study' chapters of the *OCR A level History* series (British Period Studies and Enquiries).

Understanding the wording of the question

To stay focused on the question set, it is important to read the question carefully and focus on the key words and phrases. Unless you directly address the demands of the question you will not score highly. Remember that in questions where there is a named factor you must write a good analytical paragraph about the given factor, even if you argue that it was not the most important.

Types of AS and A level questions you might find in the exams	The factors and issues you would need to consider in answering them
1 Assess the reasons why the United States was unable to defeat the Vietnamese Communists.	Weigh up the relative importance of a range of reasons as to why the United States was unable to defeat the Vietnamese Communists.
2 To what extent was the failure to win the hearts and minds of the Vietnamese people the most important cause of the American defeat in the Vietnam War?	Weigh up the relative importance of a range of reasons, including comparing the failure to win hearts and minds with other reasons.
3 'The Communist military performance was the most important reason for the American defeat in the Vietnam War.' How far do you agree?	Weigh up the relative importance of a range of reasons, including comparing the importance of the Communist military performance with other reasons, to reach a balanced judgement.

4 How successful was the Communist military performance in the years 1945–75?	This question requires you make a judgement about the Communist military performance. Instead of thinking about other reasons for the outcome of the Vietnam War, you would need to think about issues such as: • a people's war – winning hearts and minds • the importance of the Ho Chi Minh Trail • guerrilla warfare • Communist losses • the Tet Offensive • the Communist offensives of February 1969, February 1970 and Easter 1972 • the attack on Phuoc Long Province • the spring 1975 offensive.

Planning an answer

Many plans simply list dates and events – this should be avoided as it encourages a descriptive or narrative answer, rather than an analytical answer. The plan should be an outline of your argument; this means you need to think carefully about the issues you intend to discuss and their relative importance before you start writing your answer. It should therefore be a list of the factors or issues you are going to discuss and a comment on their relative importance.

For question 1 in the table (page 238), your plan might look something like this:

• Winning the hearts and minds of the Vietnamese people – including Communist policies, the behaviour and tactics of the US military, nationalism and, most importantly, the Saigon regime, the unpopularity of which (due to its corruption and evident dependence on the American foreigners) underlay all the other reasons for the failure.

• The Communist military performance – guerrilla warfare, Chinese and Soviet aid.
• The military performance of the Americans and the ARVN – including American divisions, ARVN weaknesses.
• US media coverage.

The opening paragraph

Many students spend time 'setting the scene' and the opening paragraph becomes little more than an introduction to the topic – this should be avoided. Instead, make it clear what your argument is going to be. Offer your view about the issue in the question – what was the most important reason for the Communist victory? – and then introduce the other issues you intend to discuss. In the plan it is suggested that the Saigon regime was the most important factor. This should be made clear in the opening paragraph, with a brief comment as to why – perhaps that it was considered a US puppet regime that never had popular support. This will give the examiner a clear overview of your essay, rather than it being a mystery tour where the argument becomes clear only at the end. You should also refer to any important issues that the question raises. For example:

There are a number of reasons why the Americans lost the Vietnam War: these include the greater popularity and superior military strategy of the Communists and, some say, the negativity of the American media[1]. However, the most important reason was the failure of successive Saigon governments to win the hearts and minds of the Vietnamese people[2]. This was particularly important, because, as General de Gaulle said, American domination of the Saigon regime made the Communists seem to be 'the champions of national independence' and greatly increased their popularity[3].

1 The student is aware that there were a number of important reasons.
2 The student offers a clear view as to what he or she considers to be the most important reason – a thesis is offered.
3 There is a brief justification to support the thesis.

Avoid irrelevance and description

If you use the plan effectively, it should stop you from writing out all you know about the Vietnam War. Much of that would probably be irrelevant. Similarly, the plan should help prevent you simply writing a chronological essay about the military and political situation in Vietnam during the years of US involvement. A chronological narrative would make it far harder for you to weigh up the relative importance of the reasons. Without weighing up relative importance, you would not obtain high marks.

Write analytically

This is perhaps the hardest, but most important skill you need to develop. An analytical approach can be helped by ensuring that the opening sentence of each paragraph introduces an idea, which directly answers the question and is not just a piece of factual information. In a very strong answer it should be possible to simply read the opening sentences of all the paragraphs and know what argument is being put forward.

If we look at question 2 in the table (see page 238), on the failure to win the hearts and minds of the Vietnamese people, the following are possible sentences with which to start paragraphs:

- The failure to win the hearts and minds of the South Vietnamese people was the most important factor in the American failure, because it underlay the impressive Communist military and political performance and the growing opposition to the war on the part of many in the American media, public and politicians.
- The successful Communist military performance depended to a large extent on maintaining popular support for the Communist guerrillas.
- The US military emphasised the use of superior American technology, but large-scale bombing of South Vietnam played a vital role in the alienation of the population.
- Many in the US military have blamed the American media for the loss of the war, but the media simply showed what was happening

– which was that, despite the dispatch of ever-increasing numbers of American ground troops to Vietnam, the US and South Vietnamese forces remained unable to defeat the Communists.

You would then go on to discuss both sides of the argument raised by the opening sentence, using relevant knowledge about the issue to support each side of the argument. The final sentence of the paragraph would reach a judgement on the role played by the factor you are discussing in the Communist victory. This approach would ensure that the final sentence of each paragraph links back to the actual question you are answering. If you can do this for each paragraph you will have a series of mini-essays, which discuss a factor and reach a conclusion or judgement about the importance of that factor or issue. For example:

The failure to win the hearts and minds of the South Vietnamese people was the most important factor in the American inability to win the Vietnam War[1]. Successive regimes in Saigon, from Diem (1954–63) to Thieu (1968–75), failed to offer attractive policies such as the land redistribution introduced by the Communists. Furthermore, leaders such as 'American Diem' seemed unpatriotic in comparison to 'Uncle Ho'. Sino-Soviet support for North Vietnam was never intrusive in the way that the presence of tens of thousands of American soldiers was. As Americans struggled to ascertain who was friend and who was foe, their treatment of South Vietnamese villagers, most famously at My Lai in 1968, alienated the very people they were supposed to be helping. Without the support of the population, the Saigon regime would always be dependent on large-scale American aid, and this was shown in 1975, when that aid was withdrawn and South Vietnam quickly fell to the Communists[2].

1 The sentence puts forward a clear view that the failure to win hearts and minds was the most important reason for the American defeat.
2 The claim that winning the hearts and minds was vital is proved by the speedy collapse of Thieu's regime in 1975.

The conclusion

The conclusion provides the opportunity to bring together all the interim judgements to reach an overall judgement about the question. Using the interim judgements will ensure that your conclusion is based on the argument in the main body of the essay and does not offer a different view. For the essay answering question 1 (see page 238), you can decide what was the most important factor in the American defeat, but for questions 2 and 3 you will need to comment on the importance of the named reason – the failure to win hearts and minds or the Communist military performance– as well as to explain why you think a different reason is more important, if that has been your line of argument. Or, if you think the named factor is the most important, you would need to explain why that was more important than the other reasons you have discussed.

Consider the following conclusion to question 2: To what extent was the failure to win the hearts and minds of the Vietnamese people the most important cause of the American defeat in the Vietnam War?

The Americans failed to win the Vietnam War because the military performance and political appeal of the Communists was far superior to that of the Americans and the Saigon regime. The inability of the US military and the ARVN to inflict any crushing and lasting defeat on the Communists was clearly demonstrated to the American public by the American media during the Tet Offensive. Underlying all these reasons was the failure of successive Saigon regimes to win the hearts and minds of the Vietnamese people. Clearly, the unpopularity of the Saigon regime was the main reason for the American failure[1]. Had the Saigon regime been popular, Communist guerrillas and Communist ideology would not have gained the necessary support and the United States would not have felt it necessary to bomb the territory of their South Vietnamese ally and to have 535,000 American soldiers in Vietnam by December 1967 – an obtrusive foreign presence that further increased the unpopularity of Thieu's regime[2].

1 This is a strong conclusion because it considers the importance of the named reason – winning hearts and minds – but weighs that up against a range of other reasons to reach an overall judgement.
2 It is also able to show links between the other reasons to reach a balanced judgement, which brings in a range of issues, showing the interplay between them.

How to write a good essay for the A level short answer questions

This question will require you to weigh up the importance of two factors or issues in relation to an event or a development. For example:

Which did more to bring about the end of the French colonial government in Indochina?

(i) Ho Chi Minh and the Viet Minh.

(ii) Eisenhower's policies toward Indochina.

Explain your answer with reference to both (i) and (ii).

As with the long essays, the skills required are made very clear by the mark scheme, which emphasises that the answer must:

- analyse the two issues
- evaluate the two issues
- support your analysis and evaluation with detailed and accurate knowledge
- reach a supported judgement as to which factor was more important in relation to the issue in the question.

The skills required are very similar to those for the longer essays. However, there is no need for an introduction, nor are you required to compare the two factors or issues in the main body of the essay, although either approach can still score full marks. For example, an introduction could be:

After their humiliating defeat by Germany in the Second World War, the French were determined to regain their Indochinese colonies, along with some of their national pride. However, the French colonial government was resisted by Ho Chi Minh and the Viet Minh[1]. That Communist opposition encouraged US Presidents Truman (1950–3) and

Eisenhower (1953-4) to aid the French colonial government[2]. However, as the unsuccessful American efforts under Kennedy and Johnson would demonstrate, it proved exceptionally difficult, even impossible, to defeat the Vietnamese Communists. Their strength was clearly more important in the French exit from Indochina than Eisenhower's policies were.[3]

1 The answer explains the French problems with Ho Chi Minh and the Viet Minh.
2 The implications of this development are considered.
3 Consideration is given to the relative significance of the Communist efforts as opposed to Eisenhower's policies in the French exit.

The answer could go on to argue that while Eisenhower's aid to the French was limited (as at Dien Bien Phu), the military and political strength of the Vietnamese Communists was great.

Most importantly, the conclusion must reach a supported judgement as to the relative importance of the factors in relation to the issue in the question. For example:

Both Ho Chi Minh and the Viet Minh on the one hand, and Eisenhower's policies on the other hand, had a significant impact on the end of the French colonial regime in Indochina. However, while

American policy frequently infuriated the French (Eisenhower repeatedly pressed them to grant the Indochinese greater self-government) and US assistance was limited (Eisenhower refused French requests for large-scale US airstrikes during Dien Bien Phu), the American escalation under Eisenhower's successors proved that even had Eisenhower offered greater and unqualified aid, it would have been insufficient to defeat the Communists[1]. 'Uncle Ho' won the hearts and minds of many Vietnamese people by appealing to their nationalism and the desire for a more egalitarian society. The Communist forces were not only popular amongst the majority of the Vietnamese population, but also determined and ingenious in the fight for national independence. That was well illustrated when they confounded French and American expectations by their operations on the mountainsides surrounding Dien Bien Phu. The French, like their American successors in Vietnam, were simply unable to defeat Ho Chi Minh and his followers[2].

1 The response explains the relative importance of the two factors and offers a clear view.
2 The response supports the view offered in the opening sentences and therefore reaches a supported judgement.

Interpretation guidance

How to write a good essay

The guidance below is for answering the AS interpretation question OCR Unit Y252: The Cold War in Asia 1945–1993. Guidance on answering essay questions is on page 238.

The OCR specification outlines the two key topics from which the interpretation question will be drawn. For this book these are:

- The Korean War 1950–1953 and its impact to 1977.
- Wars in Vietnam and Cambodia 1968–1993.

The specification also lists the main debates to consider.

It is also worth remembering that this is an AS unit and not an A level historiography paper. The aim of this element of the unit is to develop an awareness that the past can be interpreted in different ways.

The question will require you to assess the strengths and limitations of a historian's interpretation of an issue related to one of the specified key topics.

You should be able to place the interpretation within the context of the wider historical debate on the key topic. However, you will *not* be required to know the names of individual historians associated with the debate or to have studied the specific books of any historians. It may even be counter-productive to be aware of particular historians' views, as this may lead you to simply describe their view, rather than analyse the given interpretation.

There are a number of skills you need to develop if you are to reach the higher levels in the mark bands:

- To be able to understand the wording of the question.
- To be able to explain the interpretation and how it fits into the debate about the issue or topic.
- To be able to consider both the strengths and weaknesses of the interpretation by using your own knowledge of the topic.

Here is an example of a question you will face in the exam:

> Read the interpretation and then answer the question that follows:
>
> 'The Korean War ... is a conflict that is fundamentally Korean, but ... viewed in the United States as a self-contained story beginning in June 1950 and ending in July 1953.'
>
> (Adapted from Bruce Cumings, *The Korean War*, Random House, 2010.)
>
> Evaluate the strengths and limitations of this interpretation, making reference to other interpretations that you have studied.

Approaching the question

There are several steps to take to answer this question:

1 Explain the interpretation and put it into the context of the debate on the topic

In the first paragraph, you should explain the interpretation and the view it is putting forward. This paragraph places the interpretation in the context of the historical debate and explains any key words or phrases relating to the given interpretation. A suggested opening might be:

This interpretation puts forward the view that the Korean War was not simply a war that broke out in June 1950 and ended in July 1953, as the Americans perceived it to be. The author suggests that the war was basically a Korean civil war that began before June 1950 and remains unfinished[1]. When it refers to a 'fundamentally Korean' war, the interpretation is emphasising that Kim Il Sung and Syngman Rhee each sought to reunify the peninsula under his own rule and had taken steps prior to June 1950 to try to bring this about[2]. In contrast, many Americans saw the Korean War as a Cold War conflict generated by Kim, and more importantly by Stalin and Mao Zedong in 1950, then ended in 1953 with the restoration of the status quo thanks to the intervention of the United States and the United Nations[3].

1 The opening sentences are clearly focused on the given interpretation. They clearly explain that there are two viewpoints over the outbreak and nature of the Korean War, but there is no detailed own knowledge added at this point.
2 The third sentence explains what is meant by 'fundamentally Korean'.
3 The last sentence begins to place the concept of a 'fundamentally Korean' conflict in the wider historical debate and suggests that this historian's emphasis on it might challenge the American view that the Korean War was simply an episode in the Cold War.

In order to place Cumings's view in the context of the debate about the causes and nature of the Korean War, you could go on to suggest the importance of Soviet–American decisions over Korea at Yalta and Potsdam, of Stalin and Mao, of Truman's commitment to collective security, and of the impact of US domestic politics.

2 Consider the strengths of the interpretation

In the second paragraph, consider the strengths of the interpretation by bringing in your own knowledge that supports the given view. A suggested response might start as follows when considering the strengths of the view:

There is generally acknowledged merit in this interpretation[1]. The border clashes between North Korean and South Korean forces during 1948–9 indicated that neither Kim nor Rhee was satisfied with the status quo and that both harboured an aggressive intent toward the other[2]. The ambitions of the two Korean nationalists Kim and Rhee in 1950 had little to do with the Communist expansionism that the Americans perceived in the Communist activity in the Philippines, French Indochina, British Malaya and China between 1946 and 1949[3].

1 The answer clearly focuses on the strength of the given interpretation.
2 The response provides some support for the view in the interpretation from the candidate's own

knowledge This is not particularly detailed or precise, but could be developed in the remainder of the paragraph.
3 The final sentence links together the two viewpoints.

In the remainder of the paragraph you could show how these two factors were linked: how Kim sought approval and support from Stalin and Mao in 1949–50, before he launched the attack in June 1950.

3 Consider the weaknesses of the interpretation

In the third paragraph, consider the weaknesses of the given interpretation by bringing in knowledge that can challenge the given interpretation and explains what is missing from the interpretation. A suggested response might start as follows when considering the weaknesses of the view:

However, there are clearly weaknesses in an interpretation that suggests that the Korean War was 'fundamentally Korean'[1]. The two Koreas had been created as a result of the developing tension between the two great Cold War rivals, the United States and the Soviet Union[2]. North Korea would have been unable to stage its attack in June 1950 had it not been well armed with tanks and aircraft by the Soviets prior to that date. This 'Korean civil war' was 'self-contained' within the Cold War[3].

1 The opening makes it very clear that this paragraph will deal with the weaknesses of the interpretation.
2 It explains clearly the first weakness and provides evidence to support the claim. The evidence is not detailed and could be developed, but the answer focuses on explaining the weakness, rather than providing lots of detail.
3 Although more detail could have been provided about the development of the two Koreas, the answer goes on to explain a second weakness, the Chinese and Soviet roles in 1950, and this could be developed in the remainder of the paragraph.

Answers might go on to argue that Kim knew that Stalin's assent was essential for his attack. Throughout 1949, Kim had worked hard to try to persuade Stalin to allow an attack, and it was only when Stalin finally gave that assent in 1950 that

Kim felt able to launch his invasion. Furthermore, it was not only Stalin whom Kim felt needed to be persuaded: he thought it necessary to obtain Mao's support also. The paragraph might therefore suggest that the interpretation provides a partial answer which needs further development.

There is no requirement for you to reach a judgement as to which view you find more convincing or valid.

Assessing the interpretation

In assessing the interpretation you should consider the following:

- Identify and explain the issue being discussed in the interpretation: the outbreak and nature of the Korean War.
- Explain the view being put forward in the interpretation: the Korean War was essentially a Korean civil war rather than a self-contained episode in the Cold War.
- Explain how the interpretation fits into the wider debate about the issue: the relative importance of the Korean leaders and the Cold War context in the Korean War, but also a wider range of issues such as the need to support collective security and US domestic political considerations.

In other Interpretations you might need to:

- Consider whether there is any particular emphasis within the interpretation that needs explaining or commenting on, for example, if the interpretation says something is 'the only reason' or 'the single most important reason'.
- Comment on any concepts that the interpretation raises, such as 'total war', 'authoritarian system', 'liberalisation'.
- Consider the focus of the interpretation, for example, if an interpretation focuses on an urban viewpoint, what was the rural viewpoint? Is the viewpoint given in the interpretation the same for all areas of society?

In summary: this is what is important for answering interpretation questions:

- Explaining the interpretation.
- Placing the interpretation in the context of the wider historical debate about the issue it considers.
- Explaining the strengths *and* weaknesses of the view in the extract.

Glossary of terms

Administration   Rather than refer to a President's 'government', Americans refer to a President's 'administration'.

Agent Orange   Herbicide used by the USA in Vietnam to defoliate the trees and destroy enemy cover. It can cause illness and deformities in the descendants of those exposed.

Agrovilles   New and well-defended villages set up by Diem's regime to keep Communists out.

Air America   A supposedly civilian air carrier that the CIA used, for example in Laos during the Vietnam War.

Allies   Countries that collaborate with each other in areas such as defence and war.

Approval rating   American pollsters continually check the public's opinion (approval) of the President's performance.

Army of the Republic of Vietnam (ARVN)   South Vietnamese forces – the Army of the Republic of Vietnam.

ASEAN   Association of Southeast Asian Nations, established in 1967 to promote political and economic co-operation.

Asia-Firster   Cold War American who believed Asia should take priority over Europe in US foreign policy.

B-52s   Large American bomber planes.

Berkeley   A leading Californian university.

Berlin blockade   During 1948–9, Stalin cut off Western access by land to the Western zones of Berlin. America and Britain airlifted supplies to West Berlin, so Stalin ended the blockade.

Bill   In order to make a measure law, the suggested measure has to be presented to Congress. Once this bill is passed by both houses of Congress, and assented to by the President, the bill becomes an act or law.

Bipolar world order   In the first decades after the Second World War, the Soviet Union and the United States were by far the most powerful countries in the world and international relations were dominated by their antagonism. From the 1960s, the Soviets and Americans were increasingly unable to dominate other nations in a newly multipolar world.

Booby traps   Disguised traps.

Bugout fever   The tendency of inexperienced and frightened American troops to flee the battlefield out of formation in the early days of the Korean War.

Bunco man   A con man.

Cadres   Communist activists.

Capitalist   One who believes in a free market economy with no state intervention – the opposite of the Communist economic philosophy.

Cartels   Monopolistic associations of manufacturers.

CIA   The Central Intelligence Agency was established in 1947; it was responsible for collecting and evaluating intelligence data for the US federal government.

Cold Warrior   One who wanted the US to wage the Cold War with even more vigour.

Collective bargaining   When trade unions are able to organise and to negotiate with management over wages, hours, and so on.

Collective security   An international system whereby all countries agree to collectively protect any one of their number that is a victim of aggression. The League of Nations served as the first worldwide collective security organisation between the two world wars, and the United Nations took up the role after 1945.

Colonies   Countries/territories that have been taken over and invariably exploited by other countries.

Comecon   Soviet-dominated economic organisation for Communist nations.

Commander-in-Chief   Under the US Constitution, the President commands the US armed forces.

Commitment trap   The theory that each President after Truman was bound to continue the US involvement in Vietnam because the preceding president(s) had made Vietnam seem of increasing importance to the United States.

Communiqué   In diplomatic and military terms, a statement issued by a commander or leader.

Communists   Believers in economic equality brought about by the revolutionary redistribution of wealth.

Congress   The US equivalent of the British parliament; Congress makes laws and grants money to fund the President's policies.

Constitutional monarch   A royal head of state with real power reserved to democratically elected institutions.

Containment   The Truman administration's policy of using counterforce against Soviet expansionism.

Conventional forces   Soldiers, sailors and so on, as opposed to nuclear or high-tech weaponry.

COSVN   Central Office for South Vietnam – small, mobile Vietnamese Communist headquarters in Cambodia.

Coup   A *coup d'état* is the illegal overthrow of a government, usually by violent and/or revolutionary means.

Court-martialled   Tried by an army court for breaking army regulations.

CPK   Kampuchean (Cambodian) Communist Party from 1966.

Cross-over point   The point at which Americans anticipated that Communists would give up because they were being killed faster than Hanoi could replace them.

Cuban Missile Crisis In 1962, President Kennedy's pressure forced Soviet leader Khrushchev to remove Soviet nuclear missiles from Cuba.

Cultural Revolution   Mid-1960s' effort by Mao to revitalise and purify Chinese Communism, characterised by extremism.

Democratic Kampuchea (DK)   The name by which Cambodia was known under the Pol Pot regime.

Democrats   One of the two main US political parties; from the 1930s, favoured increased federal government interventionism to help the less privileged.

Detente   Relaxation of tension between the USA and the USSR in the Cold War in the 1970s.

Diplomatic   In international relations, 'diplomacy' means relations between nations; a diplomat represents his or her nation abroad; nations that fully recognise each other have diplomatic relations.

Domino theory   President Eisenhower's belief that if one nation fell to Communism, neighbouring nations were likely to follow.

Doves   Americans more inclined to peace during the Cold War.

DPRK   The Democratic People's Republic of Korea, also known as North Korea.

Draft   The enforced call-up of civilians to be soldiers.

Draft cards   Documents informing an American of compulsory military call-up.

Europe-Firster   Cold War American who believed Europe should take priority over Asia in US foreign policy.

Executive order   In certain areas, such as military matters, the US Constitution gives the President the power to act alone, through issuing executive orders.

Expansionism   When a country's policy is to acquire other countries/territories.

Formosa   Taiwan was more commonly known as Formosa in the 1940s and 1950s.

Fragging   When enlisted men tried to kill officers by throwing fragmentation grenades at them.

Friendly fire   When a force's own side or an ally fires on the force by mistake.

GIs   US soldiers were issued with certain equipment by their superiors. 'GI' stood for 'government issue' and was used to describe American soldiers.

Great Depression   Worldwide economic depression starting in 1929.

Great Society   Johnson programme aimed at decreasing American economic and racial inequality.

Green Berets   US Army special forces.

Ground commander   While MacArthur was in charge of US forces in the Pacific, Walker then Ridgway commanded the American troops in Korea.

Ground troops   In March 1965, President Johnson sent the first few thousand regular soldiers (rather than just 'advisers') to Vietnam.

Grunt   Ordinary ground trooper or foot soldier.

Guerrillas   Soldiers who try to avoid conventional warfare (that is, one army directly confronting another), preferring methods such as sabotage to counter the enemy's superior forces.

Guomindang (GMD)   Also known as the Kuomintang (KMT), the Chinese Nationalist Party was dominated by Jiang Jieshi from the 1920s.

Hanoi and Saigon   Nations are often referred to by the name of their capital, where the government resides, so 'Hanoi' can be used instead of North Vietnam, and 'Saigon' instead of South Vietnam.

Hawks   Militant Cold Warriors in the USA; those at the other end of the spectrum were known as doves.

Hmong   Mountain people residing in Laos, Vietnam, Thailand and China.

Ho Chi Minh Trail   North Vietnamese Communist supply route going south from North Vietnam through Cambodia and Laos to South Vietnam.

Huks   In the Second World War, Filipino resistance was led by the leftist People's Anti-Japanese Army – the Hukbong Bayan Laban sa Hapon or Hukbalahap for short, popularly known as the Huks.

Hyperinflation   When governments print excessive quantities of banknotes, the currency can become worthless.

Ideology   Set of political beliefs, for example, Communism.

Impeachment   Process whereby Congress has the constitutional power to remove an errant President.

'Imperial presidency'   Some Americans felt that under the pressure of the lengthy Cold War, the President gained greater power and became like some old European King or Emperor.

Imperialism   Territorial and/or economic and/or cultural domination of another country.

Imperialist   In this context, possessors of empires.

Internationalised Korean War   What began as a Korean civil war changed in nature when foreign nations joined in.

Iron Curtain   After the Second World War, the USSR established Communism in, and took control of, Eastern Europe. Churchill said that it was as if an 'Iron Curtain' had come down across the European continent.

Issarak   Cambodian independence movement/supporter.

Jiang Jieshi   In most books the name Chiang Kai-shek is used instead of Jiang Jieshi.

Joint Chiefs of Staff (JCS)   The heads of the American Army, Navy and Air Force.

Khmer   Ethnic Cambodian.

Khmer Rouge   'Khmer Reds', Sihanouk's name for the Cambodian Communists.

KPRP   Khmer People's Revolutionary Party, the Cambodian Communist Party, 1951–66.

Land reform   Even anti-Communist Americans saw the need for a more equal distribution of land in Vietnam: an estimated 1 per cent of the population owned all the cultivable land in the south.

Linkage   Linking US concessions to the USSR and China to their assistance in ending the Vietnam War.

Madman Theory   President Nixon's depiction of himself as an unpredictable leader in order to intimidate the Vietnamese.

Malaysia   From 1963, British Malaya and associated territories were independent and known as Malaysia.

Mandarin   A high-ranking civil servant.

Marxist–Leninist   Communist theories as established in the nineteenth century by the philosopher Karl Marx and the early twentieth century by the Russian revolutionary and then Soviet leader Vladimir Lenin.

Military Assistance Command, Vietnam   MACV was created by Kennedy to co-ordinate US efforts in South Vietnam in February 1962.

Monolithic Communist bloc   During the 1950s, many Americans believed that Moscow and Beijing were united in their foreign policies; by the 1960s, it was increasingly clear that with the Sino-Soviet split (in which other Communist nations took sides) there was no longer a united/monolithic Communist bloc.

Moratorium   In this context, suspension of normal activities, in order to protest.

Multi-party state   Nation in which voters have a free choice between several political parties.

Napalm   Flammable liquid used in warfare.

National Guard   US armed forces reservists, called up by the President in times of crisis.

National Liberation Front (NLF)   From 1960, Ho's southern supporters gave themselves this name.

National Security Council   Established in 1947 to co-ordinate US government work on internal and external security; members included the President, Vice President, Secretary of State, Secretary of Defence, and the chiefs of the CIA and JCS.

NATO   The North Atlantic Treaty Organisation was an anti-Communist Western military alliance established by the United States in 1949.

Non-Aligned Movement   Loose association of Third World nations anxious to distance themselves from Cold War antagonisms.

Non-aligned nations   Countries that remained neutral in the Cold War.

Operation Killer   Ridgway's February 1951 plan to inflict morale-damaging losses on the Chinese.

Orthodox viewpoint   Historians who see the Korean War as a war of Communist aggression and blame the Soviets for the Cold War have the orthodox viewpoint.

Pacification   Paying greater attention to the security and government of the South Vietnamese people.

Pathet Lao   Laotian Communists.

'Peace with honour'   Nixon always claimed he would get 'peace with honour' in Vietnam, by which he meant that Thieu's government must stay in power in a viable South Vietnamese state.

Peaceful coexistence   Policy of Soviet Premier Nikita Khrushchev, who said that as nuclear weapons made a US–Soviet war undesirable, there should be attempts to get along with the West.

Pentagon   Headquarters of the US Department of Defence.

People's Army of Vietnam (PAVN)   Formal name of Ho's North Vietnamese Army (NVA) by 1956.

People's Liberation Armed Forces (PLAF)   The name which Ho's southern supporters called their forces after 1960.

Politburo   The Chinese Communist government's equivalent of the British or US cabinet.

Popular mandate   Clear evidence that a political leader has the majority of the people behind him and his policies.

Post-revisionist   Following orthodox or traditional interpretations of an event such as the Korean War, historians usually come up with an opposing viewpoint – the revisionist viewpoint. Usually, the majority of historians will then combine the best of the orthodox and revisionist viewpoints.

POWs   Prisoners of war.

PRK   People's Republic of Kampuchea (1979–89).

Protocol   In this context, an agreement between signatory nations.

Pusan Perimeter   The area on the southeastern corner of the Korean peninsula, into which the US/UN/ROK forces were forced in the early weeks of the Korean War.

R&R   Rest and recuperation for American soldiers in Vietnam.

Red Scare   Period of anti-Communist hysteria.

Reparations   In this context, compensatory payments from a defeated country to victors and victims.

Republic of Korea   Anti-Communist South Korean state.

Republican   Member of one of the two main American political parties; generally opposed to federal government interventionism to assist the less privileged; many in the party were 'Asia-firsters' in the Cold War.

Revisionist   Historians critical of US motives in the Cold War as aggressive and acquisitive. The revisionist view of the Korean War is that it was a Korean civil war.

ROK   The Republic of Korea, also known as South Korea.

Rollback The Eisenhower administration verbally rejected President Truman's containment of Communism and advocated pushing back Communism in places where it was already established.

'Rolling Thunder'   Heavy, often non-stop US bombing of Vietnam.

Russian Revolution   Beginning in 1917, the Russian Emperor (Tsar) was overthrown and the nation developed into a Communist state that became known as the Soviet Union or USSR.

SCAP   General MacArthur was Supreme Commander of the Allied Powers in post-war Japan; the acronym was used to refer to MacArthur and to his administration.

Search and destroy   General Westmoreland's tactics included finding and killing groups of Viet Cong guerrillas.

Secretary of State   The US equivalent of Britain's Foreign Secretary, he had responsibility for foreign policy and was in charge of the State Department.

Security Council   The UN chamber that contained the great powers; the other members were only represented in the General Assembly.

Senate Foreign Relations Committee   Highly influential body of recognised specialists in foreign policy in the US Senate.

Sino-American   Chinese–American.

Sino-Soviet   Chinese–Soviet.

Sino-Soviet split   In the early 1960s, Chinese–Soviet mutual hostility became increasingly obvious to the rest of the world.

Southeast Asia Treaty Organisation (SEATO)   Defensive alliance between USA, Britain, France, Australia, New Zealand, Pakistan, the Philippines and Thailand, 1954.

Soviet Union   In 1922, Communist Russia changed its name to the Union of Soviet Socialist Republics (USSR) or Soviet Union.

State Department   US governmental department with responsibility for foreign affairs.

Strategic hamlets   Policy used in Malaya and Vietnam to cut off villages from Communist guerrillas by surrounding them with stockades and monitoring ingress and egress.

Summit   During the Cold War, meetings or conferences between the US and Soviet leaders were known as summit meetings.

Taiwan Strait   The stretch of water between mainland (Communist) China and Jiang Jieshi's island of Taiwan (also known as Formosa).

Tet   The most important Vietnamese festival. Americans use the word 'Tet' as shorthand for the 'Tet Offensive'.

Third World   Cold War-era name for developing nations.

Ticker-tape parade   When national heroes returned to the United States, the citizens of New York City would shower them with bits of paper (ticker-tape) as they drove through the streets of the city in an open-top car.

Truman Doctrine   Truman's declaration of Cold War on the USSR in his March 1947 speech to Congress, in which he said the Soviet threat had to be resisted.

Trusteeship   In an international context, countries that take responsibility for another country.

UNC   The United Nations Command, under MacArthur, co-ordinated the US/UN/ROK forces in the Korean War.

United Nations (UN)   The UN was set up in 1945. The 50 nations that signed its founding charter pledged to assist any other member that was a victim of aggression.

US   Pertaining to the United States.

US/UN/ROK   The forces of the United States, United Nations and Republic of Korea (South Korea) that opposed North Korea in the Korean War.

USSR   Union of Soviet Socialist Republics.

Viet Cong   After 1960, Diem called the National Liberation Front 'Viet Cong' (Vietnamese Communists or VC).

Viet Minh   Ho's Vietnamese nationalist followers were known as the Viet Minh after 1941.

Vietnamisation   A phrase/policy introduced by the Nixon administration; the idea was that the South Vietnamese government and forces should take the main responsibility for the war against Communism.

War of attrition   Westmoreland believed that US numerical and technological superiority would wear down the Viet Cong who must, after losing a certain number of men, finally decide to give up.

Watergate affair   During Nixon's re-election campaign, Republicans authorised burglary and wiretapping of Democratic national headquarters at that Watergate building in Washington, DC; the Nixon administration tried a 'cover-up'.

Western   Developed nations with democratic systems of government and white populations, for example, the United States, Britain, France and the Netherlands.

Wise Men   A group of experienced politicians, generals and others who had previously held high office, frequently consulted by Johnson over the Vietnam War.

Working Group   A group of experts brought together by President Johnson to study Vietnam and make suggestions for future policies in autumn 1964.

WPK   Workers' Party of Kampuchea or Cambodian Communist Party, 1960–6.

Zaibatsu   Industrial and financial conglomerates or cartels that emerged in late nineteenth-century Japan; under SCAP they developed into looser associations known as keiretsu.

Further reading

General

John Lewis Gaddis, *The Cold War* (Penguin, 2005)
Well-written, balanced overview

Milton Osborne, *Southeast Asia: An Introductory History* (Allen & Unwin, 2013)
Draws interesting comparisons between states and events

John Young, *The Longman Companion to America, Russia and the Cold War, 1941–1998* (Longman, 1999)
Invaluable reference work for dates, crises, individuals and their offices, treaties and summit meetings

Chapter 1

Stanley Karnow, *In Our Image: America's Empire in the Philippines* (Random House, 1989)
Lively, journalistic account

Steven Hugh Lee, *The Korean War* (Longman, 2001)
Excellent introduction

Martin McCauley, *The Origins of the Cold War* (Longman, 2008)
A Soviet specialist, with more and better insights into the Soviet viewpoint than most

Barbara Watson Andaya and Leonard Y. Andaya, *A History of Malaysia* (Palgrave, 2001)
Thorough, detailed account, especially strong on the ethnic tensions

Chapter 2

Bruce Cumings, *The Korean War* (Random House, 2010)
Fresh, revisionist viewpoint

David Halberstam, *The Coldest Winter: America and the Korean War* (Macmillan, 2008)
Account based on interesting interviews with veterans. Like many journalists, aims to hold the interest rather than to analyse

William Stueck, *The Korean War: An International History* (Princeton University Press, 1997)
Refreshing insistence upon the different perspectives of the nations involved

See Seng Tan and Amitav Acharya, editors, *Bandung Revisited* (NUS Press, 2008)
Essay collections invariably contain contributions of varied quality and usefulness, but the Introduction and the chapter on Bandung and 'Cold War International History' are helpful

Chapter 3

Stanley Karnow, *Vietnam: A History* (Penguin, 1997)
A journalist who covered the war, Karnow provides an interesting read, if a little short on analysis

Kevin Ruane, *War and Revolution in Vietnam, 1930–75* (UCL Press, 1998)
Useful, brief introduction

Vivienne Sanders, *The USA and Vietnam 1945–75* (Hodder Education, 2008)
Aimed at A-level students and geared to possible examination questions

Chapter 4

David Anderson, *The Vietnam War* (Longman, 2005)
Good, brief overview

Mark Philip Bradley and Marilyn Young, *Making Sense of the Vietnam Wars: Local, National, and Transnational Perspectives* (Oxford University Press, 2008)
Stimulating collection of essays

Timothy Castle, *At War in the Shadow of Vietnam: US Military Aid to the Royal Lao Government 1955–1975* (Colombia University Press, 1993)
Brilliantly researched account of events in Laos but a difficult read

Chapter 5

Stephen Ambrose, *Nixon: The Triumph of a Politician 1962–1972* (Simon & Schuster, 1989) and *Nixon: Ruin and Recovery 1973–1990* (Simon & Schuster, 1991)
Ambrose is a thorough, balanced biographer, who gives invaluable day-to-day accounts of the presidency

Gary Hess, *Vietnam: Explaining America's Lost War* (Blackwell, 2009)
Clearly sets out all the debates on the US involvement and failure

Melvin Small, *The Presidency of Richard Nixon* (University Press of Kansas, 1999)
Another excellent volume in the Kansas University's series. Small's loathing of Nixon cannot help but come through at times

Chapter 6

Joel Brinkley, *Cambodia's Curse: The Modern History of a Troubled Land* (Public Affairs, 2011)
Useful section on the role of the United Nations, a role that disillusioned the author

Ben Kiernan, *How Pol Pot Came To Power* (Yale University Press, 2004) and Ben Kiernan, *The Pol Pot Regime* (Yale University Press, 2008)
Detailed and so thoroughly researched that some readers might find it hard work

Philip Short, *Pol Pot: The History of a Nightmare* (John Murray, 2004)
A good general account but some readers might feel uneasy when the author attributes a great deal of blame to Buddhism for the activities of Pol Pot

Index

Acknowledgements:

American RadioWorks and Mount Holyoke College (http://americanradioworks.publicradio.org/features/prestapes/lbj_rr_052764.html and www.mtholyoke.edu/acad/intrel/vietnam/lbjbundy.htm). American Rhetoric (www.americanrhetoric.com/speeches/douglasmacarthurfarewelladdress.htm). British International Studies Association, *Still the American Century* by Bruce Cumings, 1999. Doubleday, *Years of Trial and Hope, Memoirs by Harry S. Truman*, 1965. *Foreign Affairs*, July 1947 (www.foreignaffairs.com/articles/23331/x/the-sources-of-soviet-conduct). George Washington University, National Security Archive (http://nsarchive.gwu.edu/coldwar/documents/episode-1/kennan.htm). Hodder, *Pol Pot: The History of a Nightmare* by Philip Short, 2004. *Journal of Conflict Studies*, 'Revisionism and the Korean War' by William Stueck, 2002. *Journal of Contemporary Asia*, 'From Polarisation to Integration in Vietnam' by Ngo Vinh Long, 2009. *Life* magazine, writings of Harry Truman, 1956. Michigan State University (http://coursesa.matrix.msu.edu/~hst306/documents/domino.html). Public Broadcasting Service (www.pbs.org/wgbh/amex/macarthur/filmmore/reference/primary/officialdocs02.html). Routledge, *The Origins of the Korean War* by Peter Lowe, 2014. Simon & Schuster, *Nixon: The Triumph of a Politician, 1962–1972* by Stephen Ambrose, 1989; *The Korean War* by Max Hastings, 1987. TeachingAmericanHistory.org (http://teachingamericanhistory.org/library/document/speech-on-the-far-east/). Yale Law School, Avalon Project (http://avalon.law.yale.edu/20th_century/trudoc.asp). Yale University Press, *How Pol Pot Came To Power* by Ben Kiernan, 2004; *The Pol Pot Regime* by Ben Kiernan, 2008.

Every effort has been made to trace all copyright holders, but if any have been inadvertently overlooked the Publishers will be pleased to make the necessary arrangements at the first opportunity.